The Rise of China
Implications for India

Edited by

Harsh V. Pant

Delhi • Bengaluru • Mumbai • Kolkata • Chennai • Hyderabad • Pune

Published by
Cambridge University Press India Pvt. Ltd.
under the imprint of Foundation Books
Cambridge House, 4381/4 Ansari Road, Daryaganj, **New Delhi** 110 002

Cambridge University Press India Pvt. Ltd.
C-22, C-Block, Brigade M.M., K.R. Road, Jayanagar, **Bengaluru** 560 070
Plot No. 80, Service Industries, Shirvane, Sector-1, Nerul, **Navi Mumbai** 400 706
10 Raja Subodh Mullick Square, 2nd Floor, **Kolkata** 700 013
21/1 (New No. 49), 1st Floor, Model School Road, Thousand Lights, **Chennai** 600 006
House No. 3-5-874/6/4, (Near Apollo Hospital), Hyderguda, **Hyderabad** 500 029
Agarwal Pride, 'A' Wing, 1308 Kasba Peth, Near Surya Hospital, **Pune** 411 011

First Published 2012
Reprinted 2012, 2014

ISBN 978-81-7596-895-0

Published by Manas Saikia for Cambridge University Press India Pvt. Ltd. and
printed at Sanat Printers, Kundli.

To my teachers

Contents

List of Contributors

Bibek Debroy is Professor at Centre for Policy Research, Delhi. He has earlier worked for academia (Presidency College [Kolkata], Gokhale Institute for Economics and Politics, Indian Institute of Foreign Trade, National Council for Applied Economic Research, Rajiv Gandhi Institute for Contemporary Studies, International Management Institute, National University of Singapore), industry (PHD Chamber of Commerce and Industry) and government (Department of Economic Affairs). He is the author of several books, academic papers and popular articles.

Varaprasad S. Dolla is Associate Professor in Chinese Studies, Centre for East Asian Studies at the School of International Studies, Jawaharlal Nehru University. He has published research papers in journals and books, besides presenting several papers in the international and national conferences. He was ASIA (Asian Studies in Asia) Fellow at Peking University, Beijing in 2004 and also Editorial Board member of the *International Studies* journal during 2004–09.

Ashok Kapur is Distinguished Professor Emeritus in Political Science, University of Waterloo, Canada. He is author of several major works including *India – From Regional to World Power*, is co-author of *Government and Politics in South Asia*, 6th edition and author of *India and the South Asian Strategic Triangle*.

Srikanth Kondapalli is Professor in Chinese Studies, Jawaharlal Nehru University, New Delhi. He is educated in Chinese Studies in India and China. He has been a Post-Doctoral Visiting Fellow at People's University, Beijing from 1996–98, a Visiting Professor at National Chengchi University, Taipei in 2004, a Visiting Fellow at China Institute of Contemporary International Relations, Beijing in May 2007 and an Honorary Professor at Shandong University in 2008. He has published two books, two monographs, co-edited two volumes and several articles in edited books and in journals and newspapers.

Harsh V. Pant is a Reader in International Relations at King's College London in the Department of Defence Studies. He is also an Associate with the King's Centre for Science and Security Studies and an Affiliate with the King's India Institute. His current research is focused on Asian security and defence issues. His recent books include *Contemporary Debates in Indian Foreign and Security Policy*, *Indian Foreign Policy in a Unipolar World*, *The China Syndrome* and *China's Rising Global Profile*.

D. S. Rajan held senior positions in the Government of India as China Analyst from 1964 to 2001. Post-retirement, he works as Director of Chennai Centre for China Studies, India. He is fluent in Chinese and Japanese languages and his published works include chapters on China in three recent books – *National Security Annual Review* and *New Asian Power Dynamic* (both in India) and *Political and Security Dynamics of South and South East Asia* (in Singapore).

David Scott is Lecturer in International Relations at Brunel University. He is the author of three books on China's role in the international system, published in 2007 and 2008. In recent years, he has also published various articles on Indian foreign policy, as well as articles on Sino-Indian relations.

Elliot Sperling is former Chair of the Department of Central Eurasian Studies at Indiana University, where he directs the department's Tibetan Studies Program. He has written extensively on Sino-Tibetan relations and is currently preparing a history of modern Tibet. Aside from his scholarly writings, he has provided op-ed and analytical pieces on the Tibetan situation to a number of publications.

Arthur Waldron is the Lauder Professor of International Relations at the University of Pennsylvania. He was educated at Harvard and spent a number of years studying in Asia. Before moving to Penn, he was Professor of Strategy and Policy at the US Naval War College. He is author or editor of, or contributor to, more than twenty books, of which the best known is *The Great Wall of China: From History to Myth*.

Preface

THE rise of China is the greatest geopolitical event of our times. It is being debated and analysed at various levels. In India too, it is generating a lot of excitement. At times, it is seen as an opportunity while at other times, as a challenge. Yet, there is more opinion than comprehension about the rise of China in India. To understand more clearly the implications of China's rise, we need to understand China more deeply.

This book is an attempt at exploring the multi-dimensional nature of the rise of China and its implications for India at this critical juncture when the rise of China and India is being talked about in the same breath. Not surprisingly, this project was very ambitious in scale, given the desire to examine the implications of China's rise for India along the three axes: domestic developments in China, Chinese foreign policy and India-specific issues. It was only with the help, support and encouragement of a number of people that this project could come to fruition.

First, I would like to express my deep sense of gratitude to all the contributors who, despite their busy schedules, took time off to be a part of this volume. Most of them are senior scholars of China and I have learnt a lot from their work. Therefore, it was a privilege for me when they agreed to be a part of this project. I hope they will not be disappointed with the final product.

A special note of thanks to my family and to my wife, Tuhina, in particular, without whose support none of this would have been possible. I can only hope that the abiding faith of all those who have been involved with this project in one form or another will be suitably rewarded. I hope that a better comprehension of China in India will lead to a more stable Asian strategic landscape. This book is dedicated to my teachers whose guidance over the years has been critical in shaping my thinking and academic trajectory.

Harsh V. Pant
King's College London

1

Introduction

Harsh V. Pant

CHINA looms large over the emerging strategic landscape of global politics. The rise of China as an emerging great power and as the most likely challenger to the global preponderance of the US is already having a significant impact across the globe. The rapidity of China's rising profile has surprised many though it should have been obvious to those following China's economic trajectory. As China became economically powerful, it was bound to become ambitious and assert its profile across the globe. This is a trend that all great powers have followed throughout history. China has thrived because it devotes itself to economic development while letting the US police the region and the world. Even as it decries American hegemony, its leaders envision Pax Americana extending well into the middle of the present century, at least until China becomes a middle-class society and, if present trends continue, the world's largest economy. However, while declaring that it will be focusing on internal socio-economic development for the next decade or so, China has actively pursued policies of preventing the rise of other regional powers such as Japan and India in order to attain primacy in the region.

While realising well that it would take China decades to seriously compete with the US for global hegemony, China has focused its strategic energies on Asia. Its foreign policy is aimed at enhancing its economic and military prowess to achieve regional hegemony in Asia. China's recent emphasis on projecting its rise as peaceful is merely aimed at allaying the concerns of its neighbours lest they try to counterbalance its growing influence. China's readiness to negotiate with other regional states and to be an economically "responsible" power is also a signal to other states that there are greater benefits in band wagoning to China's growing regional weight rather than opposing its rise in any manner. As has been argued by some, China's foreign policy strategy is aimed at protecting China from external threats as it pursues its geopolitical interests so as to be able to allow China to continue with the reforms of its economy, and thereby acquire comprehensive national power without having to deal with the impediments and distractions of security competition.

A growing economic power, China is now concentrating on the accretion of military might so as to secure and enhance its own strategic interests. Whatever Chinese intentions might be, consistent increases in defence budgets over the last several years have put China on track to becoming a major military power and the power most capable of challenging American dominance in the Asia-Pacific. While China's near-term focus remains on preparations for potential problems in the Taiwan Straits, its nuclear force modernisation, its growing arsenal of advanced missiles, and its development of space and cyberspace technologies are changing the military balance in Asia and beyond.

It is almost conventional wisdom now that the centre of gravity of global politics has shifted from Europe to the Asia-Pacific in recent years, with the rise of China and India, gradual assertion by Japan of its military profile, and a significant shift in the US global force posture in favour of the Asia-Pacific. Even Russia has now decided to convert its Pacific fleet into its biggest naval force, presumably to meet security threats emerging from Asia. The debate now is whether Asia-Pacific will witness rising tensions and conflicts in the coming years with various powers jockeying for influence in the region or whether the forces of economic globalisation and multilateralism will lead to peace and stability. Some have asked the question more directly: Will Europe's past be Asia's future?[1] It is, of course, difficult to answer this question as of now when major powers in the Asia-Pacific such as China, India and Japan are still rising and grappling with a plethora of issues that confront any rising power in the international system. However, what is clear is that all major powers are now re-evaluating their policy options vis-à-vis the Asia-Pacific as a new balance of power emerges in the region. China's future conduct is the great regional uncertainty and at the same time, the most important factor

---

[1] Aaron Friedberg, "Will Europe's Past be Asia's Future?" *Survival*, Vol. 42, No. 3 (Autumn 2000), pp. 147–159.

affecting regional security as well as the strategic priorities of major powers in the region.

It is in this wider context that this introductory chapter situates the present volume on the rise of China and what it means for India. First, a broad overview of the changing regional balance of power is provided underlining the manner in which major regional powers are re-evaluating their strategic options in the light of China's momentous rise. Subsequently, the focus shifts to the China-India relationship and its present trajectory followed by an examination of the growing divergence between the two Asian giants using the levels of analysis framework. Finally, the arguments presented in various chapters of this volume are summarised.

Regional Powers Recalibrate Strategies

The US Faces a Possible Power Transition

While the United States remains the predominant power in the Asia-Pacific region, its primacy is increasingly being challenged by China, making the region very susceptible to future instability. The US National Intelligence Council has made it clear that

> China will overtake Russia and others as the second-largest defence spender after the United States over the next two decades and will be, by any measure, a first-rate military power.[2]

As a response to the rising prowess of China in the Pacific, the US has commenced adjusting its defence strategy and force posture to deal with the rising dragon in Asia. The 2006 Quadrennial Defence Review (QDR) specifically called for boosting the number of naval ships in the Pacific Ocean. It decided to put six of the US Navy's 12 aircraft carriers and 60 per cent of its submarine forces in the Pacific at all times to support engagement, presence, and deterrence.[3] The Pentagon is considering buying new classes of weapons suited to a twenty-first century battle in the Pacific that would feature cyber-warfare, space weapons, satellite-guided missiles, ship-borne anti-missile defences, unmanned bombers launched from carrier decks and small, sub-hunting warships. The US is also actively expanding, diversifying and bolstering its bases in Asia

---

[2] The US National Intelligence Council Report is available at http://www.cia.gov/nic/NIC_globaltrend2020.html

[3] The 2006 US Quadrennial Defense Review Report is available at http://www.defenselink.mil/qdr/report/Report20060203.pdf

so as to move them closer to China while, at the same time, reducing their vulnerability to attack. The US Navy has accelerated its schedule for building its next generation of cruisers by seven years and is considering smaller, anti-submarine vessels. The 2010 QDR also acknowledges that "China's growing presence and influence in regional economic and security affairs is one of the most consequential aspects of the evolving security landscape in the Asia-Pacific region and globally."[4] Concerns about China's long-term intentions and future conduct in Asia are palpable throughout the document.

Theatre-range ballistic missiles, land-attack cruise missiles, anti-ship cruise missiles, surface-to-air missiles, land-based aircraft, submarines, surface combatants, amphibious ships, naval mines, nuclear weapons, and possibly high-power microwave devices have been identified by the US Congress as some of the major elements of China's military modernisation that have potential implications for the future of US naval capabilities. The primary focus of China's military modernisation is to be able to deploy a force that can succeed in a short-duration conflict with Taiwan and act as an anti-access force to deter US intervention or delay the arrival of US naval and air forces. Today, the Chinese armed forces are already considered strong enough to delay and punish the US Navy in any confrontation over Taiwan.[5] China's rapid development of cruise and other anti-ship missiles designed to pierce the electronic defences of the US vessels is specifically aimed to ensure that any US decision to intervene in a future conflict over Taiwan would be painful and fraught with risk. However, there is also a broader agenda: to attain Chinese military's dominance in the Asia-Pacific and to replace the US as the regional power, given China's rapidly expanding interests in the region and beyond. China's largely secretive military modernisation programme is producing results faster than expected and Beijing is gearing up to challenge the US military prowess in the Pacific with its aircraft carriers, rapidly growing submarine fleet, anti-ship ballistic missile (ASBM) system, and stealth fighters. This has led the US to not only adjust its force posture but to also carve a new diplomatic strategy that challenges China on its own turf. The US faces the prospect of an emerging power transition involving China, and the most consequential challenge for the US foreign policy in the coming decades will be to deal with this prospect. With this in mind, the US seems to be pursuing a policy of engaging China while simultaneously investing

---

[4] The 2010 Quadrennial Defense Review Report of the US Government can be found at http://www.defense.gov/qdr%20as%20of%2029jan10%201600.pdf

[5] Thomas Christensen, "Posing Problems without Catching Up: China's Rise and Challenges for US Security Policy," *International Security*, Vol. 25 (4) (Spring 2001), pp. 5–40.

in increasing the power of other states located along China's periphery. This has involved not only re-invigorating its existing alliance with Japan but also reaching out to new partners such as India.[6]

A More Assertive Japan

The George W. Bush Administration had backed the notion of a more assertive Japan, viewing Tokyo as an increasingly important partner at a time of dwindling support for the administration's policies among the US allies. Japan and the US signed a pact to enhance co-operation on a ballistic missile defence system in 2004 due to be fully operational by 2012. The US has also encouraged Japan to forge close political and strategic ties with neighbouring states such as India and Australia.

Japan remains wary of China's growing economic and military profile in the region and beyond. Despite significant economic and trade ties between China and Japan, political tensions have increased in recent years, especially over the differing interpretations of history by the two nations. There was a public outcry in China in 2005 when Japan's Education Ministry approved history textbooks that were said to whitewash Japan's militarism in Asia during the first half of the last century. It is argued that about 200,000 to 300,000 Chinese were killed during the Japanese occupation of Nanjing that began in 1937 and the new Japanese textbooks refered to this as the "Nanjing incident." China asked Japan to take responsibility for the unrest in Chinese cities because it had continued to rewrite the history of its World War II era occupation of China. Unrest erupted in various Chinese cities including Beijing, Shanghai, Chengdu, and Guangzhou with some subtle manipulations by China's political establishment.[7] Japan, meanwhile, asked for an apology of its own from China for violent attacks against Japanese government offices and businesses in China. It also did not help when Tokyo's High Court rejected an appeal for compensation by the Chinese survivors of biological-warfare experiments conducted by Japan during the Second World War. Relations between China and Japan took a nosedive in 2010 when China decided to cease high-level political exchanges with Japan to protest the extended detention of the Captain of a Chinese fishing trawler captured by

---

[6] Ashley Tellis, "India in Asian Geopolitics," in Prakash Nanda (ed.), *Rising India: Friends and Foes* (New Delhi: Lancer Publishers, 2007), pp. 123–127.

[7] Robert Marquand, "Anti-Japan protests jar an uneasy Asia," *The Christian Science Monitor,* April 11, 2005.

Japanese ships in disputed waters.[8] Beijing essentially bullied its way through the crisis and responded by not only threatening Tokyo but actually halting the exports of rare earth minerals to Japan underscoring China's growing economic leverage and its willingness to try to translate that into political power. In a classic case of coercive diplomacy, Beijing compelled Tokyo to release the Chinese fishing boat captain unconditionally. In this process, however, Beijing ended up damaging its credibility as a peaceful rising power in the Asia-Pacific and strengthened the military alliance between the US and Japan.

However, it would be a mistake to view these Sino-Japanese tensions merely through the prism of history or as resource competition. It is also about the future of the Asian balance of power. Both Japan and China are competing for pre-eminence in the Asian political and strategic landscape and this is producing some inevitable tensions. The spat over Japan's historical behaviour is just one of the manifestations of this dynamic. At its foundation, what is fuelling these Sino-Japanese tensions is a burgeoning sense of strategic rivalry as China's power expands across Asia, and Japan redefines its regional military role in close co-operation with the United States. Japan has made it clear that it considers China a potential military threat that would have to be faced and countered in the coming years. This was followed by Japan's announcement that a peaceful resolution of the Taiwan issue is a strategic objective that it shares with the United States, signalling to China that it might help America defend Taiwan in the event of a war.

Under the present constitution, Japan has effectively renounced virtually any form of aggression. Rules of engagement for Japanese troops on overseas peacekeeping missions are also severely limited by the constitution. As presently interpreted, they are not permitted to defend themselves or their allied troops unless directly fired upon. Because there are no ground attack units and its aircraft cannot be refuelled in flight, Japan's Self Defence Force (SDF) is restricted to home operations. Japan has gradually been trying to remove these constraints and a campaign seeking the revision of Japan's pacifist constitution is presently underway. Various Japanese governments in recent years have been keen on amending the Japanese constitution, especially Article IX, so that Japan can possess armed forces like any other sovereign country and play its rightful role as a global power. The aim is to remove

---

[8] Martin Fackler and Ian Johnson, "Arrest in Disputed Sea Riles China and Japan," *New York Times*, September 19, 2010.

constitutional constraints that would allow Japan to engage in military activities beyond its current defensive activities. The Japanese government has stressed that Japan must accept a global security role commensurate with its economic clout. Since September 11, 2001, the Japanese military has undergone its most significant transformation since the Second World War, one that has brought it operationally closer to America's military.

Japan has begun to accept more responsibility for its own national defence and is seeking a more active role as an international security actor. Authorised by the country's so-called "anti-terror" law implemented to provide logistical support for coalition forces operating in Afghanistan, Japan has refuelled US, UK and other nations' warships since November 2001. Japan's forces have been dispatched to the Indian Ocean and to Iraq as part of a more robust security policy. Japan has been providing at-sea refuelling to coalition vessels from several states performing maritime interdiction operations in the Indian Ocean. In Iraq, in accordance with a special law to aid in reconstruction, a symbolic ground force was deployed to a non-combat area in southern Iraq to engage in relief activities. After it left in 2006, Japanese planes began transporting American troops and cargo from Kuwait to Baghdad. The Japanese SDF engineering battalion is deployed in Samawah in Iraq and is working towards various reconstruction projects.[9] These Iraq missions have continued despite critics opposing these military dispatches as a violation of the country's constitution.[10] After withdrawing its military airlift mission in Iraq in the light of security improvements, the Japanese government also expressed an interest in dispatching troops to Afghanistan.[11] This military activism of Tokyo combined with a more serious outreach to other like-minded states in the region is likely to shape the balance of power in Asia in the coming years.

A "Democratic Quad" As a Trial Balloon

A triangular security dialogue between Washington, Tokyo and Canberra was initiated by Japan's former Prime Minister, Junichiro Koizumi that

---

[9] See the testimony of Christopher R. Hill, "US Relations With Japan," Senate Foreign Relations Committee, September 29, 2005, available at http://www.state.gov/p/eap/rls/rm/2005/54110.htm
[10] On the continuing domestic opposition to the LDP's plans to revise the constitution, see Leo Lewis, "Abe's Vision of a New Japan Prompts March," *The Times (London)*, May 4, 2007.
[11] "Japan Weighs Military Withdrawal From Iraq," *Associated Press*, September 11, 2008

involved regular military exchanges. Japan and Australia, with American blessings, have also signed a defence pact that further strengthens their strategic partnership by providing for the sharing of intelligence and high-level exchanges of military personnel as well as extensive co-operation in training.[12] This is the first time that Japan has signed a strategic pact with another country, apart from the US, so far Japan's only military ally. The pact aims to promote closer co-operation between the militaries of Japan and Australia through joint exercises and dialogue and this includes the establishment of joint training facilities for Japanese and Australian troops in international peacekeeping operations. The two nations have already been working in tandem for some time now. The Australian troops secured the safety of Japanese non-combatant troops when the Japanese forces were deployed in southern Iraq. The two forces also worked together to provide relief to the victims of the devastating Indian Ocean Tsunami on December 2004.

Koizumi's successor, Shinzo Abe, had made known his desire to create a four-way strategic dialogue with the US, Australia and India, a framework that Tokyo stressed would be based on their shared universal values such as freedom, democracy, human rights and the rule of law. The idea of a democratic quad, however, faded away after just one meeting of senior officials and under the Obama Administration, a new grouping has emerged – the G-3. This group, which brings together the world's three largest national economies and the most important powers in the Asia-Pacific, has trumped the idea of the Asian democratic quad, thereby underlining the centrality of China to any new global or regional arrangement. The G-3 is aimed at alleviating the fears in Tokyo that it might be marginalised amidst growing engagement between Washington and Beijing. Yet, the rise of China and Japan's increasing strategic isolation in its own neighbourhood has motivated Japan to seek closer ties with Australia and India based not only on their interests but also on their shared liberal-democratic and free market values. This focus of Japanese leaders to frame their foreign policy on the basis of values is an attempt by the Japanese elite to adopt the tools that best help them enhance their influence and shape their security environment at any given time.[13] This has allowed India to emerge as a major foreign policy priority for Japan.

---

[12] "Australia, Japan sign Landmark Defence Pact," *The Straits Times*, March 14, 2007.
[13] Michael J. Green, "Japan is Back: Why Tokyo's New Assertiveness is Good for Washington," *Foreign Affairs*, March/April 2007.

India's Balancing Act

Indian foreign policy is also gearing up with its new approach towards the US and Japan to tackle the challenge of a rising China in its vicinity.[14] If India is indeed a "swing state" in the international system, then it seems to have swung considerably towards the US. The demise of the Soviet Union liberated Indian and US attitudes towards each other from the structural confines of Cold War realities. As India pursued economic reforms and moved towards global integration, it was clear that the US and India will have to find a modus vivendi for a deeper engagement with each other. The Bush administration transformed the nature of the US-India partnership by advocating civilian nuclear energy co-operation with India, thereby incorporating India into the global nuclear order as well as declaring that the US is committed to encouraging the growth of India as a great power.[15]

The 2010 Quadrennial Defence Review (QDR) of the US also makes a very strong statement of India's importance for the US in the emerging global security architecture. While a concern with China's rising military power is palpable throughout the defence review, it is instructive to note the importance that the QDR has attached to India's rising global profile. India is described as an emerging great power and a key strategic partner of the US. Shared values such as the two states being long-standing multi-ethnic democracies are underlined as providing the foundation for increased strategic co-operation. This stands in marked contrast to the unease that has been expressed with the centralisation of power in Russia and lack of transparency in security affairs in China. It is also significant that India is mentioned along with America's traditional allies such as the North Atlantic Treaty Organization (NATO) countries, Japan and Australia. The QDR goes on to say very categorically that close co-operation with these partners (including India) in the war on terrorism as well in efforts to counter Weapons of Mass Destruction (WMD) proliferation and other non-traditional threats ensures not only the continuing need for these alliances but also for improving their capabilities.

For the US, India is now a crucial player in the emerging balance of power in the Asia-Pacific region. It would like a strong US-India alliance to act as a bulwark against the arc of Islamic instability running from the Middle East to Asia and to create a much greater balance in Asia.

---

[14] Sumit Ganguly, "India's Foreign Policy Grows Up," *World Policy Journal*, Vol. 20, No. 4 (Winter 2003–04).

[15] Harsh V. Pant, *Contemporary Debates in Indian Foreign and Security Policy* (New York: Palgrave Macmillan, 2008), pp. 19–37.

India's growing closeness to the US is also making Japan take India seriously and both are well aware of the Chinese strategy to contain the rise of its two most-likely challengers in the region. Both Tokyo and New Delhi seek to hedge against Chinese influence by trying to create stronger relations with other democracies in Asia. Both consider China a potential military threat that would have to be faced and countered in the coming years. The 2010 Defence White Paper of Japan expresses concern over the effects that the lack of transparency in China's defence policy and its military build-up will have on the regional state of affairs and on the security situation of Japan.[16] India's diplomatic and military posture is also increasingly geared towards countering China's rising profile.[17] The goal of Indo-Japanese co-operation is to ensure that China becomes less threatening and ultimately more co-operative.

India's ties with Japan have travelled a long way since May 1998 when a chill had set in after India's nuclear tests with Japan imposing sanctions and suspending its overseas development assistance. Since then, however, the changing strategic milieu in Asia-Pacific has brought the two countries together so much so that the last visit of the Indian Prime Minister to Japan resulted in the unfolding of a roadmap to transform a low-key relationship into a major strategic partnership. India and Japan have decided to invigorate all major aspects of their relationship ranging from investment, defence, science and technology to civilian co-operation in space and energy security. The rise of China is a major factor in the evolution of Indo-Japanese ties as is the US attempt to build India into a major balancer in the region. Both India and Japan are well aware of China's not-so-subtle attempts at preventing their rise. It is most clearly reflected in China's opposition to the expansion of the United Nations Security Council (UNSC) to include India and Japan as permanent members. China's status as a permanent member of the UNSC and as a nuclear weapon state is something that it would be loathe to share with any other state in Asia. India's "Look East" policy of active engagement with Association of South East Asian Nations (ASEAN) and East Asia remains largely predicated upon Japanese support. India's participation in the East Asia summit was facilitated by Japan, and the East Asia community proposed by Japan to counter China's proposal of an East Asia Free Trade Area (EAFTA) also includes India. While China has resisted the inclusion of

---

[16] Annual White Paper, Ministry of Defense, Government of Japan 2010, available at http://www.mod.go.jp/e/publ/w_paper/2010.html

[17] Harsh V. Pant, "India in the Asia-Pacific: Rising Ambitions With an Eye on China," *Asia-Pacific Review*, Vol. 14, No. 1 (May 2007), pp. 54–71.

India, Australia, and New Zealand in the ASEAN, Japan has strongly backed the entry of all three nations. As Pakistan pushed China's case as an observer to the South Asian Association of Regional Co-operation (SAARC), India pushed for the inclusion of Japan.

It is instructive that India's ties with Japan do not carry any historical baggage unlike most of the Japanese neighbours who have historical disputes with Japan. As Japan moves ahead under a new generation of political leadership to emerge as a "normal" state with legitimate security interests and concomitant military capabilities, India is more than willing to lend Japan a helping hand.[18]

Recent convergence in the strategic priorities of India and the US as well as Japan notwithstanding, it is unlikely that India would openly become a part of the US-led alliance framework against China. Like most states in the Asia-Pacific, India would not want to antagonise China by ganging up against it.

Yet, India is the country that will be and already is being significantly affected by a rising China. China is a rising power in Asia and the world, and as such, will do its utmost to prevent the rise of other power centres around its periphery like India, that might in the future, prevent it from taking its rightful place as a global player. China's "all-weather" friendship with Pakistan, its attempts to increase its influence in Nepal, Bangladesh, and Burma, its persistent refusal to recognise parts of India such as Arunachal Pradesh, its lack of support for India's membership to the UNSC and other regional and global organisations, its unwillingness to support the US-India nuclear pact – all point towards China's attempts at preventing the rise of India as a regional and global player of major import. With India's recent rise as an economic and political power of global significance, Sino-Indian ties are now at a critical juncture as India tries to find the right policy mix to deal with its most important neighbour.

China and India: Growing Divergence

At one level, bilateral relations between the two Asian giants seem very stable, perhaps more stable than they have ever been in their turbulent history. They are talking on the contested boundary issue, there are regular high-level political contacts, there have even been growing interaction between the two militaries, trade ties are burgeoning, and both have expressed their preference

---

[18] Tukoji R. Pandit, "Sun Shines on India-Japan Relations," *The Asian Tribune*, December 29, 2006.

for a multi-polar world order to the one being dominated by a single power.[19] Yet occasional rhetorical flourishes about India and China being natural partners notwithstanding, the reality of Sino-Indian relations is getting more complicated by the day as the two Asian giants continue their ascent in the global inter-state hierarchy.

China's lack of support to India in the aftermath of Mumbai terror attacks in November 2008 and its attempts at blocking the approval of the US-India civilian nuclear energy co-operation pact at the Nuclear Supplier's Group (NSG) has reinforced perceptions in India that China would do everything possible to prevent India's emergence as a major regional and global player. Meanwhile, trouble is brewing on the issue of boundary and all those years of effort at resolving the problem has come under a cloud.

The tensions over the boundary dispute between the two sides are escalating with China opening another front recently by raising objections over an area that was previously thought to have been settled. China contested Indian control of 2.1 sq km area, known as the Finger Area, in the northernmost tip of the Indian state of Sikkim in 2008. This came as a surprise to the Indians as the issue of Sikkim was widely considered to have been settled some years ago.

In 2003, when the then Indian Prime Minister A.B. Vajpayee had visited Beijing, a bilateral agreement was signed in which India recognised Tibet as a part of the territory of China and pledged not to allow "anti-China" political activities in India while China acknowledged India's 1975 annexation of the former monarchy of Sikkim by agreeing to open a trading post along the border with the former kingdom, and later by rectifying its official maps to include Sikkim as part of India. This was hailed as a major breakthrough in Sino-Indian bilateral ties though the Chinese government did not issue any formal statement recognising Sikkim as part of India. Yet, just a few years down the line, things are getting murkier with each passing day.

The Indian government informed the parliament in 2008 that the Chinese forces were stepping up regular cross-border activities. In one case, the Chinese soldiers entered 15 kilometres into India at the Burste post in the Ladakh sector along the Sino-Indian boundary and burned the Indian patrolling base. China persists in refusing to recognise the Indian state of Arunachal Pradesh as part of India, laying claim to 90,000 sq kms of its land. Even as China has

---

[19] For a detailed explication of the recent convergence and the continuing divergence in Sino-Indian relations, see Harsh V. Pant, *The China Syndrome: Grappling with an Uneasy Relationship* (New Delhi: HarperCollins, 2010).

solved most of its border disputes with other countries, it seems reluctant to move ahead with India on border issues. The entire 4,057 km Sino-Indian frontier is in dispute, with India and China the only known neighbours not to be separated even by a mutually defined Line of Control (LOC).

Despite the need for an expeditious demarcation of the Line of Actual Control, the Sino-Indian boundary talks seem to be continuing endlessly and the momentum of the talks itself seems to have flagged. China has adopted shifting positions on the border issue, time and again enunciating new principles but not explaining them. The real problem, however, is that India has no real bargaining leverage vis-à-vis China and negotiations rarely succeed in the absence of leverage. India, moreover, is not making any serious effort to get any economic, diplomatic or military leverage vis-à-vis its neighbourhood dragon. India seems to have lost the battle over Tibet to China, despite the fact that Tibet constitutes China's only truly fundamental vulnerability vis-à-vis India. India has failed to limit China's military use of Tibet despite its great implications for Indian security, even as Tibet has become a platform for the projection of Chinese military power.

Not only has China pumped in infrastructural investments in developing roads, railways, airfields, hydroelectric and geothermal stations, leading to a huge influx of Han Chinese in Tibet, it is also rapidly expanding the logistical capabilities of its armed forces in Tibet. India's tacit support to Dalai Lama's government-in-exile has failed to have much of an impact either on China or on the international community. Even Dalai Lama has given up his dream of an independent Tibet and is ready to talk to the Chinese as he realises that in a few years Tibet might get overwhelmed with the Han population and Tibetans themselves might become a minority.

Encouraged by the growing isolation of the Tibetans, the Chinese government now seems to have little interest in a genuine dialogue with the Dalai Lama. The Dalai Lama now concedes that his drive to secure autonomy for Tibet through negotiations with the Chinese government has failed, thereby strengthening the hand of the younger Tibetans who have long agitated for a more radical approach and who have demanded independence. It is a possibility that recent turmoil among the Tibetans in China may be hardening Chinese perceptions vis-à-vis India. The Chinese government continues to raise objections to the media prominence being given to the Dalai Lama and his supporters in India. Though the Indian government can do little about how the Indian media treats the Tibetan cause, it will inevitably have an impact upon Sino-Indian ties. This despite the fact that the Indian government has not been able to summon enough self-confidence to even allow peaceful protests by the Tibetans and forcefully condemn Chinese physical assaults on its Tibetan minority and verbal assaults on the Dalai Lama.

China also seems to be concerned about Indian foreign policy becoming more proactive in recent years and being able to play the same balance of power game, which the Chinese are masters of. India's growing closeness to the US and the idea that democratic states in the Asia-Pacific such as India, Japan, Australia and the US should work together to counter common threats, is generating a strong negative reaction in Beijing. Whatever the cause, the recent hardening of positions on both sides does not augur well for regional stability in Asia. Sino-Indian ties will, in all likelihood, determine the course of global politics in the coming years. The consequences of this development, however, remain far from being clear.

Explaining the Divergence: The Three Levels of Analysis

To address the ubiquitous phenomenon of multiplicity of actors, influences and processes in international politics, a Level-of-Analysis (LoA) approach is employed that analyses issues and events in international relations at three different levels: the international system level, the state level, and the individual level.[20]

The individual LoA focuses mostly on the leaders of a state, though personal characteristics of humans may also be examined. This level concerns the perceptions, choices, and actions of individual human beings. The psychological makeup of a state's leaders, the background, training, and education of the elite of the state, the ideology of the leaders, and their strategies and tactics are some of the variables that are given attention at this level.

The state LoA looks inside the states for the causes of international events. It concerns the aggregations of individuals, such as interest groups, political organisations, and governmental agencies, within states that influence state actions in the international arena. This level of causation focuses on such aspects as politics and tensions within the state, the prevailing ideologies and belief systems within the state, the groups contending for power within the state, the type of political system, and the influence of non-governmental organisations, special interest groups and public opinion on state policies. Some other variables that are considered important at this LoA are political

---

[20] For a detailed explication of this, see Kenneth N. Waltz, *Man, the State, and War: A Theoretical Analysis* (Los Angeles: California University Press, 1959).

institutions, economic structure and the level of development, history and culture.

The level of causation focused at the international systemic level examines the impact of the international systems on international outcomes. This level is particularly attentive to the structure of the international system, which is defined by the distribution of relative power capabilities among states. It is the number of great powers or polarity in the international system that defines the structure of the international system that, in turn, affects the state behaviour.

Examining the Sino-Indian ties at various levels, one finds that there are a host of reasons for the growing divergence. At the structural level, India and China are two major powers in Asia with global aspirations and some significant conflicting interests. As a result, some amount of friction in their bilateral relationship is inevitable. The geopolitical reality of Asia makes sure that it will be extremely difficult, if not impossible, for *Hindi-Chini* to be *bhai-bhai* (brothers) in the foreseeable future.[21] If India and China continue to rise in the next few years, a security competition between the two regional giants will be all but inevitable. In many ways, while globally the international system remains largely unipolar, in Asia-Pacific, a multi-polar regional order is gradually taking shape. According to a realist understanding of global politics, multi-polar systems are inherently unstable because they generate uncertainty and make it difficult for states to draw lines between allies and adversaries, thereby often causing miscalculations.[22] Any conflict between two of the powers in the system is more likely to escalate to general war as the other powers might be tempted to join in. Minor powers are also more likely to play great powers off against each other. Power imbalances are more common in a multi-polar world and tougher to predict. In a multi-polar Asia-Pacific landscape, India and China will find it much difficult to manage their relationship. Therefore, despite the occasional desire expressed by Indian political elites for a multi-polar world, Indian strategic interests, at least in the short term, are better served by an Asia-Pacific where the US retains its predominant status.

A closely related realist approach to explaining war and peace focuses less on the number of great powers in the system and more on the shifting

---

[21] "Hindi-Chini Bhai Bhai" (Indians and Chinese are brothers) was a popular slogan during the 1950s, the heydays of Sino-Indian relationship, that became discredited after the 1962 Sino-Indian war.

[22] On why multi-polar systems are more unstable as compared to bipolar ones, see Kenneth Waltz, *Theory of International Politics* (New York: McGraw-Hill, 1979). Also see John Mearsheimer, *Tragedy of Great Power Politics* (New York: W.W. Norton, 2001), pp. 138–167.

amount of power between those states known as the Power Transition theory.[23] According to one version of this approach, the largest conflicts result when a rising power is surpassing, or threatening to surpass, the most powerful state. While some argue that war results from the dominant power attempting to arrest its deteriorating position, others argue that the rising power is more likely to initiate war as it seeks to gain the influence and prestige it feels it deserves because of its increased capabilities. This again poses challenges for Sino-India ties as any attempt by India to achieve strategic parity with China might provoke reactions from China that might not be conducive for regional stability.

In one of the most detailed studies of Sino-Indian relations in a historical perspective, John Garver makes a convincing case that Sino-Indian relations have, over the years, been shaped by a deep and enduring geopolitical rivalry between the two states.[24] According to Garver, Sino-Indian rivalry is rooted in the "decades-long, multilayered, and frequently sharp conflict over the two states' relations with the lands and peoples lying around and between them."[25] Taking this structuralist approach further, Ashley Tellis has contended that China and India are rising powers in Asia and therefore, remain natural competitors, competing to increase their influence, not only in South Asia, but also outside South Asia proper. Tellis goes on to argue that Sino-Indian competition is not likely to mutate into malignant rivalry in the near-term but if Chinese and Indian economic and military capabilities continue to grow at the current pace, there is a likelihood of this relationship turning into a dyadic rivalry.[26]

This conclusion is supported by Sumit Ganguly who also contends that any dramatic improvement in Sino-Indian ties is unlikely and the relations between the two will remain competitive.[27] Mark Frazier also agrees but argues that precisely because so many sources of dispute exist between China and India, both sides have come to recognise the need to prevent tensions

---

[23] A detailed explication of the Power Transition theory can be found in A.F.K. Organski and Jacek Kugler, *The War Ledger* (Chicago: University of Chicago Press, 1980).

[24] John W. Garver, *Protracted Contest: Sino-Indian Rivalry in the Twentieth Century* (Seattle: University of Washington Press, 2001).

[25] Ibid., p. 8.

[26] Ashley J. Tellis, "China and India in Asia," in Francine R. Frankel and Harry Harding eds., *The India-China Relationship: What the United States Needs to Know* (New York: Columbia University Press, 2004), pp. 134–177.

[27] Sumit Ganguly, "India and China: Border Issues, Domestic Integration, and International Security," in Frankel and Harding eds., *The India-China Relationship*, pp. 103–133.

from leading to an overt rivalry. Therefore, according to Frazier, a quiet competition is the most likely possibility.[28] Many in India have also reached similar conclusions.[29] While there are differences on the exact nature that Sino-Indian competition might take in the future, there seems to be a broad consensus that a host of factors point towards a competitive Sino-Indian relationship.

At the state level of analysis, the varied political arrangements in the two countries make the relationship highly susceptible to mistrust and conflict. The democratic peace theory suggests that democracies do not go to war with each other but constraints that work in democracies against going to wars do not work in non-democracies. The Communist political regime in Beijing is extremely vulnerable to domestic pressures and so tends to use nationalism to divert public attention from domestic problems. With the economic crisis constraining the Chinese government's ability to provide for people's economic demands, it will be tempted to rely more in the coming years on targeting its external adversaries and India in many ways, presents an easy target.

At the individual level of analysis, the perceptual differences between the elites in India and China also present a worrisome picture of the future of Sino-Indian bilateral ties. The level of distrust of each other's intentions remains high among the elites in Beijing and New Delhi. Despite all the talk of Asian solidarity, the cultural differences between the two states remain strong. Indian political elites find it difficult to trust Beijing after the catastrophic defeat in the 1962 war, especially as it came after attempts by Jawaharlal Nehru, India's first Prime Minister, to forge strong Sino-Indian bilateral ties. The Chinese elites also distrust India, especially after recent attempts by New Delhi to forge strategic ties with Washington and Tokyo though, for a long time, India was not a priority for Chinese foreign policy. At the popular level too, negative perceptions abound. As India's former Ambassador to China, Nirupama Rao has stated, "Negative perceptions among the people on both sides about Sino-Indian bilateral relationship remains a significant challenge."[30]

The underlying thrust of the above arguments is that whether India likes it or not, the inherent competition for regional influence will always

---

[28] Mark W. Frazier, "Quiet Competition and the Future of Sino-Indian Relations," in Frankel and Harding eds., *The India-China Relationship*, pp. 294–320

[29] See, for example, Karnad, *Nuclear Weapons and Indian Security* (New Delhi: Macmillan India Ltd., 2002), pp. 540–544; Brahma Chellaney, "India, China Mend Fences," *Washington Times*, April 7, 2005; G. Parthasarathy, "Diplomacy with Dignity, *The Tribune*, May 19, 2005.

[30] Saibal Dasgupta, "India-China Relations: Rao Clears Negative Perceptions," *Times of India*, July 8, 2009.

underpin the realities of Sino-Indian relationship and therefore, India needs to shape its foreign policy accordingly. However, the Indian policy seems to be one of overemphasising the promising future potential in the Sino-Indian relationship and de-emphasising the troublesome past and present realities. It is far from clear if that approach is working and this volume is an attempt to explore the reasons why this might be the case. There are a number of volumes on the rise of China that have been published in recent years.[31] The intent behind this one is rather specific: to examine China's rise from an Indian perspective. No single volume on China's rise can be expected to cover every single aspect of this most significant geopolitical event of our time. Therefore, contributors have examined various aspects of China's rise – domestic developments, foreign policy agenda, and its positions on issues related to India – from the particular vantage point of what they mean for India. This makes this volume different from other such works in recent times.

An Overview of the Volume

This book examines the rise of China and its consequences for India along the following three axes:

Domestic Developments in China

China's economy continues to grow but fundamental vulnerabilities remain. The domestic political implications of the economic rise of China remain far from clear even as developments in the military realm continue to be opaque, generating apprehensions worldwide. The first section of the volume, therefore, focuses on the economic, political and military developments in China's domestic realm. The societal implications of China's recent economic and military rise are touched upon by the authors in so far as it directly pertains to their analyses. Overall, this section looks at domestic developments in China on various fronts and their implications for India.

The second chapter examines the developments over the last decade on the economic front in China and highlights the major trends in the Chinese

---

[31] See, for example, Susan Shirk, *China: Fragile Superpower* (New York: Oxford University Press, 2008); C. Fred Bergsten, *China's Rise: Challenges and Opportunities* (Washington, DC: Peterson Institute of International Economics, 2009); David Shambaugh, *Power Shift: China and Asia's New dynamics* (Berkeley: University of California Press, 2006); David M. Lampton, *The Three Faces of Chinese Power: Might, Money, and Minds* (Berkeley: University of California Press, 2008); David C. Kang, *China Rising: Peace, Power, and Order in East Asia* (New York: Columbia University Press, 2009).

economic thinking. It draws some implications for India of these contemporary trends in the Chinese economy. It is the economic rise of China and India that has garnered greatest attention in recent times. Even as Western economies continue to face serious problems, it is expected that Chinese and Indian economies might not fare that bad. Yet as Bibek Debroy points out, the multiple crises (food, fuel and financial) that confront the globe today will also lead to a "movement away from what was the earlier growth trajectory in China and India."

In addition, even if that growth trajectory gets back on track, the governance of international organisations and the larger global environment might be remarkably different. According to Debroy, barring some social sector indicators, China remains far ahead of India in virtually every economic indicator and the two are not in the same league. He suggests that a more useful comparison will be of China in the second half of the 1980s with "India post-2006 or thereabouts." Though Sino-Indian bilateral economic relations have been expanding ever since border trade resumed in 1992, India not only faces the issue of trade deficit vis-à-vis China but the Indian export basket to China remains extremely narrow. Moreover, as Debroy underlines, while Sino-Indian trade has increased substantially over the last few years, "bilateral investment flows haven't increased much."

Despite this, Debroy argues that bilateral economic relations, "haven't yet become inordinately strained," as "both countries are learning to adjust to each other's economic rise and the impact this is having on the global economy."

The third chapter examines the developments on the domestic political front in China over the last few decades and draws out important implications for India of these developments. The rise of China remains dependent on the smooth functioning of its political system which according to Dolla is changing in a "gradualist manner." Unlike Mao's period when socialism was at the centre of Chinese political thinking, its locus, according to Dolla, has now moved to issues, "such as nationalism, national minorities, regionalism and legalisation with critical implications for the very stability of the Chinese stability."

One of the most important means through which the Chinese political leadership has tried to retain people's faith in the political system is economic development but despite its critical importance, political reform has been ignored. As a result, serious problems continue to plague the Chinese political system. Though political institutions in China have evolved, "they are still rigid and authoritarian in their functioning."

Moreover, national minorities remain marginalised and the legal system continues to favour the state. Growing hold of the politics of resentment at the grassroots level can also undermine the future political stability of China. As Dolla argues, Chinese domestic politics are in a transitional phase. While it can safely be concluded that the institutionalisation of the Chinese government and politics will continue, the pace of this process remains far from certain. The present political leadership in Beijing seems to be cautious in approaching the restructuring of the political system and this unfinished political reform probably is the most daunting challenge for the next generation of Chinese political leaders.

The fourth chapter examines the developments on the military front in China over the last decade and its implications for India. China's dramatic rise as an economic power over the last two decades has given it an ability to develop its military might and project its power far beyond its borders. It is this military modernisation programme that is generating apprehensions across the globe and, in China's periphery in particular, about the real intent behind these developments as much of the military modernisation in China remains clouded in secrecy. What is of enormous significance for India is the fact that China's economic transformation has given it the capability to become a major military power with China spending as much as $ 65 billion a year on its military. China's enhanced military prowess will lead, as is inevitable, to an assertion of its interests more forcefully, more often than not, adversely affecting Indian interests. Srikanth Kondapalli underlines the measures that are involved in the PLA modernisation drive "streamlining and reorganising of its force structures, raising elite troops, restructuring of command and control mechanisms, restoration of the rank system and grades, emphasis on professional military education, revamping curriculum and upgrading the defence technological capabilities of the personnel." Kondapalli suggests that these measures "are meant to enhance military capabilities of China in order to overcome the perceived challenges of the state and also make China a great power."

India might not be the focus of China's military modernisation drive but this does not prevent China from deploying its assets against India if the situation demands in the future. Kondapalli underscores the increasing asymmetries between India and China, with China enjoying, "overwhelming military superiority given its higher missile inventory, arms imports and ability to spend more on acquiring advanced platforms."

More troubling, perhaps, from India's perspective is the recent evolution in China's defence strategy towards "local war under informationised conditions" with a focus on conflicts based on unresolved territorial disputes. India remains one of the only two states with which China has not resolved its territorial disputes. Kondapalli also points out the security challenges emanating for India from Chinese efforts at "border consolidation and domination efforts and improvements in military logistics in Tibet" as well as initiating "a program of selling advanced weapons" to states in India's neighbourhood. Overall, Kondapalli suggests that while China's military modernisation programme is not directed specifically at India, it has resulted in a situation where India finds itself strategically encircled.

China's Foreign Policy Agenda

Even a cursory look at global events over the last few years would reveal the growing Chinese role far and wide. China's expanding use of its soft power is evident from its resource diplomacy and the way it is attracting new partners in the developing world.[32] Asia-Pacific, of course, remains the region of prime importance where the existing dominant power and the rising power continue to jostle for influence with some long-term consequences. However, across the globe from Middle East to Africa to Latin America, China is making its presence felt. The second section of the volume examines Chinese foreign policy in the Asia-Pacific, vis-à-vis the US and in the service of its economic interests. The aim here is to examine those issues that directly impinge on Indian foreign policy. China's growing profile in the Asia-Pacific, the shifting power dynamic between the US and China, and China's global hunt for resources have a direct bearing on the trajectory of Indian foreign policy and therefore the focus of this section is on these three specific areas. Overall, this section looks at the broader foreign policy agenda of China as it has been shaping up over the last decade and its implications for India.

The fifth chapter examines the evolution in China's policy towards the Asia-Pacific over the last decade. It examines how far China has come in establishing its predominance in the region and draws out implications for India's role in the Asia-Pacific region. The region where China's rise has already started engendering appreciable changes is the Asia-Pacific and the larger Indian Ocean region. As Ashok Kapur argues in his chapter, it is China's power and influence since the 1990s that has been shaping "the strategic environment of Asia-Pacific as well as the Indian Ocean region; and China's neighbours and

---

[32] For a detailed explication of China's use of its soft power, see Joshua Kurlantzick, *Charm Offensive: How China's Soft Power is Transforming the World* (New Haven: Yale University Press, 2008).

major powers are tied to China's actions." China, according to Kapur, is not merely an economic magnet and provider of diplomatic and military support for its neighbours but "it is also a point of opposition among its rivals who fear that China's rise may not remain peaceful as it competes(or completes?) its military modernisation."

A formal balance of power does not exist in Asia-Pacific due to the constant flux in the region and the role of either China or the US as a balancer or as a power centre does not have widespread acceptance, and this allows other states some room to manoeuvre with China and the US. Kapur underlines a unique diplomatic dialectic between China and its neighbours, whereby China's method of using strategic triangles and united fronts to further its strategic agenda is now being adopted by China's neighbours and rivals vis-à-vis China. Kapur calls upon Indian practitioners to "discover the importance of triangular diplomacy and statecraft" if India is to catch up with China in so far as its regional profile is concerned. Unlike India that tends to rely on bilateral diplomacy to secure China's restraint without much success, China's neighbours in the Far East "have relied on the formation of anti-China fronts which have induced Beijing to negotiate without basis."

The sixth chapter focuses on the power transition between the rising power, China, trying to assert itself, even as the established power, the US, tries to maintain the status-quo and draws out the implications of the US-China relationship for India in the coming years. Upon assuming office, the Obama administration had famously declared that America's relationship with China is the most important one in the world and the air was thick with talks of an emerging G-2, a global condominium of Washington and Beijing, that was expected to "manage" global affairs. Though this initial optimism about Sino-US ties soon subsided under the pressure of strategic realities, the bilateral relationship between the US and China is extremely significant, not only for the two states, but for others as well and India is no exception. China seems to be making a concerted attempt to challenge America's predominant position in East Asia because as Arthur Waldron points out "the US is for China...the most worrying potential source of instability from abroad" even as China recognises that the US can also be an enabler of Chinese strategic goals, if properly manipulated. The US, on the other hand, views China as an ideal partner and this "expectation of friendship has been an enduring aspect of American foreign policy." China does not want to be a stakeholder in the international system as presently constituted, suggests Waldron, but it wants to create "a set of institutions and constituencies that will assure the survival of her regime." This involves setting up China-specific orders in politics, economics and security, and includes within it "all of her neighbouring countries, with Russia, India and Japan being, in her view, potential problems."

Waldron argues that Beijing's present policy trajectory vis-à-vis New Delhi will be counter-productive as attempts by China to intimidate and immobilise India will only lead to a more pro-active diplomatic and military response from India.

The seventh chapter examines China's hunt for resources all across the globe in support of its rapidly rising economy. It focuses on China's growing engagement with states in Africa, Middle East and Latin America, and draws out implications of this resource diplomacy for India's own policy towards these regions. In the last few years, China's voracious appetite for energy and other resources to maintain its high rates of economic growth has been one of the principal drivers of its foreign policy. This is not only changing the world energy markets but also poses a challenge to countries such as India that are also hungry for resources to sustain their own economic momentum. D.S. Rajan, in his chapter, suggests that New Delhi faces a tough challenge "against the background of its simultaneous rise along with China, a nation conducting an aggressive resource hunt backed by its active diplomacy throughout the world." As Sino-Indian competition over energy resources emerge, China seems far ahead of India. Rajan argues that this is primarily due to "the comparative inability of the Indian government vis-à-vis China in providing finances to the Indian companies to tap overseas energy markets." Moreover, Chinese attitude towards India in so far as energy relations are concerned, remain opportunistic with selective co-operation and no hesitation in edging India out if the situation so requires. India has started responding to the Chinese challenge by "projecting its own power in the region, through naval deployments and maritime diplomacy" even as its engagements with other regions of the world such as the Middle East, Africa, Central Asia, and Latin America are still at a nascent stage.

China's India Policy

Nothing will shape Indian foreign policy more than the rise of China in the coming years. Both are rising powers with a sense of their own importance in the region and beyond. Both also have some fundamental conflicting interests which are becoming more prominent by the day. The final section of the book focuses on the three main aspects of China's India policy: territorial problems between the two with a special focus on the role of Tibet and China's growing engagement in India's own background, South Asia. Overall, this section looks at the evolving policy of China towards India as both states rise in the global inter-state hierarchy and draws some conclusions about the future trajectory of Sino-Indian ties.

The eighth chapter is a detailed examination of the territorial disputes that continue to haunt Sino-Indian ties. It focuses on the claims of the two sides and the present status of the negotiations. It draws some conclusions about the effectiveness or the lack of it in so far as the Indian negotiating strategy in dealing with China is concerned as well as the factors responsible for the lack of movement on this front. As David Scott underlines, the territorial disputes between China and India continue to haunt Sino-Indian ties, with rising friction apparent in the last couple of years. He argues that these territorial disputes between India and China involve "classical geopolitics" entwined with "critical geopolitics", and their particular sense of respective "position" therein that India and China hold for themselves and for each other. Though each side argues from history, Scott suggests that in reality, the evidence from history is ambiguous and inconclusive for both sides' territorial claims. Even as the resolution of the issue seems feasible enough from the outside in terms of simple enough territorial trade offs between Arunachal Pradesh and Aksai Chin, it gets complicated by smaller issues surrounding Tawang, and wider issues surrounding Tibet, and indeed the whole balance of power in Asia between India and China.

The ninth chapter is a detailed examination of the role that the issue of Tibet has played in shaping up the Sino-Indian ties. It focuses on the historical dimension as well as the present trajectory of this dispute, and assesses if Tibet remains as important in the contemporary context as it used to be and draws some conclusions about the Chinese strategy vis-à-vis Tibet and its implications for India. Elliot Sperling argues that Tibet has played a role in Sino-Indian politics in two broad ways. One is related to India's ambiguous approach to Tibet's status, which started causing friction early on. The other relates to the still unsettled boundary question which, in addition to the conflicting territorial claims that are at its core, still has China refusing to formally recognise Sikkim as a part of India, even though China asserts no claim to it. These two aspects of Sino-Indian relations are related and still very much in play as China becomes a rising power. The question of Tibet's status influences one's approach to the border question, since acceptance of Tibet's 1914 agreement to the McMahon Line is inherently rooted in recognition of the competence of the Tibetan government to enter into international agreements. With the Dalai Lama presently presiding over a government-in-exile in Dharamsala (albeit one not recognised as such by India) the issue of status continues to interject itself into Sino-Indian relations even though India accepts Tibet as a part of the People's Republic of China. It will probably continue to do so until the passing of the present Dalai Lama. As for the frontiers, China asserts its authority with increasingly stronger formulations of its historical sovereignty over Tibet. In its most recent iteration, China now insists on unbroken sovereignty over Tibet and the frontiers it claims "since human activity began" on the Tibetan Plateau. This attitude can only signify increasing difficulty in resolving the frontier issue and increasing tension over the unresolved border issue, something that India must take into consideration as China's presence in global affairs and international economic matters becomes more consequential.

The final chapter examines the growing role of China in South Asia over the last several years. China is today more deeply involved in South Asia than it has ever been. I examine the motivations behind China's growing involvement in the region and its implications for India. As India rises in the global inter-state hierarchy, there are growing tensions between India's purported role on the world stage and demands of the challenges it faces in its own neighbourhood. South Asia is a difficult neighbourhood and India's strategic periphery continues to witness continuous turmoil and uncertainty. The instability in Pakistan, Afghanistan, Bangladesh, Nepal, Sri Lanka and Myanmar is a major inhibiting factor for India to realise its dream of becoming a major global player. India is surrounded by several weak states that view New Delhi's hegemonic status in the region with suspicion. The conundrum India faces is that – while it is seen as unresponsive to the concerns of its neighbours – any diplomatic aggressiveness on its part is also viewed with suspicion and often resentment. The structural position of India in the region makes it highly likely that Indian predominance will continue to be resented by its smaller neighbours even as instability nearby continues to have the potential of upsetting its own delicate political balance. However, a policy of "splendid isolation" is not an option and India's desire to emerge as a major global player will remain just that, a desire, unless it engages its immediate neighbourhood more meaningfully and emerges as a net provider of regional peace and stability. As I suggest in the chapter, the inability of India to assume a leadership role in its neighbourhood has been exploited by China that has made a concerted attempt over the last few years to fill the void. For a long time, only Pakistan, among India's neighbours, used China to further its strategic agenda vis-à-vis India. China-Pakistan collusion on the nuclear issue was probably the high point of this relationship. However, increasingly most of India's neighbours have made an attempt to use China as an extra-regional power in order to prevent India from asserting its regional supremacy. This strategy to use China to counterbalance India has been followed by Nepal, Bangladesh and Sri Lanka to varying degrees. And China has only been too willing to be a part of this regional manoeuvring as it not only enhances China's influence in South Asia but also keeps India bogged down in South Asian affairs, thereby preventing its emergence from the straightjacket of a mere "South Asia power" to a major global player, something that India has long desired.

Sino-Indian ties are complex and multilayered. As the contributors to this volume underline, the future trajectory of this very important relationship remains difficult to decipher. Yet as both China and India continue their ascent in global inter-state hierarchy, it will be imperative for them to build on the co-operative elements of their relationship. As of now, India is finding it difficult to cope with a rising China on various fronts. A perception is gathering momentum in India that China is becoming very aggressive in the pursuit of what it regards as its vital interests. As a result, strains in Sino-Indian ties are already visible. Rhetoric about Asian solidarity notwithstanding, the Sino-Indian bilateral relationship is becoming increasingly contentious and the trust deficit seems to be widening. As outlined in this volume, the reasons for this growing divergence are manifold and exist at all levels: structural, domestic political and individual. It is now for the Indian policy-makers to craft a policy response that, while acknowledging significant differences between the two Asian giants, is able to harness co-operative synergies between the two. If this volume is able to provoke an honest discussion on the contemporary state of Sino-Indian relationship, it would have served its purpose.

Part I

Domestic Developments in China

2

China's Economic Rise

From Hindi-Chini *Bhai-Bhai* to Hindi-Chini Buy-Buy?

Bibek Debroy

The Food, Fuel and Financial Crises

In the January 2009 update of *World Economic Outlook*, the International Monetary Fund (IMF) stated,

> Global growth in 2009 is expected to fall to ½ per cent when measured in terms of Purchasing Power Parity (PPP), and to turn negative when measured in terms of market exchange rates...Helped by continued efforts to ease credit strains as well as expansionary fiscal and monetary policies, the global economy is projected to experience a gradual recovery in 2010, with growth picking up to 3 per cent. However, the outlook is highly uncertain, and the timing and pace of the recovery depend critically on strong policy actions...The continuation of the financial crisis, as policies failed to dispel uncertainty, has caused asset values to fall sharply across advanced and emerging economies, decreasing household wealth and thereby putting downward pressure on consumer demand. In addition, the associated high level of uncertainty has prompted households and businesses to postpone expenditures, reducing demand for consumer and capital goods. At the same time, widespread disruptions in credit are constraining household spending and curtailing production and trade....Stronger economic frameworks in many emerging economies have provided more room for policy support to growth than in the past, helping to cushion the impact of this unprecedented external shock.[1]

---

[1] *World Economic Outlook Update, Global Economic Slump Challenges Policies,* International Monetary Fund, 28 January 2009, http://www.imf.org/external/pubs/ft/weo/2009/update/01/index.htm.

The decoupling argument has been done to death. In a long-term and secular sense, growth in emerging Asia (including China and India) is somewhat de-linked from secular growth in developed countries. However, that does not mean cyclical growth fluctuations in the developed world do not impact growth in emerging Asia. Nor does it mean that the real sector is decoupled from the financial sector crises. Accordingly, IMF's growth forecasts for 2009 and 2010 can be contrasted with the actual numbers for 2007 and 2008. For China, the figures are 13.0 per cent (2007), 9.0 per cent (2008), 6.7 per cent (2009) and 8.0 per cent (2010). For India, the figures are 9.3 per cent (2007), 7.3 per cent (2008), 5.1 per cent (2009) and 6.5 per cent (2010).[2] These may seem like respectable figures compared to what is happening in the rest of the world and may substantiate the quote about "stronger economic frameworks" with endogenous sources of growth based on domestic consumption and investments. To this, "strong economic frameworks" can be added limiting exposure to tainted assets by banks and financial institutions and large foreign exchange reserves. For instance, before the financial crisis broke in September 2008, Chinese reserves were 50 per cent of GDP and the figure for India was 25 per cent. However, given the growth expectations within China and India and their consequent implications for employment generation, these numbers represent significant downturns.[3] Confronted with the downturn, both China and India have eased monetary policy, India more than China.[4] In addition, both China and India have imparted additional fiscal stimuli, China more than

---

[2] Ibid.

[3] Though it does not give specific numbers for China or India, *Global Employment Trends*, ILO, January 2009, flags these employment concerns, http://www.ilo.org/wcmsp5/groups/public/-dgreports/-dcomm/documents/publication/wcms_101461.pdf. However, Responding to the Economic Crisis – Coherent Policies for Growth, Employment and Decent Work in Asia and Pacific, The fallout in Asia: Assessing labour market impacts and national policy responses to the global financial crisis, ILO, February 2009, http://www.ilo.org/wcmsp5/groups/public/-asia/-ro-bangkok/documents/meetingdocument/wcms_101730.pdf has some tentative numbers, with reverse migration flagged for both China and India. Of the estimated 130 million internal migrants in China, 20 million were estimated to have lost their original jobs. It is difficult to segregate job losses in export sectors from job losses that occurred due to industrial restructuring. For India, in addition to reverse external migration (particularly pronounced in Kerala), "workers in sectors with high exposure to the global market such as civil aviation, textiles, leather, gems, and jewellery, which employ millions of women workers, have already faced job cuts." There are issues of unemployment insurance and social security for workers who are effectively in the unorganised sector and the rural sector's capability to handle reverse migration from export-oriented urban areas. In talking about possible losses, it is necessary to distinguish between existing jobs that are lost and the counter-factual of employment that would otherwise have been created being lost.

[4] *Global Economic Policies and Prospects*, Note prepared for the G-20 meeting in London, March 2009, IMF, http://www.imf.org/external/np/g20/pdf/031909a.pdf

India, which is understandable because the fiscal balance in China is more robust. IMF estimates this additional fiscal stimulus for China at 0.4 per cent in 2008 and 3.2 per cent in 2009. For India, the figure is 0.6 per cent in both years.[5] There are, of course, legitimate concerns about what these fiscal stimuli will be used for and the capacity of the administrative system to deliver.

In a generic sense, the showdown can have different types of effects on any country. First, exports, foreign investments (direct and portfolio) and Official Development Assistance (ODA) flows suffer, reflected in slower growth. This is compounded by the erection of protectionist barriers. Second, this means poverty-reduction effects of growth also suffer. The East Asian experience in 1997–98 shows that the bouncing back varies from country to country. Korea, Thailand and Malaysia recovered faster than Indonesia did. Third, government revenue is adversely affected, limiting the fiscal space available to governments. Fourth, there are differential spatial effects, since those who are more integrated and connected with global and national markets suffer more. For example, after the Asian financial crisis, rural poor in Indonesia suffered less than the urban poor, but the rural poor in Thailand suffered more than the rural poor in Indonesia, because the rural poor in Thailand were more integrated with the urban markets.[6] Fifth, the poor are more vulnerable to shocks in the sense that if the shocks cross a threshold, there are long-lasting effects on poverty, even after the economy recovers, since debt increase, productive assets like livestock and land are sold and children are taken out of school.[7] Nutrition levels also tend to suffer. The simple point is that it is somewhat difficult to generalise, since the cushioning is a function of the public institutions and policy-making in individual countries.

The background is poverty reduction effects of growth in China and India and progress made towards the Millennium Development Goals (MDGs).[8] Until recently, the internationally accepted poverty line used to be US $ 1 per day, at constant PPP prices. PPP transformations typically increase incomes in developing countries and lower them in developed countries, since prices are lower in the former. Recently, the World Bank has recalibrated the poverty

---

[5] Ibid.

[6] See, Martin Ravallion, "Bailing out the World's Poorest," *Policy Research Working Paper*, No. 4763, World Bank, October 2008, http://www-wds.worldbank.org/external/default/WDSContentServer/IW3P/IB/2008/10/29/000158349_20081029084618/Rendered/PDF/WPS4763.pdf

[7] Ibid.

[8] The MDGs are not simply 8 goals, but there is an entire system, with 21 targets and 59 indicators. The number of targets and indicators has increased over time.

line to US $ 1.25 per day, because prices were being under-estimated in several developing countries. Following the recalibration, the percentage of people below the poverty line is 16.78 per cent in East Asia and the Pacific and 40.34 per cent in South Asia.[9] Notwithstanding China's success in reducing poverty, head-count ratios are still in the 20 per cent-plus range in rural China, and the 40 per cent-plus range in rural India (urban India is close at 36.16 per cent). Largely because of growth in China and India, the developing countries, as a group, are on track to attain the poverty reduction goal of the MDGs.[10] Even more interesting is the point made about an emerging middle class in China and India, with an exploding middle class in China between 1990 and 2005 and a similar explosion is about to occur in India by 2025.[11] This is not to deny significant intra-country differences in large and heterogeneous countries like China and India. For the period 2002–04, FAO estimated under-nourishment in the total population as 20 per cent for India and 9 per cent for China.[12] The impact on poverty reduction for China and India isn't dependent only on the financial crisis, but is also influenced by the food and fuel crises that precedes it, since food typically accounts for a disproportionately large share in the consumption baskets of the poor.

This introductory section of the chapter can be concluded with a few quick words about the G-20 and the London Summit. There are no formal criteria for G-20 membership, with the exception of G-7 and European Union (EU). However, both China and India are members. Though G-20 is supposed to be a meeting of finance ministers and central bank governors, heads of government met in Washington in November 2008 and the London meeting on 2nd April was also a leaders' summit. G-20 has no formal institutional backing. Since it has no institutional legitimacy, how has it become the main forum for discussing global issues and will it continue to do so if summits are not led by

[9] http://iresearch.worldbank.org/PovcalNet/povDuplic.html. Data are for 2005. Also see, "The developing world is poorer than we thought, but no less successful in the fight against poverty", Shaohua Chen and Martin Ravallion, *Policy Research Working Paper*, World Bank, http://econ.worldbank.org/docsearch

[10] "This picture is somewhat masked by the influence of large and better-performing developing countries, such as China and India, on aggregates," World Bank, *Global Monitoring Report 2008: MDGs and the Environment, http://web.worldbank.org/WBSITE/EXTERNAL/EXTDEC/EXTGLOBALMONITOR/EXTGLOMONREP2008/0,,menuPK:4738069~pagePK:64168427~piPK:64168435~theSitePK:4738057,00.html*

[11] Surjit S. Bhalla, *Second Among Equals: The Middle Class Kingdoms of India and China*, forthcoming, Institute for International Economics, Washington. There are issues about defining the middle class, but we can ignore those for present purposes.

[12] http://www.fao.org/es/ess/faostat/foodsecurity/Files/PrevalenceUndernourishment_en.xls

USA or UK? Will it continue to have relevance once the global downturn is over? Should G-20 replace G-8 and should that list of 12 additional countries be pruned to make the forum more effective? If such a pruning were ever to take place, China and India would certainly continue to be part of that pruned core. There is no need to recap what G-20 has accomplished. However, a few points need flagging. First, IMF reform remains high on both the Chinese and Indian agenda. Second, measures on protectionism remain high on the Indian agenda.

> For this reason, G20 leaders signed a pledge on 15 November 2008, to avoid protectionist measures. However, since then, several countries, including 17 of the G20, have implemented 47 measures whose effect is to restrict trade at the expense of other countries. While the trend is of concern, to date, these measures have probably had only marginal effects on trade.[13]

Third, China floated the idea of a new international reserve currency, as an alternative to the US dollar, an issue not addressed in the London summit. Fourth, there is continued Chinese resistance to action against tax havens.

Having said this, the food, fuel and financial crises can be interpreted as a movement away from what was the earlier growth trajectory in China and India. Eventually, that growth trajectory will resume, though the global environment might be different and the governance of international organisations might also change. The rest of the chapter thus focuses on those growth trajectories, reforms and the Indian reactions to Chinese reforms and growth experiences.

Indian Reforms and Growth

Before turning to China, it is useful to have a brief sketch of Indian economic reforms and the growth story. One should begin by asking what one means by economic reforms. Sometimes expressions like first generation and second generation are also used, suggesting that the first generation reforms were introduced in the first post-1991 flush and that the second generation is what awaits us now. Unfortunately, the expressions first generation and second generation are never very precisely defined. However, two overlapping interpretations are possible. First, first generation refers to reforms that concern

---

[13] Elisa Gamberoni and Richard Newfarmer, "Trade protection: Incipient but worrisome trends," 4th March 2009, http://voxeu.org/index.php?q=node/3183

the external sector – elimination of Quantitative Restrictions (QRs) on exports, rationalisation and elimination of export subsidies and their replacement by a system of export incentives, reduction in import duties, a market-determined exchange rate with a convertible rupee, a liberal policy on foreign institutional investments and opening up to Foreign Direct Investments (FDI). On each of these, reforms have already been introduced, or there is a time frame for their further introduction, although external sector reforms are also linked to negotiations, multilateral, regional or bilateral. They cannot always be introduced unilaterally. In contrast, second generation reforms concern the domestic economy, although a neat watertight compartmentalisation between the domestic and the external is not always possible. Understandably, political, economic considerations and vested interests are stronger in domestic economic reforms, in comparison to the external. Second, one can also interpret the first generation as reforms that concerned and were under the purview primarily of the centre, or the union government. In contrast, in a federal setup, second generation concerns reforms that have to be introduced at the state government level.[14] Thanks to the first generation having been implemented, the focus of policy change has thus shifted from the centre to the states. The cutting and the blunting edge of reforms thus lies at the level of the states and different states have reacted differently to liberalisation. What is also of note is that most product market policies are with the centre, while most factor market (labour, land) policies are with the states.

Moving on to the second generation, beyond the taxonomy, there will be a reasonable degree of consensus about what the major pending reform areas are, the so-called agenda. At best, depending on one's perspective, there may be disagreement about the priorities. The following is a list of this core reform agenda:

(1) Reforms in the rural sector – Rural/urban has a census definition and according to the 2001 census, 72.2 per cent of India's population lives in the rural areas. This is equated with earning a living from agriculture, but that is not quite true. Hence, there is an agricultural reform agenda and there is a rural reform agenda that goes beyond agriculture. Within the agriculture set, there are issues like allowing corporate sector involvement in agriculture, removal of government imposed restrictions on production, marketing and distribution, refocus of public expenditure away from input subsidies to infrastructure

---

[14] The Seventh Schedule to the Indian Constitution sets out a union list, a state list and a concurrent list.

and extension services, dis-intermediation of distribution chains, forward markets, contract farming, revamping credit and insurance, and freeing up of land markets. All these are linked to encouraging commercialisation and diversification. There is also an issue of encouraging off-farm employment and this is where rural sector reforms kick in, through provision of physical and social infrastructure. Out of India's 600,000 villages, there are around 100,000 where both are hardly present.

(2) Taxation reforms – These have both a direct and an indirect tax component, and the latter includes import duties. Barring agriculture, which is in a category of its own, the timeline for reduction in tariffs on industrial or manufactured products, is reasonably clear. The broad shape of indirect tax reform is clear and has been set out. There should be a combined Goods and Service Tax (GST), with service sector taxation integrated into a Value Added Tax (VAT) framework instead of being a tax on turnover. This will be accompanied by a withdrawal of all other taxes like central excise, central sales tax, octroi, state-level sales tax, entry tax, stamp duties, transportation taxes, and so on. All that has happened now is a limited VAT, in the sense of unification of state-level sales tax, and the time frame for introduction of GST is 2011 onwards. GST is also required to make the export incentive system World Trade Organization (WTO)-compatible, introduce appropriate countervailing duties and allow better defence against anti-subsidy and anti-dumping investigations. Unfortunately, the mindset of allowing discretions and exemptions get in the way of standardisation and harmonisation. That apart, there is an even more serious issue of lack of financial devolution within the states, down to urban local bodies and *panchayat*s. In its absence, it becomes impossible to eliminate local taxes. There is a parallel exemption issue for direct taxes, both for personal income taxes and corporate taxation.

(3) Public expenditure reforms – This has a centre, state and even local body aspect. Although the importance of each element is a function of the level of government that one has in mind, a substantial chunk of public expenditure is on interest payments, wages and salaries, and pensions. In the short run, these expenditures are inflexible, although in the long run, one can borrow less, employ fewer people and enter into new pension arrangements with new entrants into the civil service. Compared to a work force of 385 million (the labour force is slightly larger at 420 million[15]), 18.5 million people work for

---

[15] These are 2004–05 figures from *Economic Survey 2007–08,* Department of Economic Affairs, Ministry of Finance, Government of India.

the government, including 3.5 million who work for the central government and 6 million who work for the public sector. If one includes those who work for quasi-government bodies, the number increases to around 30 million. On reforming civil services in India, several recommendations have been made. The issues of downsizing, identifying surplus manpower, retraining, Voluntary Retirement Schemes (VRS), contractual appointments, lateral entry and evaluation and vertical mobility keep recurring and the reform agenda is also known. In addition to borrowing and expenditure on the administrative machinery of the government, public expenditure also includes public services. These are not necessarily in areas where market failure exists, so that the classic public good argument has doubtful validity nor can a merit good argument be used, since subsidies are never targeted. That apart, expenditure is never linked to tangible improvement in outcomes and administrative costs of delivery are extremely high. This is the right place to mention why this paper will not list out two commonly cited issues in the core reform agenda – budgetary deficits and infrastructure. The former is indeed important and there is a Fiscal Responsibility and Budget Management Act (FRBM). However, deficits (fiscal or revenue) are symptoms rather than the disease and in the absence of revenue (tax and non-tax) and expenditure reforms, talking about deficit reduction is neither here nor there. The second commonly cited reform area that will not be listed separately is infrastructure, although there are estimates that if all infrastructure is available efficiently, the increment to GDP growth will be of the order of 1.5 per cent. There are different kinds of infrastructure and what works for one kind of infrastructure, may not work for others. Some parts of infrastructure are central government subjects, while others are state or even local body subjects. However, the reason for not listing infrastructure separately is a different one. In the absence of resolving the subsidy issue and appropriate user charges, the infrastructure problem will remain. That too, is a symptom rather than a disease.

(4) Law reforms – This category subsumes several different elements – statutory law reform, faster speed of dispute resolution and reforms of administrative law, so that procedural costs are eased. Within statutory law reform, there are issues of rationalisation and harmonisation across statutes that have been enacted at various points in time, eliminating old laws that serve no purpose, junking unnecessary state intervention in many of these statutes and even introducing new legislation where none exists. On faster dispute resolution, a new Arbitration Act has been in place since 1996, but conciliation/mediation is still not credible. Within the court system, there

is an estimated backlog of 28 million cases stuck in courts, not including those that are stuck in quasi-judicial forums. On the third strand of law reform, beyond civil service reform, the broader agenda of administrative law reform involves two kinds of relationships that can overlap – dealings between the citizen and the government and dealings between an enterprise and the government. The latter can again be divided into three phases of an enterprise's existence – entry, functioning and exit. The former involves birth certificates, death certificates, land titles, assorted requirements of establishing one's own identity and issues connected with accessing public services. For both the citizen and the entrepreneur, the years since 1991 have witnessed the exertion of countervailing pressure, documenting corruption and inadequate delivery of services, even if this countervailing pressure tends to be located in certain geographical parts of the country. Partly as a result of such pressure, a central Right to Information Act (RTI) has now been passed. Two commonly cited items are again not being listed in this paper in the core reform agenda and an explanation is again in order. First, there is no separate listing of labour law reform, because that has been subsumed in this heading of law reform. Second, there is no separate listing of governance as a heading, even though that is a buzzword. While governance means different things to different people, this deliberate exclusion is because most items included in governance, unless one has in mind electoral processes, civil rights and a free press, have already been included elsewhere.

While there is no disagreement about these reform areas being important, why have the required reforms not been implemented? This is because of the political economy, not because these areas are unimportant, but because there is lack of consensus. Moreover, if one tracks the debate and distils out where there is lack of consensus, the debate boils down to one simple issue, regardless of the reform area. There is a lack of consensus about the role of the government and core governance areas. The core governance areas for any state ought to be ensuring law and order, an efficient dispute resolution mechanism and intervention in some areas of physical and social infrastructure, sometimes through financing rather than through actual provisioning. It is because the Indian state is asked to do many more things that these four core reform agendas continually get stuck.

Notwithstanding this lackadaisical movement on most domestic reforms, barring the financial sector, there is no dearth of reports that are bullish about Indian growth prospects, some external, others internal or endogenous. Some of these are not concerned with the overall economy, but concentrate instead on segments like outsourcing and software exports.[16] Since reforms are equated with post-1991 developments, most external projections assume that 6 to 6.5 per cent is the base-line rate of growth now. The key question is whether there has been another structural break in 2003–04, with a base-line trend growth of 8.5 per cent or thereabouts. There are several reasons for such a belief. First, the savings rate has increased and so has the investment rate, leading to convergence between East Asian (and Chinese) investment rates and those in India. The earlier compartmentalisation assumed between consumption-led growth in India and investment-led growth in China is no longer true. Second, the Incremental Capital/Output Ratio (ICOR) is now around 4, which suggests that real growth of 9 per cent is eminently doable. There is yet another change that is sometimes ignored, at least in this context. The share of agriculture and allied activities in GDP is declining and that of services is increasing. What is pertinent is that the service sector tends to have a lower ICOR. That apart, if agriculture is growing relatively slowly and services is growing relatively fast, the sectoral shift from agriculture to services itself jacks up GDP growth as a statistical inevitability. Third, the effect of export growth on GDP growth is perhaps not always explicitly recognised. Fourth, while the demographic dividend and India's demographic transition is recognised, its impact on GDP growth is not always factored in, the Brazil-Russia-India-China (BRIC) report being an exception. Growth projections are thus based on capital inputs, ignoring the labour component and the Indian labour force is expected to grow at just below 2.5 per cent a year between now and 2020. This labour contribution should itself add a clear percentage point to GDP growth, problems of education, skills and morbidity notwithstanding. Fifth, the population is young, with a median age of 24. This does things to entrepreneurship that we imperfectly understand. One should not therefore be surprised if GDP growth turns out to be something like 9 per cent between 2010 and 2015 and accelerates to 10 per cent between 2015 and 2020, ignoring the effect of exchange rate changes.

Chinese Reforms and Growth

However, the Indian reform and growth story gets conditioned by what China has been able to achieve. Table 2.1 illustrates the comparison across

---

[16] Thomas Friedman's *The World is Flat: A Brief History of the Twenty-first Century,* 2005, is an example.

Table 2.1 *The China-India Comparison*

	China	India
PPP GDP, US $ billion, IMF, 2007[17]	7035	299
PPP per capita GDP, US $, IMF, 2008	5943	2787
Human Development Index (HDI), UNDP, 2008	0.781	0.609
Life expectancy at birth, years, UNDP, 2008	72.7	64.1
Adult literacy rate, UNDP, 2008	93.0%	65.2%
Combined enrolment ratio, UNDP, 2008	68.7%	61.0%
Population below US $ 1.25 a day poverty line, UNDP, 2008	13.4%	41.6%
Global Hunger Index, IFPRI, 2008	7.1	23.7
Under-5 mortality rate, IFPRI, 2008	2.4%	7.6%
Under-nourishment in population, IFPRI, 2008	12%	20%
Doing Business Rank, World Bank, 2009	83rd	122nd
Global Competitiveness Index Rank, World Economic Forum, 2008	30th	50th
Index of Economic Freedom score, Heritage Foundation and Wall Street Journal, 2009	53.2	54.4
Corruption Perception Index score, Transparency International, 2008	3.6	3.4

assorted yardsticks, making the point that regardless of how India may have performed post-1991 in absolute terms, in the relative comparison, India falls behind. Several more variables can be added to those included in Table 2.1, but they all reinforce the same general picture. Barring some freedom and governance-type indicators, China is far ahead of India, including virtually every economic indicator.

First, there are understandable questions about the quality of Chinese statistics.[18] However, even when attempts have been made to correct data, they, at best, scale down Chinese achievements a bit. Subject to subjectivity in all such corrections, even with corrections, the Chinese track record remains impressive. Second, barring some social sector indicators, the Chinese and Indian base lines were roughly similar in the second half of the 1970s. At least a comparison was possible in 1978–79, which is when China started the economic reforms. Since then, China and India are clearly no longer in the same league. Third, for a while, there were reactions

---

[17] As was mentioned in Section 1, the PPP estimates have been recalibrated subsequently.

[18] This should not be taken to mean that there are no questions about the quality of Indian statistics.

in India that China had started economic reforms in 1978–79, while India initiated reforms in 1991.[19] China, therefore, had a head start of almost 15 years and one ought to compare China in the second half of the 1980s, not with India in the second half of the 1990s, but with India post-2006 or thereabouts.[20]

Reforms in China date back to 1978, with a switch from a centrally planned system to a more market-driven one, the accepted phrase being one of "socialism with Chinese characteristics" (*Juyou Zhongguo tese de shehuizhuyi*). These reforms started at the 3rd Plenary Session of the 11th Central Committee of the Communist Party of China (CPC) in December, 1978 and were subsequently reconfirmed at the 3rd Plenary Session of the 12th Central Committee of the CPC in October, 1984 and the 14th National Congress of the CPC in October, 1992.[21] These are also reforms identified with Deng Xiaoping. Specifically, these reforms decentralised control over State-Owned Enterprises (SOEs) by increasing the authority of local authorities and plant managers, privatised SOEs, dismantled the rural commune system and replaced it with a household responsibility system, increased use of material incentives, allowed small-scale enterprise in services and light manufacturing, opened up to foreign trade and investment and improved economic infrastructure.

Within the labour market, the metaphor for reforms was an end to the "iron rice bowl" (*tie fan wan*) system. A porcelain or clay rice bowl breaks when it is dropped, thus rendering it useless. In contrast, when an iron rice bowl is dropped, it does not break and can be used repeatedly, the metaphor being that an employee is not punished despite repeated mistakes. The iron rice bowl system meant guaranteed job security and steady income and benefit flows, an implementation of "from each according to his ability and to each according to his needs" principle. In the urban segment, this led to perverse incentives and there was an estimated over-manning of between 20 and 30 per cent in SOEs. However, in the rural segment, many benefits associated with the "iron rice bowl" were excluded and migration was

---

[19] This is a simplification. There were pre-1991 reforms in India too but they are not as systematic and comprehensive as those that have occurred since 1991.

[20] While still not comparable, GDP growth rates picked up in India from 2003–04, a fact already mentioned. Again, though not comparable with Chinese figures, FDI inflows began to pick up in India from 2006–07.

[21] In 1997, the 15th National Congress of the CPC effectively sanctioned privatisation of SOEs.

tightly controlled through the household registration system (*hukou*). This created perverse incentives of a different kind and 30 per cent of the rural labour force was estimated to be surplus and prevented from playing a role in the industrialisation process. The point to note is that the labour market reforms must also be understood against the backdrop of this rural/urban segmentation, instead of as an unified whole that cuts across an integrated labour market. There were bits of urban labour market reform. There were bits of rural labour market reform. Moreover, in the process, as the *hukou* system was loosened, but not completely relaxed, large segments of migrant populations were left dangling. In urban areas, with a focus on SOEs, the major milestones are the following: First, grant SOEs autonomy in determining wages, with incentives like bonuses and over-time thrown in, implemented through a labour contract system, thus negating the earlier principle of lifetime guaranteed employment. This also led to an increase in inter-enterprise wage differentials. Second, allow SOEs to be converted into joint stock companies, with workers acquiring shares and becoming stakeholders. Third, allow redundant workers from SOEs to be retrenched, necessitating retraining and redeployment for such laid-off workers (*xiagang*). Unemployment in SOEs increased because of several reasons – competitive pressures, elimination of unwanted workers and competition that rural migrants brought into the urban labour market. Fourth, introduce a system of unemployment insurance. Unemployment insurance comes from three sources – enterprises of former employees, the government at the centre and local levels, and unemployment insurance fund. Fifth, introduce social security (medical insurance, disability insurance and pensions) reforms, since loss making and bankrupt enterprises were no longer in a position to fund guaranteed payments. If Article 70 of the National Labour Code of 1994–95 is taken as a yardstick, social security covers five heads – unemployment, pensions, sickness, industrial (workplace) injury and maternity. Sixth, as a fallout of the SOE reform, there was a switch in employment from SOEs to Township and Village Enterprises (TVEs). Subsequently, a new labour law was implemented from January, 2008. In contrast, in rural areas, the major milestones are the following: First, grant rural households autonomous decision-making rights by allowing collective and shareholder-based co-operative enterprises, enabling diversification away from classic agriculture. Second, loosen *hukou* and allow rural workers to work in urban enterprises. Third, and this is a point that sometimes does not receive adequate attention, encourage entrepreneurship in rural China.

Quite often, Indian reactions to Chinese reforms hinge around Chinese successes in introducing flexible labour markets. The following quote from a government document is symptomatic:[22]

> Indian labour market is characterised by a sharp dichotomy. A large number of establishments in the unorganised sector remain outside any regulation, while the organised sector has been regulated fairly stringently. It can be reasonably argued that the organised sector has provided too much of job security for too long, while the unorganised sector has provided too little to too many. Various studies indicate that Indian labour laws are highly protective of labour, and labour markets are relatively inflexible. These laws apply only to the organised sector. Consequently, these laws have restricted labour mobility, have led to capital-intensive methods in the organised sector and adversely affected the sector's long-run demand for labour. Labour being a subject in the concurrent list, state-level labour regulations are also an important determinant of industrial performance. Evidence suggests that states, which have enacted more pro-worker regulations, have lost out on industrial production in general. Perhaps there are lessons to be learnt from China in the area of labour reforms. China, with a history of extreme employment security, has drastically reformed its labour relations and created a new labour market, in which workers are highly mobile. Although there have been mass layoffs and open unemployment, high rates of industrial growth especially in the coastal regions helped their redeployment. In spite of hardship, workers in China seem to have benefited from wage growth, additional job creation and new opportunities for self employment.

However, the labour market is only part of the story. There are similar reactions to China's success in becoming a manufacturing hub, fuelled largely by FDI inflows, with better infrastructure and simplified procedures and indirect tax structures thrown in:

> The manufacturing sector in India, for all these reasons, grew annually only at an average of 6.3 per cent during 1991 to 2003 as against over 12 per cent in China. For instance, many studies argue that total taxes on manufactured goods are 25 to 30 per cent of the retail price in India, compared to 15 per cent in China. FDI inflow figures are 3.40 billion US dollars in 2001, $ 3.45 billion in 2002, $ 4.27 billion in 2004 and $ 7.5–8 billion in 2005, there being a gap between approvals and inflows. This is still a far cry from China's $ 53.51 billion in 2003. The average manufacturer in India loses 8.4 per cent a year in sales on account of power outages as opposed to less than 2 per cent in China and Brazil.[23]

[22] *Economic Survey 2005–06*, Department of Economic Affairs, Ministry of Finance, Chapter 10.
[23] *National Strategy for Manufacturing*, National Manufacturing Competitiveness Council, Government of India, 2006, http://nmcc.nic.in/pdf/strategy_paper_0306.pdf

Nor is this an argument about organised manufacturing alone. There are similar laudatory references to China's success in reforming SOEs and transforming agriculture and creating rural industrialisation,

> We need to learn from the Chinese model of rural business hubs that add value to agricultural produce within the rural area.[24]

Understandably, this appreciation also extends to social and physical infrastructure and China figures prominently in all benchmark comparisons, including government documents. The following quotes, all from India's 11th five-year plan document, are illustrative:[25]

> Life expectancy at birth has increased from approximately 32 years for both males and females in 1951 to 63.9 years for males and 66.9 years for females in 2001–06. Yet this is well below the life expectancy of around 80 years in industrialised countries and 72 years in China.
>
> The GER[26] for higher education (percentage of the 18–23 age group enrolled in a higher education institution) currently is around 11 per cent whereas it is 25 per cent for many other developing countries. China has increased its GER in higher education from 10 per cent in 1998 to 21 per cent in 2005.
>
> China has achieved growth rates exceeding 9 per cent for two to three decades.

On skills,

> One reason for this poor performance is the near exclusive reliance upon a few training courses with long duration (2 to 3 years) covering around 100 skills. In China, for example, there exist about 4000 short duration modular courses which provide skills more closely tailored to employment requirement. India currently ranks 13th among the top 38 countries in terms of number of publications in SCI journals; China ranks 9th. On the other hand, India ranks 2nd after China, among the top 23 developing countries. However, the productivity of Indian science as a measure of dollars spent per publication in Science Citation Index (SCI) journals is comparable with other countries.
>
> As far as trade is concerned, we need to exploit export opportunities opened by access to global markets by expanding our export of goods and services thus generating high quality employment. Countries such as China have exploited these opportunities very well and we need to learn from their experience.

[24] Prime Minister's speech, delivered to a conference of Chief Ministers on Panchayati Raj, June 2004.

[25] *Eleventh Five-Year Plan (2007–2012), Inclusive Growth*, Vol.1, Planning Commission, Government of India, Oxford University Press, 2008.

[26] Gross enrolment ratio.

A.T. Kearney FDI Confidence Index 2006 based on a 7-year survey of top 1000 firms, covering 68 countries receiving 90 per cent of the FDI has rated India ahead of the US in terms of business confidence index. The top honours go to China.

In a subsequent volume of the same plan document, there are the following quotes:[27]

> Yet, only about 2 per cent of these fruits and vegetables are processed as against 23 per cent in China." The comparatively low share of India in the world export of manufacturers is reflected in its low share of manufacturing value added in GDP compared to countries in South East and East Asia (15.9 per cent of India against China (34.5 per cent) in year 2000.
>
> The Yiu Lian Dockyard Ltd, the biggest shipyard in China, has steel renewal capacity of 250 mt per day as against 5 mt per day at best in India, and sand/grit blasting capacity of over 15000 sqm per day against around 1000 sqm per day in India. It takes 6 to 7 days in India to blast the outer hull of a 30000–40000 DWT ship and 50 days to replace 250 mt of steel in India against just one day in China for each of these operations. Since the time taken for ship repair (is) of the essence for competitiveness, the longer time taken by the Indian ship-repair industry makes it less competitive.
>
> The main reason for India to be well behind China in textiles and clothing is the absence of economies of scale in the manufacturing enterprises in the country.... The result is that the industry is fragmented and is unable to respond to the large volumes of orders that are placed by the retail chains in the industrial economies.
>
> The real importance of the SMEs, however, can be seen in China where over 68 per cent of the exports come from the SMEs.

Hence, there is a recognition that China has handled labour and land markets better,[28] including issues of land acquisition, compensation, rehabilitation and resettlement, all important in questions related to infrastructure development and even rural transformation, setting up small-industry clusters and urbanisation. Most India-based statements about a China-India comparison are indeed, invariably centred on infrastructure, especially power and transport. For instance, the point is often made that China spends around 12 per cent of the GDP on infrastructure, compared

---

[27] *Eleventh Five-Year Plan (2007–2012), Agriculture, Rural Development, Industry, Services, and Physical Infrastructure*, Vol. III, Planning Commission, Government of India, Oxford University Press, 2008.

[28] Beyond the point that there is an enormous amount of state intervention and lack of transparency in China, the argument cannot be advanced for capital markets.

to around 3.5 per cent for India.[29] Especially on power therefore, Indian manufacturing has had to resort to inefficient solutions like captive generating sets. A World Bank survey found that 61 per cent of India's manufacturing firms own captive generating sets, compared to 27 per cent in China.[30] India's urbanisation levels are lower than in many other developing countries and the rate of urbanisation has slowed over time. However, with higher growth, there are urbanisation pressures and issues of acquiring and converting agricultural land to non-agricultural use. This has been a controversial issue, and not just in the context of Special Economic Zones (SEZs). For both infrastructure and urbanisation, and reforms in general, comparisons are thus made about the political economy of resistance in China, as compared to India. There is a narrow point about Chinese decision-making being much more decentralised, even before the 1978–79 reforms. In contrast, Indian decision-making is much more centralised, notwithstanding some devolution to states and the constitutional sanctity given to *panchayat*s and urban local bodies. However, the broader point is about democracy and its lack. Thus, arguments are advanced about a "democracy tax" in India.[31] It is doubtful that this trade-off exists. Assuming it does, it is unlikely that any Indian would wish to give up India's democracy.

Bilateral Economic Relations

From the general aspects of reform experiences and contrasts, let us now move on to the specifics of bilateral economic relations. Despite frictions, such as those on border issues, on both sides there has been a recognition that bilateral economic relations can expand. The trade agreement granting Most Favoured Nation (MFN) status goes back to 1984. However, the improvement in relations is usually dated to Prime Minister Rajiv Gandhi's visit in 1988, followed by the Chinese premier's visit in 1991 and the Indian president's visit in 1992. Border trade resumed in 1992 and an additional trading post was opened in 1993. Unfortunately, bilateral trade data is available only till 2007–08. In that year, bilateral trade was US $ 37.8 billion, with India exporting US $ 10.8 billion and importing US $ 27.1 billion. Before the global

---

[29] This partly explains China's higher incremental capital/output ratio.

[30] *Private Sector Strategy for the World Bank Group,* http://siteresources.worldbank.org/INTINDIA/Resources/Annexure7.pdf

[31] In cross-country correlations, it is impossible to establish a link between GDP growth and democracy. The relationship is simply not robust enough, especially if one excludes natural resource-based economies.

slowdown hit, there was a bilateral trade turnover target of US $ 60 billion set for 2010. Apart from India's trade deficit issue, the Indian export basket to China is extremely narrow – with ores, cotton yarns and fabrics, organic and inorganic chemicals, precious stones, and metals and machinery. India's import basket from China is broader – with electrical machinery, organic chemicals, iron and steel, mineral fuel and fertilisers. To put some kind of perspective to these numbers, in 2007–08, China accounted for 5.3 per cent of India's exports, Hong Kong chipping in with another 4.0 per cent. Barring the US (13.7 per cent), no other country had such a large share. China's share in India's import basket was 11.2 per cent, the largest for any country.

This is the right point to mention the South Asian Association for Regional Cooperation (SAARC) and India's Regional Trade Agreements (RTAs). There are several reasons why the SAARC and South Asian Free Trade Area (SAFTA) process is becoming somewhat irrelevant. First, customs duties on manufactured products are not really the issue, which is what SAFTA liberalises. They have been, and will be reduced, because of unilateral liberalisation, apart from the Doha Work Programme eventually resurfacing. Second, given this liberalisation thrust, the timeline of 2016 is too long. Third, this liberalisation will be circumvented by Non-Tariff Barriers (NTBs), standards, sensitive lists, rules of origin, safeguards, and anti-dumping, apart from issues of revenue compensation to Least-Developed Countries (LDCs). Fourth, India is now a party (existing or proposed) to several other sub-regional RTAs – the Bay of Bengal Initiative for Multi-Sectoral Technical and Economic Co-operation (BIMSTEC), Chile, Singapore, Thailand, ASEAN, Japan, South Korea, United States, EU, GCC, Andean Community, Brazil, South Africa, Southern Common Market between Argentina, Brazil, Paraguay and Uruguay (MERCOSUR), South African Customs Union between Botswana, Lesotho, Namibia, South Africa and Swaziland (SACU), China, Afghanistan, Sri Lanka and Bangladesh are examples. These overtake SAFTA and also strain the limited negotiating capacity and manpower resources that the Commerce Ministry possesses. In addition, they lead to allegations of circumvention of rules of origin. Fifth, as is but obvious, any process of bloc formation has to be cross-subsidised by the larger country, in this case, India. Even if there is no actual cross-subsidisation, the relative gains accrue more to smaller countries, theoretically, as well as empirically. If there is subsidisation by India, should that be in the area of classic trade liberalisation? Sixth, studies establishing the great potential that exists in free trade within South Asia are neither here nor there.[32]

---

[32] This statement should not be interpreted as a dismissal of studies that estimate illegal cross-border trade between India on the one hand and say, Bangladesh, Sri Lanka and Pakistan on

The results are tautological, since any process of liberalisation will lead to welfare gains in a net sense. The key question to ask is, what are the trade liberalisation gains within SAARC, as compared to trade liberalisation gains with other parts of the globe, especially those parts that are economically more important – North America, Europe and ASEAN along with South Korea, Japan and China added? Resources have opportunity costs. Seventh, as the focus of some of India's recent RTAs indicates, India needs to move away from classic free trade agreements in manufacturing to those in services (such as through comprehensive economic co-operation agreements), including agreements on freer cross-border movements of labour and capital. Does the existing SAARC trade agenda fit into this? Eighth, given the large and heterogeneous country that India is, is the idea of regional trade integration at all appropriate? Alternately, does one have in mind economic integration between the southern parts of India and Sri Lanka and Maldives, and between the eastern parts of India and Bhutan, Nepal, Bangladesh, Myanmar, Thailand and China or even between the northern parts of India and Pakistan? Apart from the tactical intent, is there thus an economic rationale to sub-regional integration too? Should one therefore encourage direct interaction between India's states and neighbouring countries, rather than pushing everything at an all-India level?

The point of this is that India has begun to look beyond SAARC and beyond WTO too, in driving RTAs, with a specific focus on East Asia. This derives additional impetus from the fact that the Doha negotiations are presently stagnating. There is also recognition that many of India's backward regions are towards the east and the Northeast and these need economic integration with neighbouring countries, including China. An India-China friendship year was celebrated in 2006, with youth exchange programmes. Bilateral tourist flows have increased, including the tapping of the Buddhist circuit in India. More pertinently for present purposes, there is a Joint Study Group (JSG), which will eventually lead to some kind of RTA between India and China. There are several reasons why this has not proceeded faster. First, there is the matter of inadequate transport infrastructure on the Indian side of the border. Second, there is the overwhelming impression that Indian manufacturing is not cost competitive and will be deluged by Chinese imports, an impression apparently reinforced by India's bilateral trade deficit. The current global slowdown has

the other. However, one must be careful. What goes by the name of illegal trade is sometimes third-country trade and actual cross-border illegal trade is not entirely informal trade and, as the experience with Sri Lanka demonstrates, cross-border trade does not occur only because trade policy imposes customs duties. A large contribution is also due to high procedural costs associated with formal trade.

only compounded these fears, since there are suggestions that Chinese exports will now be re-routed to the Indian market. Indian manufacturing is indeed not cost competitive. However, the fears about India being deluged by imports from China, especially in consumer goods, has been over-exaggerated, though such fears have been around for at least a decade now. Being cost competitive is not quite the same thing as dumping. The latter has a technical definition under General Agreement on Tariffs and Trade (GATT)/WTO agreements. Having said this, the bulk of India's anti-dumping investigations have been directed against China.[33] In addition, there was a temporary ban imposed against Chinese toys on safety grounds. This was not WTO-compatible and was soon lifted.

Other than trade, there is the cross-border investment issue. Too often, the China-India comparison has been posed as competing destinations for inward FDI flows and as mentioned earlier, China and India aren't quite in the same league, though their location advantages should not be posed as an either/or choice. In 2007, FDI inflows into China were US $ 83.5 billion and those into India US $ 13.7 billion.[34] However, more interestingly, FDI outflows from China were US $ 22.5 billion and those from India were US $ 13.6 billion,

An increasing number of developed countries are also attracting FDI from economies in the region, and some of their Investment Promotion Agencies (IPAs) are establishing offices for this purpose, including in China, India and Singapore. India is now among the top investors in the United Kingdom. China is rapidly becoming a leading investor in many developing countries, including some African LDCs. Chinese and Indian firms were particularly active investors in extractive industries, both within and outside the region. China, India, the Republic of Korea and Thailand introduced or adapted their outward FDI policies and regulations. The objectives of such measures have been primarily to enable these countries to increase the competitiveness of their firms, including to secure access to natural resources. For example, China expanded its support to investments in Africa, by providing loan finance

[33] See, *Annual Report, 2005–06,* Directorate General of Anti-dumping and Allied Duties, http://commerce.nic.in/traderemedies/ANNUAL_REPORT_2005_2006.pdf?id=1. China accounts for almost 50 per cent of India's anti-dumping investigations. There is a problem with matching Indian data on anti-dumping investigations with WTO data, since the classifications are different. There is greater leeway with anti-dumping procedures against China, since China's accession agreement to WTO does not allow it to have "market economy" status until 2016.

[34] *World Investment Report, Transnational Corporations and the Infrastructure Challenge,* UNCTAD, 2008, http://www.unctad.org/en/docs/wir2008_en.pdf. The definitional base for FDI classification is not the same in the two countries. In general, there is over-estimation in China and by the same token, relative under-estimation in India.

through the Export-Import Bank of China and establishing the China-Africa Development Fund to support African countries' investments in agriculture, manufacturing, energy, transportation, telecommunications, urban infrastructure and resource exploration. It also supports the development of Chinese firms' activities in Africa.[35]

While trade between China and India has increased fairly fast, though on a low base, bilateral investment flows have not increased much. Indian FDI in China is largely restricted to the IT sector. Chinese FDI into India is often constrained by Indian concerns about security.

However, in the bilateral economic relations category, relations have not yet become inordinately strained. The odd friction over some issue or the other is understandable. In international forums like IMF, World Bank, WTO and even the G-20, China and India have not yet adopted conflicting positions, unlike in non-economic domains like the UN, specifically the Security Council, on nuclear issues. The core of the developing country coalition in WTO, also named G-20, consists of China, India, Brazil, South Africa, and to a lesser extent, Argentina. Obviously, with growth in both countries, there will be tensions over competitive access to natural resources, commodities and energy. The Africa problem is symptomatic, where there is Indian concern that Chinese FDI and Chinese aid are being used to address such strategic issues. The Indian overseas aid is largely in the form of credit lines and is not classic foreign aid. That apart, the scale of Indian FDI outflows and aid is not commensurate with Chinese levels. Beyond Africa, some such strategic conflicts are also visible in South Asia or East Asia. However, stated in simple terms, both countries are learning to adjust to each other's economic rise and the impact this will have on the global economy and there is quite a bit of mutual respect.[36] To use two clichéd expressions made popular in the Indian press, India provides much of the software and China provides much of the hardware. China is the manufacturing hub, while India is the services hub. This is clichéd and a gross over-simplification, but there is some truth in the assertion. Second, from Hindi-Chini *bhai-bhai*, we have now moved to Hindi-Chini buy-buy.

---

[35] Ibid.
[36] The rather unhappy expression Chindia has been coined.

3

Domestic Politics in Contemporary China

Ideas, Institutionalisation and Issues

Varaprasad S. Dolla

The significance of domestic politics can never be underestimated because if there is one dimension that could potentially threaten the current phase of China's rise it is this. Conversely, the rise of China is equally dependent, if not more, on the smooth functioning of the political system. These two processes are interrelated and in turn dependent on the current political leadership as well as people. Since the stability of Chinese political system is critical to its rise, there is an imperative to gauge the contemporary domestic politics as accurately as possible eschewing any kind of ideological or any other lenses. The enormity of the complex nature of Chinese political system is captured best by Michel Oksenberg when he posited that it "defies encapsulation in a single short phrase. Such previous depictions as "totalitarianism", a "Leninist party state", "fragmented authoritarianism", "soft authoritarianism", or "bureaucratic capitalism", miss the complexity of Chinese state structure today."[1]

Given this complexity, this chapter focuses primarily on three central themes of ideas, institutionalisation and issues that have been determining the dynamics of Chinese polity in the last three decades. It also offers some concluding remarks highlighting the problems and future of domestic politics

---

[1] Michel Oksenberg, "China's Political System: Challenges of the Twenty-first Century," *The China Journal* 45 (2001), p. 21.

in China and their implications for India. What is distinctly common to these three is the continual change that has been taking place in a gradualist manner.[2] Equally interesting is that they have been changing both well beyond, for some, and below for others, of any conceivable imagination of several shades of sinologists, thus making the existing analytical tools inadequate thereby requiring us to be flexible as Tony Saich quite aptly compares the Chinese political system to a moving target.[3] A moving target, therefore, requires a flexible approach that facilitates a better understanding of the changes that have been taking place in contemporary Chinese domestic politics.

Ideology to Ideas

Two pertinent issues of divergent *perspectives* and the *process* are factored into the analysis of the shift from ideology to ideas. First, the divergent *perspectives* on ideology that came to be part of the intellectual attempts at understanding the political changes that have been taking place in China since 1978 have exclusively focused on ideology rather than on the shift from ideology to ideas, which this study identifies as a critical gap and endeavours to fill it. Second, the *process* of shift was essentially led by the state though the Chinese society occasionally and indirectly contributed to it. These two - perspectives and process - are weaved to form a rich tapestry of a dispassionate analysis of the Chinese contemporary domestic politics, particularly in the realm of ideology that is increasingly transforming into variegated ideas.

Perspectives on Ideology

In analysing the shifting sands of ideology in China, a number of sinologists shed light from different spectrums. Four distinct perspectives can be gleaned from this body of literature. First perspective highlights the decay of ideology in China. For instance, Hong Yung Lee argues that reforms in the post-Mao period in a way undermined the role of ideology, making it more or less lose its relevance, lacking coherence in terms of vision, goal and strategy, not being able to answer the question of how far the reforms can go without diluting the official claims that China is, indeed, a socialist country. He even

---

[2] Deng Xiaoping, a firm believer in the ancient wisdom of "cross the river while feeling the stones", followed it despite certain challenges on the way.

[3] Tony Saich, *Governance and Politics of China* (New York: Palgrave, 2001), p. 205.

goes to the extent of saying that the declining relevance of ideology in daily life, bureaucrats in the party's propaganda apparatus are so demoralised that they do not want to do any ideological work. A supreme irony with the party, he says, is that the party workers find themselves preaching the very ideas that they had condemned earlier as capitalist ideology.[4] The changes in ideology have led another scholar to conclude that

> ideology has been stretched to breaking-point and both leaders and followers talk of "crisis of faith" leading to the weakening process of the government's legitimacy while the people's response to the government's authority has become increasingly cynical with general acceptance on the surface but private reservations combined with a touch of anger.[5]

Gordon White postulated that the leadership in post-Mao China has initiated a three-fold process of repudiating ideological distortions of Mao's period, reviving a healthy ideological heritage and adapting the existing ideological framework to the new economic environment of market socialism in relation to ideology. And "the net result was ideological decay, a loss of political faith and direction, not merely among the general population, but also among the political elite in the Communist Party."[6]

The second perspective goes a step further arguing that "ideology is dead and has no place and plays no substantial role in the Chinese society."[7] Cheng Li pronounced the death of ideology in China based on his analysis of reform and its impact on the Chinese society and polity. In a similar vein, while writing about ideology Roderick MaqFarquahar states that "Deng's support for reform formula left no room for ideology."[8]

The third perspective, in complete contrast to those advocating the decay and end of ideology in China, argues that ideology continues to play a crucial role in Chinese politics and economy. For Sujian Guo ideology operates in a new form and framework under Deng and Jiang Zemin. He assumes that the post-Mao regime continued to claim the absoluteness of communist ideology and reaffirm

---

[4] Hong Yung Lee, "The Implications of Reform for Ideology, State and Society in China," *Journal of International Affairs* 39.2 (1986), pp. 77–89.

[5] Lucien W. Pye, "The State and the Individual: An Overview of Interpretation," *The China Quarterly* 127 (1991), pp. 457–58.

[6] Gordon White, *Riding the Tiger: The Politics of Economic Reform in Post-Mao China* (London: Macmillan, 1993), p. 150.

[7] Cheng Li, *Rediscovering China: Dynamics and Dilemmas of Reform* (Lanham, Maryland: Rowman and Littlefield Publishers, 1997).

[8] Roderick MaqFarquahar, *The Politics of China: The Eras of Mao and Deng* (Cambridge: Cambridge University Press, 1997), p. 3.

the inevitability of socialism. While acknowledging incoherence among the components of the regime's ideology and related behaviour, the post-Mao regime never abandoned the "hard core" of their incredible goals and fundamental principles and norms, but only made adjustments to achieving them.[9]

The fourth perspective espouses a new role for ideology as Bill Brugger and David Kelly argue that "Ideology still functions, but in the mode described by Alain Besancon, where it becomes equivalent to the regime."[10] The implication of this assessment is that ideology will continue to be a part of Chinese political system as long as this regime remains in power in its current avatar. In agreement with this line of argument Joseph Fewsmith succinctly and appropriately suggests that "Deng sought to 'refunctionalise' the ideology…by moving away from the radical, dysfunctional ideology of Mao…."[11] This view suggests that the function of ideology in the post-Mao period is to legitimise the communist rule in China besides providing sustenance to the economic reform carried by the leadership.

While the second and third perspectives take two extreme positions, which one finds to be far removed from the current reality, the first and fourth perspectives come close to representing the existing reality of the place and the role of ideology in China. But these two perspectives are problematic in the sense that they represent only partial reality. The most plausible explanation that represents more than partial reality is what can be called a combination of "refunctional-dysfuntional" process wherein ideology is vital to the ruling class which uses it to legitimise the changes it brings in various segments of the Chinese society but it is also slowly vanishing from the day-to-day lives of the majority. More importantly, a phenomenon that is glaringly absent in these scholarly analyses is the shift from ideology to ideas, which the following section delineates.

Process of Shift from Ideology to Ideas

In contrast to the above scholarly analyses, this study posits that one of the first major changes that occurred in the post-1978 Chinese political system is

---

[9] Guo Sujian, *Post-Mao China: From Totalitarianism to Authoritarianism* (Praeger: Westport, Connecticut, 2000).

[10] Bill Brugger and David Kelly, *Chinese Marxism in the Post-Mao China* (Stanford: Stanford University Press, 1990), p. 170.

[11] Joseph Fewsmith, "Reaction, Resurgence and Succession in Chinese Politics since Tiananmen," in Roderick MaqFarquahar, ed., *The Politics of China: The Eras of Mao and Deng* (Cambridge: Cambridge University Press, 1997), p. 470.

the paradigmatic shift from one overarching ideology that dominated Chinese politics under Mao to several ideas that came to form the broad framework within which the subsequent political processes have been evolving. What is distinctive about this shift is that these new ideas have, in many ways, provided a new twist to the very ideology that they came to redefine. In other words, these ideas are essentially new interpretations of the old political ideology of socialism. To begin with, it was Deng Xiaoping who set in motion this process by bringing in his own unique facets to the issue of ideology emphasising that this ideology is not static but dynamic with two dimensions of theory and praxis. For him, the efficacy of an ideology needed to be judged on the basis of its praxis using one of the most often quoted adages "seek truth from facts" which came to be some sort of Biblical truth. However, in China ideological correctness is still an issue that cannot be discounted despite the fact that ideology has lost its earlier sheen and impact in shaping its polity, economy and society. In other words, a public policy, say for example, rural democracy, has to be ideologically palatable to the leadership.

In so doing the Chinese state has been trying its best to keep ideological fervour alive and kicking, chiefly to legitimise its continuation in power. One of the ways in which the Party and the government has been doing this is by advancing new interpretations of ideology of socialism. The government felt the need to further improve and strengthen ideological and political work, primarily to meet the situation in reform and opening to the outside world.[12] Following this felt need government's interpretation of ideology underwent profound changes during the leadership of Deng Xiaoping, thus forcing communist ideology to make a paradigm shift moving away from Mao's version of ideology of "politics in command" to Deng's version of "economics in command." Thereafter, it witnessed two more major shifts from "economics in command" to "socialism with Chinese characteristics" and to "market socialism" based on the principle of "practice is the sole criterion." Deng, by emphasising "practice is the sole criterion," had introduced a new focus to the issue of socialist ideology. The opening of Marxism, Leninism and Mao's Thought for a wider interpretation in the context of reform programme and its aftermath has led to a process of being termed as "an intermediate ideology", "one that strategically appeals to a number of constituencies and whose ambiguities as much a strength as a weakness."[13]

---

[12] Summary of World Broadcasts, FE/7878/B11/2–3.

[13] David Kelly, "Guest Editorial Introduction," *Chinese Law and Government* 29. 2 (1996), p. 7.

Though the shift from ideology to ideas was a top-down one, it was facilitated by a variety of institutions ranging from Party school to think tanks to universities.[14] This process has been highly successful in meeting the immediate requirement of continuing the reform programme and maintaining political and social stability.

Deng and some of the liberal minded leaders like Zhao Ziyang[15] were more interested in the material well-being than in ideological well-being which is why "the ideological and political discourse in most of the 1980s had been conducted relatively freely, except during the brief anti-rightist campaigns in 1981, 1983 and 1987."[16]

They were not obsessed with ideological purity but deeply committed to economic development. For them, ideological poverty was acceptable but not economic poverty. In fact, it was the immediate imperative to rescue China from a deep economic crisis that influenced Deng to initiate economic reform which in turn necessitated ideological reform that began at the Third Plenum of the 11th Party Congress in 1978. Apart from this, Deng's moderate approach to economic restructuring right from the beginning of the 1950s, which salvaged China from a deep economic crisis after 1959, was the main factor for such a change both in ideology and economic reform. For Deng, it is the efficacy of policies and programmes that was more important than revolution and mass mobilisation.

This, however, did not mean that Deng had completely abandoned the need for ideological progress. In fact, he called for clarity in the ideological line as being essential to establishing a correct political line.[17] Deng supported criticising wrong ideologies whether they were "Left" or "Right." In his analysis, he equated this with emancipation of the mind.[18] In other words, he called for some kind of balance in his approach to ideology. Since it is the Chinese Communist Party which sets the tone for any change in the ideological line, he tried to bridge

---

[14] Joseph Fewsmith, "Where Do Correct Ideas Come From?: The Party School, Key Think Tanks, and the Intellectuals," in David M. Finkelstein and Maryanne Kivlehan, eds., *China's Leadership in the 21st Century: The Rise of the Fourth Generation*, (Armonk, New York: M. E. Sharpe, 2003), pp. 152–64.

[15] Zhao Ziyang, "Report to the Thirteenth CCP Congress," *Beijing Review* 9.15 (1987), pp. xxiv–xxv.

[16] Merle Goldman, "The Potential for Instability among Intellectuals and Students in Post-Mao China," in David Shambaugh, ed., *Is China Unstable?: Assessing the Factors* (Armonk, New York: M. E. Sharpe, 2000), p. 115.

[17] Deng Xiaoping, *Selected Works of Deng Xiaoping*, vol. II, second edition (Beijing: Foreign Languages Press, 1995) p. 197.

[18] Ibid, p. 373.

what he was doing with the principles of the Party which was why he said in another speech that "the people who are not on track ideologically are those who make statements contrary to Party principles…."[19] Deng also tried to link material progress with cultural and ideological progress. He said in another speech "material progress will suffer delays and setbacks unless we promote cultural and ideological progress as well."[20] Deng wanted economic reform and ideological and political work to go hand in hand given the unfolding of Chinese economic and political scenarios. However, the reality was in favour of economic reforms rather than being able to maintain a perfect balance. Changes in the ideological realm followed economic reforms as Joseph Cheng points out "major economic reforms in a Marxist-Leninist state certainly call for justifications in the ideological sphere."[21] Economic reform programme, in fact, necessitated reform in ideology-reinterpretation of ideology. In other words, changes in ideology followed changes in the economic structure initially and later they went hand in hand reinforcing each other. Deng can undoubtedly be called the harbinger of this "revolution in ideology," a silent revolution which led to profound changes in polity, society and leading to large-scale prosperity of the largest group of people in the shortest span of time. A popular saying captures the credibility of this analysis: "Mao gave us liberation (add ideology to it) and Deng gave us food." The nature of ideology in post-Mao China is akin to the proverbial new wine in the old bottle or old wine in new bottle conundrum. The recent changes in the ideology resemble the former rather than the latter. These radical changes in ideology have proven Gresham's law wrong: bad ideology drives out good ideology. Deng's good ideology, in fact, drove out "bad" ideology of Mao's period.[22] The summation of Deng's ideas came to be called the Deng Xioaping's Thought which was also incorporated into the 1982 Constitution of China and thus elevated it to be the basis of the political, economic, social and cultural changes that are presently unfolding in China.

Leaving an indelible imprint on the ideological trajectory of China, it became a political tradition in China since 1978 beginning with Deng Xiaoping. In line with this tradition, Jiang Zemin left his imprint on the process of shift from

[19] Ibid, p. 384.

[20] Deng's speech at the CPC national conference. *Beijing Review* 28. 39 (1985), pp. 15–18.

[21] Joseph Y. Cheng, "Introduction: China's Modernization Programme in the 1980s," in Joseph Y. Cheng, ed., *China: Modernization in the 1980s*, (Hong Kong: The Chinese University Press, 1989), p. ix.

[22] Occasionally Mao turned good ideology into bad ideology by personalising it whereas Deng turned bad ideology-Mao's ideology-into good ideology by de-personalising it.

one overarching ideology to multiple ideas by laying the foundations for a new framework of what came to be called Three Represents[23] [*sange daibiao lilun*], which was written into the Chinese Communist Party constitution at the 16th Party Congress in 2002 thus signalling its relevance and importance to the Chinese polity. The Three Represents[24] cover three issues: the development of the advanced productive forces, orientation of China's advanced culture and fundamental interests of the overwhelming majority of the Chinese people. The development of the advanced forces of production is a clear reflection and reiteration of Deng's thrust on economic development. The orientation of Chinese advanced culture is some sort of revival of Chinese culture that includes Confucian philosophy and ethics as is being strengthened and promoted by the state across the globe, by establishing Confucius Study Centres and thereby allowing it to impact its polity besides attempting to use it as a source of Chinese soft power. The third component of fundamental interests of the overwhelming majority of the Chinese people is rather problematic in the sense that it deflects the real problem that the Chinese state is faced with the issue of minorities in China by focusing on the overwhelming majority.

In carrying forward this political tradition, Hu Jintao, the present Chinese President from the fourth generation with his own contribution to the ideological discourse by introducing the framework of Scientific Outlook on Development [*kexue fazhan guan*] consisting of two major components of development and harmony, takes the trajectory of shift from ideology to ideas to a different level. This framework "takes development as the essence, putting people first as its core, comprehensive, balanced and sustainable development as its basic requirement...."[25]

He views this framework as a cure for all the political, economic and social challenges that China has been facing. By doing so, he not only neutralised some of the complicated issues in Jiang Zemin's formulation but also made it much more contemporary given the present focus on sustainable development and peace, in the context of terrorism at the global level. A more important

---

[23] Jiang Zemin, *Full Text of Jiang Zemin's Report at the 16th Party Congress* presented on November 8, 2002. http://www.fmprc.gov.cn/eng/37815.html; accessed on 17 November 2002.

[24] Manoranjan Mohanty argues that they "are a package of economic, social and political guidelines which rationalise some of the policies that the CPC has already begun to pursue in the past two decades." However, linking the Third Represent to the political aspect of democracy seems to be rather problematic given the inadequate theoretical underpinnings to that effect. For more on Mohanty's views, see his article "Three Represents: Ideology of the Fourth Generation," *China Report* 39. 2 (2003), pp. 242–44.

[25] Hu Jintao, *Report to the Seventeenth Congress of the Communist Party of China*, October 15, 2007.

reason for emphasising harmony is the domestic dissatisfaction emerging as a result of the kind of development agenda being followed currently.

The cumulative impact of the introduction of economic reforms and the consequent reinterpretations of ideology is that the Chinese of all strata have been left free to be preoccupied with their respective professions and the struggles that have come about with the reforms. They, in turn, have made both the Party and more importantly the common people less ideological in their orientation and approach with major implications for the ideology of Marxism, Leninism and Mao's thought.[26] In the lives of the majority of the Chinese, ideology, in a sense, is being replaced by economic realism and development. Most Chinese are more concerned about livelihood than ideology. Except among the Party cadre and the ruling class, ideology hardly figures in the imaginations of most Chinese. If at all it does, it is primarily to be wary of any ideological disputations with some conservative elements in the ruling class. Recognising this phenomenon, the Chinese Communist Party (CCP) in one of its resolutions had admitted the weakening and scaling down of its ideological and political work, particularly in the universities and colleges.[27] Furthermore, it also expressed concern that the content, form and methods of conducting ideological and political work also grew out of sync with the needs and demands of the new conditions.[28] This occurred despite the Party's attempt at raising the ideological and political consciousness of the broad masses of its members. The process of shift from ideology to ideas could eventually change the very face of ideology provided it continues in the same direction and at the same pace.

Both the *perspectives* on ideology and the *process* of shift from ideology to ideas will continue to unfold in future with all their complexities. Interestingly, the ideology as well as its interpretations have kept pace with the changing context and time.[29] In the arena of the *process* of shift from ideology to ideas, the ideas that came to shape the Chinese political system may mean very little in bringing substantial changes but their utility is in being used as a source of justification for the multifaceted reforms being introduced by the leadership

---

[26] Hong Yue Lee, "The Implications of Reform for Ideology, State and Society in China," *Journal of International Affairs* 39.2 (1986), pp. 77–89.

[27] SWB: FE/7849/B11/1.

[28] Zhang Gang, "Mistaken Ideas Dictated by Interests," *Chinese Law and Government* 29. 2 (1996), pp. 44–47.

[29] Yin Jizuo, "The Party's Ideology Keeps Pace with Time," *SASS Papers (9),* (Shanghai: Shanghai Academy of Social Sciences Press, 2003), pp. 1–9.

in China since 1978. As the *process* changes, so do the *perspectives* as this section added a new perspective on the changing face of ideology in China in the last three decades. Currently both the Chinese integration, in its economic as well as cultural forms, with the global community and the present phase of globalisation are further making the phenomenon of shift from ideology to ideas much more complex thereby requiring further analysis.

Institutions to Institutionalisation

While most of the institutions that continue to operate since 1978 were of Mao's epoch, their mode of functioning, however, has been radically different. During Mao's era various political institutions were subjected to the vagaries of political and ideological winds and movements like Hundred Flowers, Great Leap Forward and Cultural Revolution. But with the exception of Anti-Rightist movement of 1983, we do not notice such a phenomenon during Deng's leadership. In fact, what distinguishes the political institutions from Mao's period was the process of institutionalisation. Once again it was Deng who began a gradual process of institutionalisation of Chinese political institutions by bringing in a number of norms and rules thereby providing a considerable degree of stability in the system. The institutionalisation is common to almost all the political institutions beginning from the highest and powerful state to the lowest and weakest Villagers' Committees. The other institutions such as party and government are not entirely outside the purview of institutionalisation. The degree of institutionalisation varies from institution to institution given their predisposition and willingness to change. Another phenomenon common to these institutions is that they are open to adapt themselves only to the changing economic architecture centred on reform and not to the Western liberal political traditions.

The State

Since the institutionalisation was an initiative led by the top echelons of the ruling class, they began it with the Chinese state, the most powerful and the highest institution, perhaps to ensure smooth facilitation of the same at the lower levels. The end result of this process is that the Chinese state has transited from being more repressive to less repressive with occasional deviations. This transition led a number of scholars into characterising the Chinese state in quite diverse ways. For instance, Dorothy Solinger described it as "totalitarian, authoritarian, semi-authoritarian, party-state and developmental."[30] Similarly, Richard Baum and Alexchenko list about 28 facets of the Chinese state.[31] Much more recently, Jude Howell, after mapping perspectives of various scholars, concludes that the "Chinese state is best understood as polymorphous, assuming multiple, complex forms and behaviours across time and space, and defying any definition which reduces it to a single actor."[32] While these perspectives of Chinese state are insightful, the focus here is on how the Chinese state transformed over the years locating it within the broad framework of institutionalisation. A major shift occurred in the functioning of the Chinese state is in the realm of from being the vanguard of ideology to being the pioneering agent of economic development which led to some of the above characterisations. The end result of this change is more predictability and stability of the political system and less instability. The political logic of economic development is to derive legitimacy to its continuation in power. The state's successful track record of achieving over 9 percent GDP growth rate over the last three decades is used to sooth its conscience given its occasional authoritarian and undemocratic use of power.

As a result of these changes in the character and functioning of the state, we notice another interesting phenomenon of the changing dynamics between the state and society wherein there has been a steady retreat of the state in regulating society. The exact nature of the retreat of the state is highly debatable. One of the views is that both the state and society came to acquire new meanings given the changes that were made possible by the reform and restructuring process. It was more of a transition of both the state and society. But for Gordon White this process, particularly an uneven redistribution of economic power, led to the strengthening society while undermining the state and its ancillary agencies.[33] In contrast, Dorothy Solinger argues "what appears as the liberation of society has actually…been an incorporation of society."[34] Another view espouses that the withdrawal of the state is partial and it led to the revival of many traditional practices.[35] Deng Xiaoping was the architect of this process who initiated a new

---

[30] Dorothy Solinger, China's *Transition from Socialism: Statist Legacies and Market Reforms, 1980–1990* (Armonk, N.Y.: M.E. Sharpe, 1993).

[31] Richard Baum & Alexei Shevchenko, "The State of the State," in Merle Goldman and Roderick McFarquhar, eds., *The Paradox of China's Post-Mao Reforms* (Cambridge, MA: Harvard University Press, 1999), p. 333.

[32] Jude Howell, "Reflections on the Chinese State," *Development and Change* 37. 2 (2006), p. 275.

[33] Gordon White, *Riding the Tiger: The Politics of Economic Reform in Post-MaoChina* (London: Macmillan, 1993), p. 198.

[34] Dorothy Solinger, *China's Transition from Socialism: Statist legacies and Market Reforms, 1980-1990* (Armonk, N.Y.: M.E. Sharpe, 1993); p. 259.

[35] Tony Saich, *Governance and Politics of China* (New York: Palgrave, 2001), pp. 1–2.

path of relations between state and society in contemporary China. This path has neither been easy nor without problems. The Chinese state, in carrying out a sustained rapid economic reform, had to share some of its power and responsibility with the society, which is seen by many as a process of weakening of state's reach and power. This is a welcome phenomenon for many Chinese, but is seen by some as a major threat to the authority of the Chinese party and the state. What has changed in the dynamics between state and society is not the substance but the style. The communist state in China continues to wield power over society. It continues to be authoritarian especially while dealing with dissent. While it is a bit soft on "social dissent", a dissent concerning social issues; it is not so in regard to political dissent and internet freedom. The Chinese state is also quite wary of various forces of democracy both from within and without given the 1989 legacies. Moreover, the state is aware of the potential of new communication technologies of Internet, mobile, text messages that were put to effective use during the 2008 Tibetan and 2009 Xinjiang unrests. This is largely because it is unduly perturbed by the possibility of a potential threat to its own power. Its focus is on development without democracy rather than development and democracy. However, it has been more responsive to some of the demands of the society. One of the demands of the Chinese society is that the state should be more open in its approach to sharing information pertaining to various social issues. A case in point was the 2003 Severe Acute Respiratory Syndrome (SARS) crisis. Though the Chinese state refused to acknowledge the extent of the crisis initially, it conceded eventually and came forward to divulge the number of people affected by SARS and initiated a several measures to contain and improve healthcare, another clear departure from Mao's period.

The Party

CCP is the dominant and the most powerful one among the nine parties in China. With 73.36 million members as of 2007 holding diverse views about reforms, state and society, it is a formidable force to reckon with. However, the CCP has been going through a process of transition and transformation gradually though at a snail pace. This gradualist process is much slower than the economic reform that China has been witnessing. Once again it was Deng Xiaoping who began this process when he said:

> We hope every Party committee and every Party branch will encourage and support both inside and outside the Party to dare to think, explore new paths,

and put forward new ideas, and that they will urge the masses to emancipate their minds and use their heads.[36]

Deng did follow-up the tenor and intent of the essence of this broad direction he set as we saw in the realm of ideology in the previous section. However, so far as the issue of daring to think in the area of political institutionalisation, particularly pertaining to the Party, his track record has been wide off the mark. With the exception of a few minor changes, he ensured that the Party retained its control of the polity, economy and society. Some of the changes that the Party has witnessed over the last three decades form part of the discussion below.

Ever since the Chinese Communist Party's position and power was institutionalised into the 1982 Constitution in the form of Four Cardinal Principles – pursuing the socialist path, commitment to Marxist, Leninist and Mao Zedong's thought, upholding people's democratic dictatorship and leadership of the Party – thereby consolidating its leadership, it has been functioning as the vanguard and the fundamental political institution providing the broad framework within which the state, government and society operate. In other words, the locus of real power is the party and it endeavours to maintain its monopoly over the entire edifice of the Chinese polity, economy and society. However, in the recent past it has also come under immense pressure to transform itself in line with the changing contexts of economic development, social change and internationalisation of its foreign policy. One of the first changes that came about was the transition it had been making from being a *revolutionary* party to being *reform* party. Under Deng, the Party was no longer required to carry out communist revolution and instead lead reform from the front. This process has not been easy both for those who wanted to see it changed. A major step in the process is the amendment of its constitution. Simultaneously the Party carried out an internal and systemic change by moving from being a Party of the farmers and workers to becoming a Party of the educated and the elites. It attempted to recruit many members from the colleges, universities and other institutions. Today its composition, though still dominated by the farmers and workers, is changing with about 14 percent constituting the intellectuals and the educated who are actually shaping the Party's architecture to a considerable degree.

Moreover, continuing the post-1949 tradition of consultation in the form of Chinese People's Political Consultative Conference, the leadership

---

[36] Quoted in John Gittings, *China Changes Face: The Road from Revolution, 1949–1989* (London: Oxford University Press, 1989), p. 180.

under Hu Jintao attempted to promote a more formalised, institutionalised and effective consultative interface between the CCP and the other eight parties in China. CCP is more open to receive research-based inputs from these parties. Despite the consultative nature of this exercise, the positive dimension is that it is infusing some broad consensus on issues confronting the Chinese political system. Another radical change that occurred in the party was in its perception of the business community, its arch enemy during Mao's period, when it opened its doors for them in 2001. The outcome of this change in its perception is partly to incorporate the business community into its fold and also to recognise their contribution to the economic development of China. A major factor that facilitated this kind of internal opening policy to businessmen is that many party members themselves own some of these businesses while several others are owned by their kith and kin.

In addition, CCP's relations with the society have also undergone several changes over the last three decades. The gulf between the party and society has widened in the context of reforms wherein the latter perceives the former as a hub of corruption since the economic reforms are carried under the aegis of the Party. This occurred despite the fact that the Party tried to use impressive economic growth as a major source of its legitimacy for its continuation in power. Many Chinese tend to have mixed response to see the connection between the Party and economic development. While some attribute the rapid economic development to the Party there are several others who do not share this view. For them economic growth is occurring in spite of the Party. Besides this, CCP's relationship with the PLA is also critical for its survival as it operates as an institution throwing up new ideas to sustain the state and government and the latter as a source of raw power to support all the three in times of crisis as it happened during the 1989 students movement. As a token of gratitude, the Party has been a robust supporter of modernisation of PLA, particularly since the 1991 Gulf War when the Chinese state realised the gap between PLA and the American defence forces.

The real question is whether CCP would be able to maintain its hold over the Chinese political system in the years ahead. This is subject to its willingness to change with the changing social, political and economic realities. There are some indications of CCP moving in that direction but they are too little and too late. One will have to wait and see whether these realities will overtake them or CCP will be able to keep them under its control and continue its political hegemony.

The Government

The Chinese government, which had been under the shadow of the Party until 1978, began to move away from it with the efforts of the leadership at the highest level. In order to make the government more effective in ensuring sustained economic growth, the leadership endeavoured to separate it from the Party. The very attempt to do so suggests that the Party had been a stumbling block to what the leadership at the top echelons and government wanted to accomplish. Of the two institutions, the Party and the government, it is the latter that is credited with the accomplishment of remarkable economic development. The nodal agency of the Chinese government is the State Council with the Premier as its head. The Chinese government under the leadership of the Premiers like Zhao Ziyang in the 1980s, Li Peng and Zhu Rongzhi in the 1990s and now Wen Jiabao has been the pivotal catalyst of change in various political processes beginning from strengthening the legal system, centred around the Constitution, to initiating various administrative reforms. One of the most complex issues that Deng managed to accomplish was the introduction of the retirement age of 75 for those in political authority. This has facilitated the process of phasing out the old and conservative leaders in the government besides minimising the succession struggles that many see as a major "Achilles heel" of the Chinese polity. Though internal squabbling continues to plague the succession process, it is kept away from the public view thereby limiting the adverse ramifications.

But the critical issue with the Chinese government is that it tends to exercise political power with minimal accountability. The issue of accountability is rather weak in Chinese polity. Unlike in the liberal democracies where the government is responsible to the public, the Chinese government is responsible to the Party. Therefore, one notices a strong imprint of the Party on the government and its functioning. In an interesting article Susan Shirk described the relationship between the CCP and Government as the principal and the agent wherein the latter functions within the broad framework set by the Party.[37] As has been indicated, though the government has been *agent of the Party* it has also been the *agent of change* within the Party mainly due to the credibility that it gained as a result of the remarkable success of reform programme. It was the government that worked out the finer details of a number

---

[37] Susan Shirk, "The Chinese Political System and the Political Strategy of Economic Reform," in Kenneth Lieberthal and David Lampton, eds., *Bureaucracy, Politics and Decision Making in Post-Mao China* (Berkeley: University of California Press, 1992), pp. 59–91.

of institutional and bureaucratic changes such as decentralisation of decision making power to the provincial and county levels and superannuation age for both the political leaders and bureaucrats, which were permitted by the Party. In one sense, the government and Party worked together thereby mutually reinforcing and consolidating the changes that they brought about. The lead in initiating these changes is taken by the government.

A much more recent phenomenon is the steady shift of focus from government to governance in the global context has its resonance in China wherein the government has been quite focused on governance and the *quality* of delivery of various administrative functions pertaining to environment and education rather than *quantity* of control. This trend has had a sobering impact on the very nature of government making it much more accountable to the people. This can particularly be seen in the government's policies towards layoffs either from PLA or from industries wherein it has been providing training for those being laid off to be absorbed into the newly emerging professions and industries such as information and communication technologies (ICTs) and tourism. Despite some of these positive changes there have been a number of protests both in urban and rural China. According to some estimates, there are as many as 90,000 protests annually in different parts which indicate that there is much to be desired in the realm of good governance being delivered by the government.

People's Liberation Army

People's Liberation Army (PLA), the real power wielding or more accurately power tilting institution, particularly during a political crisis, has a considerable role in determining and maintaining political stability of the Chinese state and society. Though PLA had a very diverse social base at the time of its inception it remained under the control of the CCP and the state since the establishment of PRC. Its role was decisive both during the Cultural Revolution as well as the 1989 Tiananmen Square crackdown. The increasing professionalisation and a systematic and gradual deceleration in its budget allocation, particularly in the 1980s and bringing together the defence and civilian production processes through technology transfer that Deng brought within the institution undercut some of its earlier sheen and political clout. Steady economic development brought to the Chinese leadership an awareness about the technological backwardness of its defence forces during the Gulf War, thus a greater emphasis was placed on the need to modernise its defence system, which eventually led to various measures of increased budget allocation further leading to greater sophistication (though China lags far behind the US). This phase of modernisation of PLA during the 1990s re-energised it, making it a formidable force both in the Chinese politics as well as in the realm of military prowess in the international context.

As indicated, its usefulness and power are generally demonstrated in the event of any political crisis. So long as there is no threat to the stability of the state it will remain in the barracks. Nevertheless, it continues to be a potent force in the Chinese political system with the ability to tilt the political tides in favour of the one who cultivates and maintains control over the PLA. The fissures in the PLA come to the fore, particularly during political succession, when who actually wields control over PLA is proven with utmost subtlety. In this regard, there were some anxious moments during the leadership transition from Jiang Zemin to Hu Jintao when the former wanted to retain control over the PLA by extending his chairmanship of the Central Military Commission (CMC), but he was slowly divested of this within two years after Hu Jintao became the General Secretary of the Party and President of China. Currently Hu Jintao holds complete control of the CMC and PLA without any major threats to his position from any quarter. It remains to be seen whether this tradition will continue in the future.

Villagers' Committees

While the above discussed political institutions are legacies of Mao's era, Villagers' Committees (VCs) are entirely the products of Deng Xiaoping period and the reforms he introduced since 1978. Rural China has witnessed several path breaking changes over the last three decades. One of them is that it traversed from *Fanshen* [turnover] during Mao's period to *Shenfan* [Incompatible] under Deng's rule.[38] Today's rural China is incompatible with Communism and more compatible with capitalism as much as the urban China is. The period from 1978 to 1988 was a transitional period in which the stage for the political reforms in rural China was prepared. In this, the economic freedom that was given to farmers in agricultural production came to pave the way for change in rural politics.

---

[38] These two seminal works by William Hinton depict the changes that rural China witnessed since 1949 with admirable finesse and a great deal of accuracy. Following are the more details of the two books: *Fanshen: A Documentary of Revolution in a Chinese Village* (New York: Vintage Books, 1966); *Shenfan: The Continuing Revolution in a Chinese Village* (New York: Vintage Books, 1984).

Like the dismantling of commune system was initiated by Anhui province, the change in rural politics was led by Guangxi Zhuang Autonomous Region in the late 1970s but thereafter it has been approved, appropriated and controlled by the state. The initial purpose was to address the decline in social order and broader political crisis which was created in the wake of the dismantling of commune system and the emergence of Household Responsibility System (HRS). It took about four years for the Chinese leaders to allow it as a new political institution in rural China. Peng Zhen, National People's Congress (NPC) Vice-Chairman was a staunch supporter of the VCs. He sent several delegations to study how they function and encouraged other provinces to experiment. Thereafter, he got it incorporated into the 1982 constitution thereby providing legal validity. In addition, a special Central Committee Circular was issued in 1983 giving it official sanction.[39]

All these efforts culminated in the formalisation of Villagers' Committees in 1988 through the legislation of Organic Law.[40] As part of this process grassroots elections were also introduced to be conducted every three years, thus sowing the seeds of gradual change in the rural political system with an inbuilt hope that this would be slowly taken to the higher levels. More importantly, the Villagers' Committees are in a way non-party institutions erected between the state and the people. It is a system of accountability outside the purview of the state. In the process, party and government officials' direct decision making powers are weakened making rural politics much more complex. One of the consequences was that the prestige of the party cadre plummeted quite sharply.[41] The state views the Villagers' Committees as a buffer structure to receive all the criticism from people that otherwise would have been directed to it. Village elections make the elected leaders, and not the government, responsible to the electorate.[42] The Law of the Villagers' Committee was amended in 1998 with more changes streamlining the election process. Though there are several skeptics who doubt the future impact of these initiatives translating into grassroots democracy, there are others who are hopeful of these elections transforming rural China into

---

[39] Kevin Brien J. O. and Liangjiang Li, "Accommodating "Democracy" in One Party-State: Introducing Village Elections in China," *The China Quarterly* 162 (2000), pp. 465–489.

[40] People's Republic of China, *Organic Law of the Villagers Committee of the People's Republic of China*, http://www.china.org.cn/english/government/207279.htm; accessed on 3 March 2007.

[41] Jean C. Oi, "The Role of the Local State in China's Transformation," *The China Quarterly* 144 (1995), pp. 1132–49.

[42] John James Kennedy, "The Face of "Grassroots Democracy" in Rural China: Real versus Cosmetic Elections," *Asian Survey* 42. 3 (2002), pp. 456–482.

a genuine democracy in due course. Brien and Li further argue that some villagers including local leaders, who began to see the elections as a quick means to dislodge corrupt officials, were robust supporters of China's tryst with democracy. They, therefore, demand free and fair elections. Sometimes they even boycott and occasionally complain to the higher authorities. They also identified a phenomenon of the officials of the Ministry of Civilian Affairs (MCA) being adept in using international support. For instance, Ford Foundation granted a substantial amount for its Research Society of Basic Governance. Asia Foundation, International Research Institute, United Nations Development Agency (UNDA), European Union (EU) have joined Ford Foundation in supporting local governance in China. Moreover, though rural democracy in China is evolving into "crony democracy" like "crony capitalism", it provides some sort of legitimacy to Villagers Committees besides functioning as checks and balances on the local officials. What one, however, can surmise at this stage is that it is too early to pronounce a final verdict on the utility of elections in Chinese villages. With all the complexities and problems with village elections such as no national standardised procedure, no exact idea of how many of 930,000 villages in China hold elections (Brien and Li estimate that only 10 percent of the villages hold well run elections, ¼ to ⅓ villages have conducted the elections according to the rules and 60 per cent of all the villages holding elections) and several methods of nomination in China,[43] many local administrators being loathe to villagers electing their leaders with the view that they would interfere with the local administration's policies and compete with their decision making powers, opposition from township administration, delay or rigging the elections, and monopolising nominations (Brien and Li), the democracy movement at the village level led by the state is slowly inching forward with the hope of strengthening representative democracy in China.

The steady shift from institutions to institutionalisation has, apart from transforming the very face of the Chinese political system to a considerable extent, led to several other changes. One of the changes as Gordon White points out is the emergence of an embryonic civil society.[44] Though the nature of civil society in China, like its political institutions, is highly appropriated and controlled by the state yet it is slowly making an impact on some less sensitive issues such

---

[43] Robert A.Pastor and Qingshan Tan, "The Meaning of China's Village Elections," *The China Quarterly* 162 (2000), pp. 490–512.

[44] Gordon White, *Riding the Tiger: The Politics of Economic Reform in Post-Mao China* (London: Macmillan, 1993), p. 199.

as environment, poverty and education leaving out out the more touchy issues such as human rights and legal and prison reforms. Secondly, the Chinese society has been evolving as a more complex one with a vibrant intellectual community, students and media with immense potential for political and social change. Thirdly, Elizabeth Perry observes another interesting change occurring beyond the state-society paradigm and finds that a number of processes that are unfolding in the provinces and counties need to be factored in our analysis of Chinese political system for a better understanding.[45] Fourthly, public discourse, which is quintessential for any political change, is more open than ever before. Compared to Mao's period there has been considerable openness among different sections of the Chinese society to debate and critique various policies of the government. But there are certain restrictions on what they can and cannot speak vis-à-vis the state. Anything too critical of the state is met with serious consequences thus putting breaks on the freedom of the individuals making it more of a restricted and qualified freedom.

Issue to Issues: Widening Horizons

The hub of domestic politics in China since 1978, unlike during Mao's period where the central focus was essentially on socialism, has been centred on many issues such as nationalism, national minorities, regionalism and legalisation with critical implications for the very stability of the Chinese polity. However, one should not assume that these issues were completely absent during Mao's period. Indeed they were not. But they were essentially overshadowed by one overarching issue of socialism whereas during the post-Mao's period they have began to overshadow socialism in the wake of the waning of its place and role. This process, in a way, unleashed a new sense of diversity and plurality into the Chinese political system despite the homegenising attempts by the state, party and government.

Nationalism

China has moved from being called a nation without nationalism by Sun Yat-sen[46] to becoming an ultra-nationalist one in a span of one century. The issue

---

[45] Elizabeth Perry, "Trends in the Study of Chinese Politics: State-Society Relations," *The China Quarterly* 139 (1994), pp. 704–13.

[46] Sun Yat-sen, *The Three Principles of the People*. Translated into English by Frank W. Price. Abridged and edited by the Commission for Cultural History of Kuomintang. (Taipei: China Cultural Service, 1953).

of nationalism also saw another major change as Prasenjit Duara highlights. Stating that "China chose the territorial model of civic nationalism as a against the ethnic-cultural nationalism to be the most suitable to realise its emancipatory goals as well as ameliorate the inequalities among its citizens across regions, class and gender" during Mao's period, Duara articulates that "there has been a de-territorialisation of the ideology of nationalism which becomes increasingly disarticulated from the model of territorial civic nationalism and turns to cultural-ethnic models more attuned to the intensified quest for global competitiveness"[47] in the wake of the new globalisation since 1980. This coincided with the process of nationalism reemerging as a major political issue and a force in the wake of erosion of communist ideology. The concept of nationalism moved from being a mere sense of belonging to one nation to being seen as an ideology wherein it is used as a political tool to remain in power and accomplish certain national and international goals. For both the leadership as well as the majority of the Chinese, ideology of nationalism appealed more potently than the communist ideology since it is other-directed without major implications for themselves unlike the latter.

Nationalism in China has developed two facets, a domestic and an external. In its domestic facet, the kind of nationalism that is being promoted was questioned by some of the liberal minded Chinese. A robust manifestation of this could be seen in the popular TV serial *River Elegy* which critiqued the version of nationalism that the party had promoted in the 1980s. At the same time, nationalism came quite handy in resolving some of its historical legacies of colonialism, particularly in the context of reunification of Hong Kong in 1997 and Macao in 1999. Nationalism is also used extensively in the area of maintaining stability in regard to the national minorities such as Tibetans and Uighurs when they began to question nationalism enunciated by the state and party. The minorities wanted the Chinese version of nationalism to be revisited. But the state views these assertions with immense potential for destabilising and dismembering China. There are others who see this rather differently and believe that those who triumph in this contestation will determine the nature of nationalism in China in the years to come. Nationalism with its two variants of ethnic and cultural dimensions is used as a major force to unite and ensure the stability of China. It also took another interesting dimension of being used in the context of economic development wherein China began to

---

[47] Prasenjit Duara, "Nationalism and Transnationalism in the Globalization of China," *China Report* 39. 1 (2003), pp. 12–14.

evaluate its economic development juxtaposing to that of the Japanese and the Newly Industrialising Economies (NIEs) of East Asia.

In its external dimension, the Chinese state used nationalism in gaining a number of advantages in the bilateral, regional and international arenas. For instance, nationalism was evoked in its relations with Japan over its PM's visits to Yasukuni shrine and the text book controversy. A number of cyber attacks were launched by the Chinese on Japanese websites causing considerable damage to the Japanese Internet network. The use of nationalism in the context of Belgrade bombing of the Chinese embassy in 1999 was a major reflection of the aggressive Chinese nationalism that rattled the international community. Interestingly enough, the state that evokes these nationalistic passions also has the ability to contain them when they become too dangerous. Blazing the fires of nationalism and dousing them suggests an element of state orchestration. This kind of orchestration of nationalism may not be beneficial to Chinese polity in the long run.

National Minorities

A closely related issue is that of national minorities and their place and role in Chinese domestic politics. This is one of the most delicate issues in the Chinese politics, primarily because the stability of the Chinese political system is directly linked to this and can be disturbed by any mishandling of the issue. The significance of the issue can be better appreciated only when one considers the following details. There are 56 recognised nationalities with 55 being called national minorities and one majority nationality-Han. About 400 minorities are waiting to be recognised by the government. The recognised 55 national minorities constitute about 8.2 per cent of the total population, with 18 per cent of the arable land and 38 per cent of the forest land and 60 per cent of the total Chinese territory under their control. 18 of these national minorities have more than a million population. The largest is Zhuang concentrated in Yunnan and Gguanxi Autonomous regions with more than 15 million, while the smallest national minority-Lhoba has only about 3000 people. Majority of them inhabit in the five autonomous regions and 659 autonomous cities and counties. Most of these regions share borders with several countries, making them strategically significant for China in its domestic, regional and international politics.

Three issues of past, present and future of the minorities in China are relevant to put the relations between minorities and Han majority in perspective.

On the issue of the relations between minorities and majority in the past, Dick Wilson asserts that the historical legacy of these national minorities dominated regions seems similar to that of the former colonies of the West.[48] On the present context, June Teufel Dreyer considers the relations between the two as "a major problem of integration, jurisdiction and loyalties besides economic disparities creating mote complications and the solution for this seems to be more elusive than before."[49] On the issue of the future of minorities vis-à-vis majority, Katherine Palmer is of the view that they are "more likely to resemble minority relations in the United States rather than that of former Soviet Union."[50] While the three views have some grain of truth, they fall short of the total reality of the issue as the following discussion highlights.

The Chinese leadership, in their policy towards national minorities has moved from one end of the spectrum of advocating a level playing field in the 1930s to the other end of assimilation during Mao's era. Since 1978, there has been marked improvement in the treatment of national minorities in contemporary China. The 1982 Constitution targets both Han and minority chauvinism. Article 4 reads: "All nationalities in the PRC are equal. The state protects the lawful rights and interests of the minority nationalities and upholds and develops the relationship of equality, unity and mutual assistance." It further states:

> Discrimination is prohibited; Any acts that undermine the unity of nationalities or instigate their secession are prohibited; Speed up economic and cultural development; Regional autonomy is practiced; Self government is promoted; All the minority nationality dominated areas are deemed to be inalienable parts of China; Freedom to develop their own spoken and written languages and to preserve or reform their customs is given to them.[51]

From the standpoint of unification, these constitutional provisions enable the leadership to strengthen national unity and maintain territorial integrity.

But from the perspective of the minorities, though the 1982 Constitution espouses such excellent principles, there are certain problems in implementing them on the ground. One of them is lack of genuine autonomy. Some of

---

[48] Dick Wilson, *China, the Big Tiger: A Nation Awakes* (London: Little Brown, 1996).

[49] June Teufel Dryer, *Chinese Political System: Modernization and Tradition* (London: Macmillan, 2000).

[50] Katherine Palmer, "China's Nationalities and Nationality Areas," in Christopher Hudson, ed., *The China Handbook* (Chicago: Fitzroy Publishers, 1997), p. 283.

[51] People's Republic of China, *The Constitution of the People's Republic of China* (Beijing: Foreign Languages Press, 1982).

the minorities firmly maintain that the various political processes in their autonomous regions are still dominated and controlled by the Han nationals, be it party or administrative processes. They are also critical of the state-orchestrated influx of Han Chinese into the national minority regions that has been changing the demographic composition in these regions besides undermining the local economic and cultural dynamics. For these reasons, besides others, some minorities like Tibetans and Uighurs continue to struggle not only for autonomy but also for independence. While the question of independence seems herculean, at least for now, their movement for autonomy is genuine. The recent attempts by Tibetans in 2008 and Uighurs in 2009 to internationalise their concerns are indicative of the enormity of the issue.

The onus of allowing the national minorities to exercise genuine autonomy in their regions without changing the demographic composition is entirely with the Chinese leadership. So long as this is neglected, the issue of national minorities will continue to haunt China.

Centre-Province Relations

Another issue is Centre-Province relations which came to occupy a significant place in Chinese politics in the wake of the institutional changes and economic reform that began in the early 1980s. The manner in which this issue is managed would also have serious implications for the future of the Chinese political system. It can either break or further unify China. Therefore, the Chinese leadership at the Centre is quite concerned about this and tries to balance development and stability besides strengthening the centripetal forces. In doing so, the Centre has been attempting, with some degree of success, to draw legitimacy from the economic development that the provinces have been accomplishing. Centre needs them as much as they need it in maintaining the current rate of growth. The dynamics of Centre-Province relations are viewed by both the parties involved as mutually beneficial.

However, after the Tiananmen Square crackdown there has been a resurgence of centrifugal forces as the central government has tightened its control over the allocation of resources, and the widening of market oriented reforms. Centre began to tighten the noose on the economic freedom granted to the provinces in order to maintain political unity. For instance, the Centre imposed a number of restrictions such as the need to take permission for undertaking large-scale projects. Though there are some exceptions to this.

Shanghai, for example had no such restrictions. Decline in state revenues from 36 per cent in 1978 to 14.2 per cent in 1999 is seen as a process of weakening of the centre vis-à-vis the provinces. Though several scholars see this as a new trend wherein the centre delegating the responsibility to the provinces to manage various economic issues locally, there are others who approach this as a new phenomenon of provinces becoming stronger vis-à-vis the centre.

Further compounding the Centre-Province relations is the issue of regional trade protectionism that came to the fore as certain provinces in the interior and western parts of China felt that provinces such as Guangdong, Fujian, Zhejiang and Jiangsu on the east coast are given more preferences. As a result, they began demanding similar preferences in order to boast their local economies. In responding to this the Centre introduced the Western Development Project aiming at the development of these regions. But this had limited impact on the development of these provinces and autonomous regions primarily because the state is not as committed to their cause as it is to the coastal provinces.

In addition to the economic imperatives, the Chinese leadership has been keen on balancing centralisation and decentralisation of decision making process. Unlike in Mao's period, Deng and his followers did not want to control every part of an average Chinese. They have been more concerned with the *quality* of control rather the *quantum* of control. This approach and policy, in a way, led to qualitative change in the decentralisation of decision-making process in China. The provinces, autonomous regions and counties have been allowed to make decisions pertaining to the local development and various political and social issues. In this context, in order not to lose complete control over the provinces the Centre came up with indirect means to control them by developing rules and regulations for the provinces, better auditing, improving administrative monitoring and collection of information, and thus making them dependent on the Centre. The Centre deems the relationship with the provinces as not necessarily one of a zero-sum game.

According to Jae Ho Chung provincial-international relations further makes the analysis more complex due to provinces being integrated to the global economy. Moreover, the most recent phenomenon of sub-provincial cities emerging as powerful competitors to the provinces is further making the dynamics between the provinces and the Centre more complicated.[52] Despite

---

[52] Jae Ho Chung, "Studies of Central-Provincial Relations in the People's Republic of China: A Mid-term Appraisal," *The China Quarterly* 142 (1995), pp. 487–508.

all these processes, as long as the twin goals of stability and development are being accomplished the Centre has no problem in sharing a part of its power and responsibility with the lower levels. This process is likely to continue in the foreseeable future.

Legal System

The legal system is another significant issue that has come to occupy central place in Chinese polity in the recent past. While the new leadership felt the need for a balanced and fairly developed legal system, it was economic reform programme that played a critical role in its growth. This legal system is economic development-centred rather than individual-centred. In other words, it is economy-driven rather than freedom-driven. When the legal system began its new journey in post-1978 China, it was essentially one of "rule by law" [*yi fa zhi guo*] and ever since it has been moving slowly and steadily towards "rule of law" [*fa zhi guo jia*]. "Rule by law" and "Rule of Law" are two key concepts in the lexicon of Chinese legal system. In the former, there is no primacy of law over other institutions. For instance, the state is not subjected to law rather law serves the state. Law is intended to serve socialism rather than individual. The latter, "rule of law", wherein the state and other institutions are under the law on the lines of the Western concept of rule of law has still not taken strong roots in China. The silver lining, though, is that China's pre, and post-entry into the WTO has further expedited the institutionalisation of legal system in China. According to Liu Ji, the development and amendment of a series of criminal laws, civil laws and economic laws, and especially the fact that their enforcement is now based on the "presumption of innocence" rather than the "presumption of guilt", represents progress in the development of the rule of law in China.[53]

Though human rights issue deserves special focus given its importance, it is discussed under the broad rubric of legal system because both are closely related in the sense that an efficient legal system paves the way for better human rights record. Human rights issue does not figure in the Chinese domestic politics as majority of its domestic constituency is largely silent on it, under the influence of Confucian and communist traditions of passive

---

[53] Liu Ji, "The Reform of the Chinese Political System," Address to Europe-China Forum on September 23, 2003. http://www.ceibs.edu/ase/Documents/EuroChinaForum/liuji.htm; accessed on March 25, 2009.

political culture rather than in the "let hundred schools of thought contend" tradition. However, it is one of the most contentious issues that not only unnerved China in its endeavour to integrate with the global economy but also brought a new focus to the universal human rights debate led by the Western countries including the UN Declaration of Human Rights. While the human rights debate led by the West exclusively centered on civil and political facets, the Chinese emphasised on the economic and social dimensions. The Chinese leadership had generally replaced *human rights* with *human development*. For them so long as human development is taken care, human rights issue is addressed. In their perspective individual rights do not matter much and they are subsumed in the rights of the community and the state. Chinese *White Papers* on human rights highlight the issue in greater detail.[54] While some of the Western countries use human rights violations in China as a tool to contain China's rise, China focuses on social and economic components of human rights to deflect the West's concern for human rights in China. The pertinent issue is that the human rights framework constitutes both the Western and Chinese versions of civil, political and economic, and social foci. They are two sides of the same coin. China tends to neglect the former while addressing the latter. It must strike a balance by focusing on all the dimensions. This can be possible only by strengthening legal system.

Of all the issues relating to the legal system in China, enforcement has been rather problematic as Tony Saich argues that "legal system is simply one specific cog in a bureaucratic machine that is built to achieve state objectives."[55] Neither the state nor the government is keen on enforcing legal processes pertaining to the individual since it is perceived as an extra burden. They, however, are not found wanting in enforcing legal procedures pertaining to economic development. In comparison to many developing countries, legal education and training is quite underdeveloped. In addition to this, there is too much of official interference in the legal proceedings. As a result, there is a lack of judicial independence. Despite these problems, Chinese legal system has come a long way from its near extinction during Mao's period to gaining public confidence in the recent past given the number of cases wherein the victims won legal suits over copyright infringement, officials who levied exorbitant fees being punished, a writer getting damages from a state-run

---

[54] People's Republic of China, *White Papers of the Chinese Government 2* (Beijing: Foreign Languages Press, 2000).

[55] Tony Saich, *Governance and Politics of China* (New York: Palgrave, 2001), p. 123.

publishing house, an actress over a magazine. The number of legal cases which increased from 3 million in 1990 to 5.3 million in 1996 is an indication of the improving face of Chinese legal system. At the 17th Party Congress Hu Jintao, while claiming that China has "made steady progress in implementing the rule of law as a fundamental principle", acknowledged that "efforts to improve...the legal system fall somewhat short of the need to expand people's democracy and promote economic and social development."[56] Thus the legal system in China has a long way to cover in becoming more and more people-centred rather than being party-oriented, controlled and dominated.

Democracy

Though the issue of democracy has been on the periphery of the Chinese political agenda for the last three decades, one can glean three distinct paths being pursued by three different sections to introduce some sort of democracy in post-1978 China. First, *top-down path* pursued by the Chinese state. Deng Xiaoping delved on the issue for a while, particularly in the early 1980s. However, he gave it up towards the end of that decade primarily due to the immense resistance from the conservative leadership. Since then this has been put on the back burner. Moreover, though the Chinese leadership claims that Chinese state adheres to the Democratic Dictatorship, one of the four cardinal principles providing a broad framework; and as Randell Peerenboom articulates that China will evolve its own version of democracy on its terms and at its own pace, which is different from the Western liberal democracy;[57] there are no concrete steps being taken in that direction. One could, however, point out the October 2005 government document of *Building of Democracy in China* as an evidence of some concrete steps being taken by the state on this issue.[58] While this is a positive sign, in essence it is to appropriate and shape non-state attempts of introducing democracy in China.

Second, *bottom-up path* initiated by the people from Guangxi province when they, for the first time, initiated some form of local democratic governance. Unfortunately, like civil society, this bottom-up initiative of democracy was appropriated by the state and took control of it before it posed any major threat

---

[56] Hu Jintao, *Report to the Seventeenth Congress of the Communist Party of China*, October 15, 2007.

[57] Randell Peerenboom, *China Modernizes: Threat to the West or Model for the Rest* (London: Oxford University Press, 2008), p. 244.

[58] People's Republic of China, *Building of Political Democracy in China* (Beijing: The State Council Information Office, 2005).

to its dominance in general and to its version of democracy in particular. Like the household responsibility system (HRS), there is every likelihood of it moving to the core of the Chinese political system as some movement towards it is already in operation through the Villagers' Committees.

Third, *middle path* pursued by the Chinese intellectuals and students who attempted to bring Western style democracy to China in the 1980s.[59] The intellectuals and students could think of democracy only after 1975 when the Chinese state took several measures directly relating to them. Of the two, the intellectuals received enormous support from the state in anticipation of their contribution to economic development. One of the first steps that Deng Xiaoping took was to recognise them as an integral part of the working class when he said: "Chinese intellectuals including the overwhelming majority of the old intellectuals from the pre-Liberation society have become part of the working class and now serve the cause of socialism consciously and actively."[60] This radical change provided a great deal of freedom compared to that of Mao's period. It restored their political status and they were no longer called the ninth stinking category. Moreover, they were not required to be ideologically oriented. This was a major step that gave intellectuals more time for intellectual pursuits. Their social status and economic conditions have also enormously improved with the success of economic reforms. Intellectuals, with this renewed position and favourable conditions, began to press for changes not only in social but also political arenas right through the 1980s. Quite interestingly scientists[61] such as Fang Lizhi and several others, as a sub-class of the intellectuals played a commendable role in trying to bring Western liberal democracy to China. But the state and the party were keen on gradual reforms and insisted that they be confined to economic and social realms. Following the pace set by the intellectuals, several reform-minded students shared the views of the intellectuals and tried to take it to its logical conclusion through protests and hunger strikes which culminated in the democracy movement and the subsequent Tiananmen Square crackdown that suppressed the voices of freedom. Since then the intellectual and student communities began to be quite cautious of the state. This lull had given the state and the

---

[59] Merle Goldman, ed., *China's Intellectuals and the State: In Search of a New Relationship* (Massachusetts: Harvard University Press, 1987).

[60] Deng Xiaoping, "Concerning Problems on the Ideological Front," *Selected Works of Deng Xiaoping*, vol. II, 2nd ed., (Beijing: Foreign Languages Press, 1995), p. 192.

[61] For more on this, see Lyman H. Miller, *Science and Dissent in Post-Mao China: The Politics of Knowledge* (Seattle: University of Washington Press, 1996).

government some breathing space to concentrate on various developmental issues. However, the present absence of democracy movement is not to be construed as the death of the *middle path* to democracy. There has been a subtle and indirect support for democracy emerging at various levels. For instance, we notice some sort of revival of the democracy movement in the Chinese cyber world despite all attempts of the government to nip it in the bud. The rise of another phase of democracy movement depends on the functioning of the state and the intellectual and student communities. The Chinese intellectuals and students are waiting for an opportune time to initiate what they firmly believe to be their fundamental right. It remains to be seen which of these three paths to democracy will see fruition in the years to come.

Concluding Remarks

In one of the passionate and insightful discourses when Tzu-kung, one of the 36 disciples of Confucius, enquired about the nature of good government, Confucius, the wise and thoughtful Chinese political philosopher, said, "Food enough, troops enough, and the trust of the people." Tzu-kung said, "If it had to be done, which could best be spared of the three?" "Troops", said the Master. "And if we had to, which could better be spared of the other two?" "Food", said the Master. "From of old all men die, but without trust a people cannot stand."[62] Following this ancient intellectual discourse between the most influential Chinese political philosopher and his disciple, giving preeminence to people's faith in the leaders vis-à-vis food and security, the leadership since 1978 has been striving to retain people's faith in the Chinese political system through various means and methods. One of the means is through economic development. The method of gradualism is seen to be the most viable and pragmatic way. But building people's faith through political reform is right at the bottom of this process despite its critical role in it. Unless Chinese leaders address this issue their vision of peaceful rise would remain rather problematic.

Problems

Contemporary Chinese domestic politics is inextricably linked to the way Chinese society and economy have been evolving in the last three decades.

---

[62] Confucius, *The Sayings of Confucius*. Translated by Leonard A. Lyall. (London: Longmans Green and Co., 2007).

This continuum between politics, economy and society has been shaping the rise of China. The Chinese leadership is quite determined to ensure China's peaceful rise through four modernisations of agriculture, industry, science and technology and defence. The track record so far has been impressive and beyond the predictions of most scholars of all hues and shades. Despite this determination and fairly successful track record so far, there are some serious problems that persist in the realm of Chinese domestic politics. First, the gulf between ideology and praxis is a critical problem for the Chinese leadership. Deng Xiaoping managed it with certain dexterity despite several challenges. Jiang Zemin and Hu Jintao have carried forward the process. The three leaders have added their bit to the ever evolving Chinese political philosophy through their socialism with Chinese characteristics, market socialism, Three Represents, Building Harmonious and Well-off Society, and Scientific Development. In all these innovative ideological conceptualisations there is lurking a clear disconnect between political pronouncements and practice. Though the Chinese leaders claim that the Chinese polity is still on the road to socialism, the reality on the ground is slowly moving in the opposite direction. The outcome of this process could be the beginning of a political reality that the Chinese state and party have been attempting to thwart. Another ground reality is that the locus of real power is shared between the Centre and provinces, which might weaken the former. Except from the national minority dominated regions and provinces the Centre has not faced any threat to its stability so far. However, there is no guarantee that this would continue in the future.

Second, though political institutions have been "bending without breaking" as Jean Oi aptly puts it,[63] they are still rigid and authoritarian in their functioning. Some sort of governance with iron hand has been in operation. This is possible largely because people are passive, waiting and watching how the political processes are unfolding. As I found in my own interaction with some of the intellectuals in China during 2004, there is a palpable fear among them, particularly while expressing their frank opinions about the functioning of the government. Generally there are two kinds of opinions that many Chinese hold to their chest, one critical and private that they strongly believe and the other pragmatic and public, less critical and less

---

[63] Jean Oi, "Bending without Breaking: The Adaptability of Chinese Political Institutions," *Working Paper No. 61*, October 2000, (Center for Research on Economic Development and Policy Reform, Stanford University), pp. 1–26.

truthful primarily for public consumption. There is real tension between the two waiting to burst forth.

Third, though there has been considerable improvement in the development of legal system, it continues to be weak and pits the relations between the citizen and the state in the latter's favour. Individual is severely subjected to the community and its goals. The Chinese state's contention that community and its goals being more important than the individual goes against the universal rights of individual. This is something that the state and the Chinese people will have to resolve and the sooner they do it the better both for the individual as well as the society and the state.

Fourth, ensuring a genuine autonomy to the minority nationalities continues to be a problem for the Chinese government. The objective of genuine autonomy can be realised only when the minorities genuinely feel part of China without being forced. And this cannot be accomplished without granting them comprehensive, and not partial, autonomy as has been the case for the last three decades. This requires some sort of trust-building between the majority Han and the minorities, both nationally and locally. This needs to be seen not just in pronouncements but in reality. Their representation in various political processes is quite dismal. For example, in the 17th CPC National Congress there are only 14 out of 204 members from the national minorities. There is only one member from the minority communities in the Standing Committee and no minister representing them. Their representation is a shade better among the Alternate members with 23 out of 167. This is not enough. Much more needs to be done.

Fifth, social conflict and politics of resentment at the grass-roots level has the potential to undermine the political stability and derail the current peaceful rise of China. In order, partly to make the villages and counties self-sufficient and reliant and partly to deflect the growing crisis emanating from the reform process, the state allowed and supported Villagers' Committees which are seed-beds for democratic system to evolve in China. In this realm, like in regard to socialism, the Chinese leaders are desperately trying to give a Chinese touch to the very institution of democracy which may have serious implications for both state and society in China.

Finally, a highly neglected issue is the representation of women in various political processes. For example, in the 17th CPC National Congress they are only 13 out of 204 "from the other half of the sky" that Mao so fervently used to say of women. Their representation is a shade better among the Alternate members with 24 out of 167. This is an issue that the Chinese women along with their representative body All China Women's Federation (ACWF) and the leadership will have to grapple with and ensure that there are constitutional and political measures to facilitate women to participate in the political processes.

Future

Given these problems persisting with the Chinese political system, what is its likely future is a critical issue that one must be concerned about. Any discussion on the future of Chinese government and politics needs to begin with a caveat: none can project the developments in China with any amount of certainty. Domestic political system in China has been witnessing significant changes since 1978. However, there is enormous scope for further changes in the realm of Chinese political institutions and processes. Given the recent trajectory of a growing institutionalisation of Chinese government and politics, it can be safely argued that this process could continue. But one can never be certain about the pace of such a process because of the persisting tension between the radical and conservative reformers. In contrast to the Western conventional argument that characterises the changes occurring in China as economic reform without political reform, China has seen several political changes and the gamut of political reform could widen in the years to come. Introduction of grassroots democracy is a clear indication in this direction. With the slow withdrawal of state from a number of social spaces has created avenues for their expansion in the future. Globalisation as a social, economic and political process will have serious implications for the Chinese government and politics. For instance, ICTs, which are the driving forces of globalisation, will continue to play a critical role in further transforming the domestic politics in China despite the Chinese state's attempts to contain and limit their impact on various political processes.

Chinese domestic politics are in a transitional phase wherein one observes the policy of crossing the river by feeling the stones in practice, a policy that would continue in the days ahead. Deng Xiaoping is undoubtedly the architect of these changes. However, he carried out only partial changes leaving the rest for his successors to do the rest beginning with a process of reinterpreting socialism. The successive leaders, Jiang Zemin and Hu Jintao, did contribute to this based on the changing domestic realities. There is much that could be done. The plausibility of a continual reformulation of socialism, under the broad rubric of fresh and new ideas, is likely to continue in the foreseeable future. While Hu Jintao's recent acknowledgment that political restructuring has to be deepened is encouraging, but not being specific about what that deepening of political restructuring involves is rather disappointing. He seems to be cautious about the extent to which he can go in deepening the restructuring of the political system. Being too cautious does not help the common Chinese to be able to participate in various political processes meaningfully. There is, therefore, enormous scope for a number of changes in the Chinese domestic politics, whose future is dependent on the both the leadership and the led and more importantly on how they approach them. The unfinished political reform underscores the daunting challenge ahead for the next generation leaders. One will have to wait and watch closely how the Chinese political system will unfold in future.

Implications for India

The political changes that have been unfolding in contemporary China will have both positive and negative implications for India. Let us turn our attention to the positive implications. First, the current shift from ideology to ideas is good for India because the eventual outcome of this process is that China would cease to be an authoritarian state slowly moving towards a much more benign power and therefore easy to deal with. Second, the focus from institutions to institutionalisation also bodes well for India as this further transforms and consolidates the various reforms that came about in the institutional structure of the Chinese political system be it the state, government, party, PLA and Villagers' Committees. Of all these, positive changes in the two institutions of the CCP by opening its doors for businessmen and Villagers' Committees moving closer to the Indian Panchayati Raj system, have the potential to bring the two neighbours closer to each other in being similar in their political institutions. Moreover, it is also good for India if China manages to handle the simmering tensions among its provinces over various issues of resource allocation and development vis-à-vis the Centre because there will be one issue less to use as an excuse against India to turn its people's attention from its domestic crisis. In addition, slow and steady progress being made in the realms of legal system, as it inches towards individual-centred, and democracy, regardless of whichever path triumphs, will bring the two systems to a common ground, thus minimising the differences in their respective political systems to adversely impact the relations between the two.

In regard to the plausible negative implications, the manner in which Chinese nationalism, with all its complexities, evolves in the future will have serious implications for India. In the event of nationalism taking a virulent form, say for example, on the border issue between India and China, it could seriously strain the relations at some point. This requires some sort of serious thinking on the part of the Indian government to be able to deal with such a scenario. In fact, one can trace two strands of Chinese, one striving for better relations and cooperation with India, while the other trying to demonstrate their "Middle Kingdom" syndrome. The Indian foreign policy making structures must endeavour to cultivate and strengthen the former while isolating the latter for better relations as the two Asian giants are rising simultaneously. The other issue that could have a bearing on India relates to Chinese policy towards its national minorities. If China manages to handle the issue without letting it threaten its internal stability and territorial integrity then it lessens its impact on India. In case, things go out of hand, this could have its rippling effect on Indian unity. Therefore, both the countries have to be more inclusive by granting genuine autonomy and thereby assuaging the concerns of the minorities while dealing with them in their respective political systems since both have minority-related issues to grapple with.

4

China's Military Modernisation

Dragon Fire on India

Srikanth Kondapalli

CHINA has initiated a concerted military modernisation programme in the last few decades, the impact of which is being felt in the neighbourhood, including on India. An important dimension of China's rise recently is its military modernisation programme, which was enhanced after the People's Liberation Army (PLA) suffered losses in the 1979 Vietnam War. The 1985 "structural reorganisation" plan had relatively succeeded in putting the rank and file of the PLA on the road to a "lean and mean" armed forces. Hardware and software modernisation of the PLA and double-digit increases in the defence budget allocations, in the last two decades, were to make it one of the major forces to contend with in the region. It is generally recognised that by 1999, the PLA was making a turnaround from large infantry-based armed force to that of gradually acquiring the potential to project power abroad. This was part of the strategy to transit from mechanisation to information-based warfare.

The transition in the PLA are clearly visible. On January 11, 2007, China conducted an anti-satellite test with a ground-based missile destroying one of its retired Fengyun satellites located at about 860 km in orbit. Three years later, the same day in 2010, China conducted successfully an interceptor missile test. The Chinese air force has unveiled newer versions of multi-role aircraft (J-10), while acquiring others from Russia (Su-27 and Su-30). In October 2006, a Chinese conventional submarine trailed *USS Kittyhawk* near Okinawa. In December 2006, the PLA also indicated in its white paper on national defence that China would increasingly deter regional conflicts from breaking up and would manage conflict in short to medium term. Further instructions for Revolution in Military Affairs (RMA) applications were issued through the January 2009 white paper on national defence. China in April 2009 also organised an international fleet review – underlining the global tasks of its naval forces.[1] Indications of these were made in December 2008 when the Chinese navy despatched two vessels to the pirate-affected Somalia coasts. During the October 2009 Beijing parade, China had displayed 52 weapons – including DF-31 inter-continental ballistic missiles, DF-21, 11 and 15 series of short and medium range ballistic missiles, DH-10 cruise missiles, Marine Corps, J-10, J-11 (Su-27) multi-role aircrafts, Kongjing-2000 Airborne Early Warning and Control (AEWC) system, unmanned aerial vehicles, infantry fighting vehicles, etc.

The above measures underline the successes in PLA modernisation, which involved streamlining and reorganising its force structures, raising elite troops, restructuring of command and control mechanisms, restoration of the rank system and grades, emphasis on professional military education, revamping curriculum and upgrading the defence technological capabilities of the personnel. These are meant to enhance military capabilities of the country to overcome the perceived challenges of the state and make China a great power. Several factors have influenced such modernising efforts, viz., changes in the nature of warfare, technology, ability to divert precious budgetary and human resources, political leadership's choices and outlook, and the like. The actual modernising efforts of the PLA were carried out by different defence industrial, staff and other related military establishments. This chapter traces the main features of PLA modernisation in the last one decade and reflects on its impact on India.

Roadmap for Modernisation

Specific measures in this direction were made by the leadership. In the 1990s, Central Military Commission (CMC) of the PLA reportedly projected a

---

[1] On the occasion, President Hu Jintao stated that the Chinese Navy is "a service arm of strategic nature, a comprehensive nature, and an international nature, and the Navy has an important place and role in defending the nation's sovereignty, security and territorial integrity, and in protecting the nation's maritime interests and developmental interests". Hu cited at Chen Wanjun et al, "Party Central Committee and Central Military Commission's Concern for the Construction and Development of the People's Navy," *Xinhua Domestic Service,* April 25, 2009, NewsEdge Document Number: 200904251477.1_305e109b5cc757f2.

three-stage modernisation programme for the armed forces – viz., an initial modernisation of the three branches from 1992 to 1996; a second phase of "fundamental modernisation" by 1998; and a third phase of "basic advanced modernisation" completed by 2001.[2] The late 2002 16th Communist Party Congress emphasised on mechanisation and informationisation to be pursued for the next two decades. Subsequently, the December 2006 white paper on national defence outlined the roadmap of such modernisation as:

> (the) first step is to lay a solid foundation by 2010, the second is to make major progress around 2020 and the third is to basically reach the strategic goal of building informationised armed forces and being capable of winning informationised wars by the mid-twenty-first century.[3]

The 2006 white paper reiterated that mechanisation would be the "foundation" and informationisation as the "driving force" of the PLA modernisation. This meant a gradual increase in the mechanised platforms like tanks, armoured personnel carriers, naval ships, fighter aircraft, etc. while information technology related platforms would be gradually increased in the PLA inventory. The October 2007 17th Communist Party Congress as well as the 2008 6th white paper on defence, issued in January 2009, reiterated these points.

Force Structure Reform

One of the first measures in the direction of modernisation is the force structure reform. Among the organisational structures, the ground, navy, and air force, the Second Artillery of China has grown into the 3rd largest of such forces in the world. After the 1979 Vietnam War, they were subjected to several bouts of reform and reorganisation following changes in the defence strategy of the country, from people's war under modern conditions to local war under high-tech and then to informationised conditions.[4] Changes in military personnel

---

[2] See *Cheng Ming* March 1, 1992, in *Foreign Broadcast Information Service: Daily Report, China* (hereafter *FBIS-CHI) FBIS-CHI-92-045*, March 6, 1992 p 37 and David Shambaugh, *Reforming China's Military* (Berkeley: University of California Press, 2003). See also the United States Department of Defense annual reports on the PLA at <http://www.defenselink.org>.

[3] See "China's National Defense" White Paper issued by the state council on December 29, 2006 at <http://english.peopledaily.com.cn>.

[4] See Ku Guisheng, "The New Change in Military Affairs Calls for the Renewal of the Organizational Setup of China's Military," *Liaowang* July 28, 2003 in FBIS-CHI-2003-0805 August 15, 2003.

profile (in terms of technical and command qualities and preference to younger personnel), role of Non-Commissioned Officer (NCO) corps, re-introduction of military ranks and grades, enhancing professionalism, demobilisation, raising elite and rapid response forces, reduction in Military Regions (MRs), infusing high-tech weaponry, digitalisation, revamping training programmes, integration of forces, setting up theatre command posts, etc. are all part of this effort.

Internally, the PLA is in transition with the reform and modernisation process. Introduction of age limits up to 65 years of service (specifically at the campaign levels), professional trends, NCO system, higher educational requirements, etc. are some of the recent measures. By the end of 2006, nearly 70,000 NCOs were assigned to about 70 jobs in the technical and administrative streams

> including supply chief, aviation technician, captain of small-sized transportation boat, electric and mechanic chief, observation and communication chief, navigation chief, small warehouse chief, confidential archives keeper, club director, auto service unit head, driving instructor, head of soldiers training unit, nurse and managing personnel of logistics of the people's armed force department.[5]

From 2007, the PLA members started wearing a new uniform. This was to be implemented across the rank and file in about three years.[6] The PLA soldiers' salaries have also been doubled from 2006 – thanks also to the defence budget rise. Emphasis on RMA necessitates enhancing talent pool in the military through collaboration with the hi-tech civilian sector.[7]

Troop Demobilisation

More visible than all these measures was the ten demobilisation efforts, with the last three announced in 1985 (one million demobilisation of troops), 1997 (half-a-million demobilisation) and in 2003, having a lasting impact. In the 1985 efforts, the officer-to-soldier ratio was lowered from

---

[5] Yang Yangshen and Li Junping, "Nearly 70,000 NCOs Replace Officers in 70-odd Positions," *Liberation Army Daily* January 8, 2007 File Number 985 Accession Number 237800100.

[6] "Chinese President Stresses Party Loyalty And Modernization at PLA Birthday Rally," *Xinhua* August 1, 2007 OSC Transcribed Text File Number 985 Accession Number 248050319.

[7] "Chinese President Approves Military Talent Retention Rules" *Xinhua* August 2, 2007 at BBC Selected World Broadcasts.

1:2.45 to 1:3.3, strength of technical personnel was increased and military academies were reorganised.[8] In the 1997 reorganisation, ground forces' strength was further reduced while navy, air force and rocket forces' strength were enhanced, in addition to creating a new armaments department. The first tri-serve integrated services system was also formed. In the last reorganisation in 2003, joint operations command institutions were formed and command structures were simplified.[9]

With these reorganisations, the number of group armies was brought down from 24 to 21 and then to the current 18.[10] Efforts were on to downsize the strength of the group army from nearly 50,000–70,000 troops a unit to brigade level for rapid response.[11] Relatively, the mechanisation levels of the Beijing, Shenyang and Jinan MRs are higher as compared to the other MRs.[12] Further, at the 80th anniversary of the foundation of the PLA in 2007, Hu Jintao said that the military should

> strike a sound balance between speed, quality and efficiency in its modernisation drive and must be integrated into the country's overall modernisation strategy and serve the interests of national security and development.[13]

RMA

All the above measures of reform and reorganisation of the PLA structure are a part of the drive towards RMA, although initially this may not have been

---

[8] Currently, 117 military academies have been brought down to 67. See Hu Chunhua and Zou Weirong, "PLA Establishes New Type Military Personnel Cultivation System," *Liberation Army Daily* October 23, 2008 World News Connection File Number 985 Accession Number 270450109. In addition, after 30 years of reform, it was stated that currently 66 per cent of cadres in the PLA have obtained undergraduate and above academic qualifications. See Zhou Ben and Bao Guojun, "Overall Quality of Ranks of Cadres in Our Army Sharply Rises by (a) Great Margin," *Liberation Army Daily* October 31, 2008 World News Connection File Number 985 Accession Number 270850547

[9] This is based on Zhang Lishe and Liang Pengfei, "Reform Organization and Composition and Accelerate our Military's Pace toward Fewer but Better Troops," *Liberation Army Daily* October 31, 2008 World News Connection File Number 985 Accession Number 270851569.

[10] Robert SaeLiu, "The Great Chinese Puzzle," *Jane's Defence Weekly* September 24, 2003.

[11] John Hill, "China's PLA Reform Success," *Jane's Defence Weekly* December 1, 2003.

[12] This is based on International Institute of Strategic Studies, *The Military Balance 2007–2008* (London: Oxford University Press, 2007)

[13] Hu cited at "President Says China to Build "Slim but Strong" Armed Forces," *Xinhua* August 1, 2007 at BBC. At the speech, he stressed the formula of "revolutionary, modern and regularised" armed force. See "Chinese Agency Depicts Beijing Meeting on Army Anniversary," *Xinhua* August 2, 2007 at BBC.

the agenda.[14] China's interest in the RMA aspects like Information Warfare (IW), Electronic Warfare (EW), Command, Control, Communications and Computers, Intelligence, Surveillance and Reconnaissance (C4ISR) and space warfare dates back to the 1980s and predates the post-Gulf War 1991 debates on the subject. However, these remain elementary in nature. From the mid-1990s, there has been a growing Chinese interest in studying, adapting and implementing RMA aspects suitable to the country. Termed as "military revolution" [*junshi geming*], but more aptly updated as "new military revolution" [*xin junshi geming*], RMA debates have been vibrant in China.[15] These have had an impact on the preparations for forming different doctrines, organisation, equipment/systems, training and the likes.

A journey towards RMA implies a paradigm shift from continental and territorial focus to five-dimensional (land, air, sea, space and electro-magnetic) spectrums, from traditional warfare modes based on quantities of infantry, armour, artillery, ships, aircraft and other related aspects to qualitative technological and information-based superiority in combat and agile organisational set-up, from relying on experience to scientific and systematic management, etc. No contact, zero casualty war, rapid response elite units, battlefield digitalisation, long-range, terminally guided precision strikes, Beyond-Visual Range (BVR), etc. are some of the other features of the RMA.

Impact on the Organisation

Drastic changes in the organisational structure of the armed forces are expected once RMA is initiated across the board. Such changes are visible in not only a different professional military outlook but also in a "lean and mean" armed force.[16] Specific aspects of the impact of PLA modernisation efforts are felt in the following fields.

[14] For the latest reiteration of this aspect at the highest level, the 17th Party Congress held on October 15, 2007 stated:

> We must build strong armed forces through science and technology. To attain the strategic objective of building computerised armed forces and winning IT-based warfare, we will accelerate composite development of mechanisation and computerisation, carry out military training under IT-based conditions, intensify our efforts to train a new type of high-calibre military personnel in large numbers and change the mode of generating combat capabilities.

[15] See Liang Biqin, ed. *Junshi Geming Lun* [Theory of Military Revolution] (Beijing: Academy of Military Science Publications, 2001) and Zhang Huaibi (ed), *Junren Shouce* [Soldier's Handbook] (Beijing: NDU, 2005) p. 212.

[16] Zhang Huaibi (ed) *Junren Shouce* [Soldier's Handbook] (Beijing: National Defence University, 2005), pp. 227–29.

Quality

The PLA traditionally had emphasised on numbers in combat operations. In most of the military campaigns that the PLA fought in the past involved hundreds of thousands of troops, mainly infantry forces. However, the advent of modern concepts meant introduction of qualitatively better troops than quantitatively higher numbers. In this context, the Chinese leader Deng Xiaoping in 1975, while attending an enlarged meeting of the CMC as the then chief of general staff, criticised the PLA as guilty of "bloating, laxity, conceit, extravagance and inertia and that this over-expanded and inefficient army is not combat-worthy."[17]

Theatre Commands

As a part of the effort to enhance efficiency in C4ISR, China is toying with the idea of making the MRs into US-type theatre command posts with proper integration of various services. The key question in the MR reorganisation still remains on how to make the command structures function in an efficient manner by integrating all services in both peacetime and during warfare.[18] According to a PLA officer, as cited by You Ji,

> The revolution in information technology changes with each passing day the battleground structure, operation modes and concepts of time and space, which dictates overhaul of the traditional "centralised" and "tier-by-tier" administrative/command structure.[19]

---

[17] Deng Xiaoping, *Selected Works of Deng Xiaoping* (1975–82) (Beijing: Foreign Languages Press, 1984) pp. 91 and 11.

[18] See Andrei Pinkov, "How Is Reform Carried Out in the Chinese Military Command System?," November 7, 1998 at <http://www.kanwa.com/english/981210a.html>. According to a September 1987 definition of a "theatre of war" [*zhanqu*], it is "a strategic region mapped out by a country, starting from overall strategic needs, and based on geography and the direction of strategy. Generally speaking, each theatre is an independent, or relatively independent, battlefield." See Editorial Committee of *Inside Mainland China*, *A Lexicon of Chinese Communist Terminology* 2 vols. (Taipei: Institute of Current China Studies, 1997) [hereafter *The Lexicon*] vol. 2 p. 458. It was reported that Nanjing MR has been upgraded to a theatre command post for operations against Taiwan, a process initiated with the "Strait 96 Number One" joint exercises of 1996.

[19] See You Ji, "Revolution in Military Affairs – A New Guide for China's Military Modernisation" accessed on February 23, 2004 at <http://idun.itsc.adfa.edu.au/ADSC/RMA/RMAPAPERS/Ji.htm>.

Nanjing and Guangzhou MRs are likely to be the first candidates if these commands are created in China.

Rapid Response Forces (RRFs)

China has started raising RRF units after the 1991 Gulf war in the three armed services and the 2nd Artillery Forces.[20] Of the original 24 group armies, 7 are of the rapid response [*kuaisu fanying*] type and form the "main" aspects of the Chinese ground forces' combat capabilities. These 7 are the numbered group armies 1, 13, 21, 27, 38, 39 and 54 – all designated as Type A.[21] RRFs were instituted in the 15th airborne army, marines and other forces. Beijing MR reportedly formed a special reconnaissance troop on the pattern of the US Green Berets.[22] In addition to the RRFs in the main armed services of the country, the PLA has also started establishing 18 rapid reaction engineer units to counter natural disasters. These are to be converted into "task forces".[23]

Command and Control

Chinese military and strategic level communication networks and automation is the responsibility of General Staff Department's (GSD) Communications Department that is considered to be the Signal Corps headquarters.[24] The Command, Control, Communications and Intelligence C3I system [*sanxi xitong*] has received considerable attention from September 1982 when the People's Republic of China (PRC) had ordered all the armed services

---

[20] See Andrew ND Yang and Milton Wen-Chung Liao, "PLA Rapid Reaction Forces: Concept, Training and Preliminary Assessment," in James C. Mulvenon and Richard H. Yang Eds. *The Peoples Liberation Army in the Information Age* (Santa Monica: RAND Corp, 1999) pp. 48–58; and "China's Rapid Reaction Force and Rapid Deployment Force" at <http://www.ndu.edu/inss/China_Center/chinacamf.htm>. According to one version, all Type A group armies located in the north, northeast are of rapid response capable. See Chinese Military Digest, 1999 at <http://www.gsprint.com/cmd/cmd.htm>.

[21] See *"Junshi Kongjian"* at <http://www.tl.ah163.net/personalhomepage/aaa/aaa/lj/s-lj.htm>; and International Institute of Strategic Studies, *The Military Balance 2002-2003* (London: Oxford University Press, 2002) p. 139.

[22] Li Chengfeng "Challenging the Limits of Survival: Record of a Certain Beijing MR Special Reconnaissance Force's Wilderness Survival Training," *Xiandai Junshi* [Contemporary Military] No. 260, September 11, 1998, pp. 19–22 in *FBIS-CHI-98-296* October 26, 1998.

[23] Xinhua cited by "PLA Forms Disaster Response Units," *Jane's Defence Weekly* April 26, 2000 p. 14.

[24] This is based on David Finkelstein, "The General Staff Department of the Chinese People's Liberation Army: Organization, Roles & Missions" in Mulvenon and Yang Eds. *The People's Liberation Army as Organization*, pp. 160–66.

to introduce and improve the rapid transmission of battle commands.[25] In 1993, a pan-China fibre-optic cable system was reportedly laid with the help of relevant civilian organisations.[26] Developments in modern military communications of China are reportedly seen in six areas:

1. Analogue technology is being replaced by digital technology;
2. Electrical cables by optical fibre cables;
3. Electro-mechanical switches by computer-controlled switches;
4. Single-purpose terminals by multipurpose terminals;
5. Single-tasking networks with multitasking networks; and
6. Manual management is being replaced by automated and intelligent management.

These are said to have contributed to the relative digitisation of the forces.[27] The civilian sector's advances came to the PLA's rescue in this effort as well. The Shenyang MR, for instance, has utilised civilian Information Technology (IT) assets to develop its field command automation system given the MR's specific technical problems related to operations in freezing temperatures.[28] By establishing regular co-operative ties with a number of network technology companies in Beijing's IT-hub Zhongguancun, this MR reportedly solved 100 technical problems related to information drive.[29] Nevertheless, progress in IW and automation of field command of PLA appears to be slow and patchy. Several articles in the *PLA Daily* have referred to this process, and evidence as such advertised, is by fits and starts rather than consistent or extensive in different services and branches of the PLA, though it should be pointed out that a beginning has been made in the process.

Chinese writings obliquely refer to future plans to set up a "network force" and "sky troops" but there is no concrete evidence of any such formal units. In 1996, China reportedly established "Information Security and Research and Development Laboratory at Beijing with an advanced IW team for "organised software combat'."[30]

---

[25] Editorial Committee of Inside Mainland China, *A Lexicon of Chinese Communist Terminology*, 2 vols. (Taipei: Institute of Current China Studies, 1997), vol 2., pp. 62–63.

[26] David Finkelstein, "The General Staff Department of the Chinese People's liberation Army: Organization, Roles and Missions," in James C. Mulvenon and Richard H. Yang (eds) *The People's Liberation Army in the Information Age* (Santa Monica: RAND Corp, 1999) pp. 161–62n.

[27] See Li Xuanqing and Ma Xiaochun, "Armed Forces" Communications Become "Multidimensional," *Xinhua* July 16, 1997.

[28] However, in another case, such field command systems malfunctioned. See "Armoured Regiment Under Beijing Military Region Integrates Automatic Field Command System With Various Squads, Command Systems," *Liberation Army Daily* March 4, 2004 in FBIS-CHI-2004-0405 April 6, 2004.

[29] An Puzhong and Song Yuangang, "Specialists in China's "Silicon Valley" Contribute to Military Informationization Drive," *PLA Daily* February 24, 2004.

[30] See "Chinese Plan Cyber Warfare" August 4, 1999 at <http://www.newsmax.com>.

In 1999, the *PLA Daily* reportedly announced a campaign to recruit computer hackers to be trained as "cyber warriors" at PLA schools.[31] However, to guard against cyber-warfare attacks, the PRC in April 2000 enacted a National Defence Information Security Act (NDISA), after reports indicated that Taiwan was beefing up its information warfare task force following attacks from computer hackers in the mainland in August 1999 on Taiwanese government-run websites.[32] On February 10, 2001 the CMC issued provisions to the four general departments on "Security and Confidentiality of Computer and Information Systems" for strengthening security procedures within the PLA. Subsequently, it was reported recently that sensitive German, US, Indian and Japanese websites were reportedly frequented by the Chinese hackers.[33]

Logistics

Logistics' modernisation is another area the PLA has been stressing to meet future warfare needs. According to the 2000 white paper, logistics' modernisation is geared to provide "…flexible and effective field facilities for logistical supply, sustenance support, medical aid and emergency repair, surface replenishment, air refuelling and manoeuvrability support for the second artillery force."[34] The PLA in this regard has introduced three major reforms to their logistics units: "linking the logistics work of the three services, carrying out socialised logistics support, and improving the ability of field operation mobile support."[35]

In early 2000, China introduced the system of joint logistics by integrating facilities at the MR and local levels. The contract system was introduced and a military insurance system was instituted among the ranks. The roads and railway networks that China has been planning or developing in various regions of the country needs to be stated here.

[31] "Chinese Army Recruits 'Hackers'" August 4, 1999 at <http://www.newsmax.com>.

[32] Wendel Minnick, "Taiwan Upgrades Cyber Warfare, *Jane's Defence Weekly* December 20, 2000 p. 18.

[33] According to Ron Deibert and Rafal Rohozinski 1295 computers in 103 countries were hacked in 2007–09 by operations originating mostly from China. See "Investigating a Cyber Espionage Network" March 28, 2009 at <http://www.scribd.com/doc/13731776/Tracking-GhostNet-Investigating-a-Cyber-Espionage-Network >.

[34] "China National Defense in 2000" at <www.fmprc.gov.cn/eng/32221.html#2>.

[35] See *Xinhua* June 14, 1999 in *SWB FE/3564 G/10* June 18, 1999.

Current Force Levels

China currently has nearly 1.9 million armed force personnel divided among the ground, air, navy and strategic forces. In the ground forces, there are about 18 group armies directing manoeuvre forces of about 44 infantry divisions (including 5 mechanised infantry divisions with two amphibious assault units and 24 motorised infantry divisions), 3 rapid response units at national and 9 RRF units at regional levels. A 15th airborne army (with plans to raise the 16th in the offing) provides for limited airborne missions. Two amphibious assault units and the strengthened Marine Corps provide for the amphibious operations of the PLA forces.

China's ground forces command about 7,580 main battle tanks and 1,000 light tanks in addition to 4,500 armoured personnel carriers, 14,000 towed artillery, 1,200 self-propelled guns, 2,400 Multiple Rocket Launcher (MRLs) and 381 helicopters although most of these are obsolete.

Relatively, the mechanisation levels of the Beijing, Shenyang and Jinan MRs are higher as compared to the other MRs. Shenyang MR, with an estimated 250,000 troops, has 4 group armies, 1 mechanised brigade, 2 armoured, 4 motorised, besides others. Beijing MR, composed of 300,000 troops, has 5 group armies with 2 armoured, 1 mechanised, and 5 motorised divisions, besides others. Jinan MR has 190,000 troops with 3 group armies, 2 armoured, 1 mechanised infantry and others. Nanjing MR, with focus on Taiwan operations, has 2 armoured brigades. Other MRs have either 1 or no armoured units and are relatively less mechanised. The white paper pondered the ways to transit from this mechanisation towards information platforms.

China's naval forces consist of about 255,000 personnel, with one strategic and 54 tactical submarines, 29 destroyers, 45 frigates, 331 patrol and coastal combatants, 52 amphibious vessels, and about 700 naval aviation aircraft.[36] New warships are under construction including Yuan class submarines, new nuclear attack SSNs and Strategic Nuclear Submarines (SSBNs), with the latter poised to enter the Yulin base in southern Hainan

---

[36] See International Institute of Strategic Studies, *The Military Balance 2008* (London: Routledge, 2009) pp. 383–84 and *US Department of Defense, Annual Report To Congress: Military Power Of The People's Republic Of China* 2009 pp. 48–49 accessed at <http://www.defenselink.org> See also Srikanth Kondapalli, *China's Naval Power* (New Delhi: Knowledge World, 2001) and Bernard Cole, *The Great Wall at Sea: China's Navy Enters the Twenty-First Century* (Annapolis, MD: Naval Institute Press, 2001).

province. It is estimated that a quarter of the capital expenditure of the country's defence budget is allocated each to the naval and air forces. With China's GDP becoming the 3rd largest in the world at about $ 4.8 trillion and a majority of this coming from maritime export and import routes, the role of the naval forces is clear. Again, China had imported nearly 200 million tonnes of oil in 2009, 80 per cent of which came through the Straits of Malacca's. Of these, West Asia (which constitutes nearly 56 per cent of oil flows to China) and Africa (which constitutes nearly 26 per cent of China's oil imports) predominate in the Chinese calculus. Hence, the current Chinese focus on the naval forces. To enhance its naval prowess, China had conducted joint naval exercises with more than 10 countries in the last few years.[37] By September 2009, China had conducted 29 joint military exercises with several countries, mostly related to counter-terror or counter piracy exercises.[38]

China's air force has about 400,000 personnel, with 6 bomber regiments, 39 fighter regiments and 24 regiments for ground attack missions, 290 planes for reconnaissance or ELINT roles, one A-50 I AEW, 513 transports and about 100 helicopters. Major modernisation efforts have commenced in this force as well which the 2009 white paper considers as "strategic". Confirming this view is the statement of the Chinese air force commander Xu Qiliang's comments in early November 2009, that China will develop space capabilities and that "only power could protect peace."

While moving away from the declared Chinese official position on opposing outer space weaponisation, Xu advocated the "historical inevitability" of militarisation of space and that the PLAAF is moving in this direction.

In addition, the strategic weapons programme of China (including nuclear and ballistic missiles) has shown improvements in quantitative and qualitative terms. With an estimate 48 Inter-Continental Ballistic Missiles (ICBMs) and 1700 Intermediate Range Ballistic Missiles (IRBMs), China is emerging as a major force in international strategic relations. Its January 11, 2007 test of an anti-satellite weapon, by knocking off one of its own Fengyun satellites

[37] Cited at Chen Wanjun et al, "Party Central Committee and Central Military Commission's Concern for the Construction and Development of the People's Navy," *Xinhua Domestic Service* April 25, 2009 NewsEdge Document Number: 200904251477.1_305e109b5cc757f2.

[38] Li Yun, Bai Ruixue, Wang Tiande, and Yue Lianguo, "('Peace Mission-2009') United Strength-Complete Record of 'Peace Mission-2009' China-Russia Joint Anti-Terror Military Exercise (Parts One and Two)," *Xinhua Domestic Service* August 9, 2009 NewsEdge Document Number: 200908091477.1_ad39291972e4c08c Accession Number 284950609.

through a ground based missile (possibly DF-21), indicated its capabilities in this crucial field.

Implications for India

Not all the above efforts of the PLA, however, are directed against India, although any of these military assets could be pitched if need be. For instance, while the current PLA focus is on Taiwan, Senkaku Islands/East China Sea and South China Sea area, it should be noted that any of these assets could be redeployed to other theatres of war if the situation arises. For, in 1962, nearly 6 months before the border clashes between India and China, the latter redeployed some units/troops from the Taiwan front. With the cross-Straits relations improving with the introduction of *santong* (3 communications, viz., post and telecommunications, shipping and air travel), China can indeed shift some of its military capabilities against other perceived adversaries, especially Vietnam and India.

Overall, Indian concerns on the PLA modernisation currently are conventional in nature – related to immediate national security needs of the country in relation to the border areas, concerns on China's transfers of military equipment to Pakistan, Bangladesh, Nepal, Myanmar and Sri Lanka.[39] It is possible that this conventional nature of Indian concern could graduate to that of strategic dimensions if China – as a part of its strategic rise – intends to restrict Indian space and its freedom of judgment and action initially in the immediate Indian neighbourhood, and in the long term at international strategic environment, including that of countering United States-India partnership. However, since mutual attention has not been sharply drawn at each other for several decades (excepting in 1998–99 and in the last two years), differences of perceptions and capabilities have not been directed against each other in a concerted manner so far. This situation may be changing recently with differences between New Delhi and Beijing mounting.[40]

---

[39] See Srikanth Kondapalli's, "Chinese Military Eyes Southern Asia," in Andrew Scobell and Larry Wortzel eds. *The PLA Shapes the Future Security Environment* (Carlisle Barracks, PA: US Army War College & The Heritage Foundation, October 2006) pp. 197–282 at http://www.strategicstudiesinstitute.army.mil/pdffiles/PUB709.pdf.

[40] The Indian Military Operations Directorate reportedly conducted a simulated war game in March 2009 with a scenario of confrontation with China in 2017. See Rahul Singh's, "Indian Army fears China attack by 2017," *The Hindustan Times* March 26, 2009 at <http://www.hindustantimes.com/StoryPage/StoryPage.aspx?id=1d63761b-88eb-4f69-b5a8-ce512c6e32cc >.

The PLA modernisation programme is a concern for India in a number of ways. First, in the backdrop of strained relations between the two following the war in 1962, the PLA's concerted modernisation in land, air, naval, strategic frontiers and in electromagnetic spectrum, could have the effect of further increasing asymmetries between the two countries. In the comprehensive national (hard and soft) power indicators, although China and India had started almost at the same level of development in late 1940s, China has enhanced its cumulative strength (military included) in the last few decades. While Indian military achieved parity in certain sectors of conventional military strength, including qualitative indicators like professionalism, higher training levels, air-to-air missiles, re-fuelling, interdiction, high altitude combat, interdiction on high seas, etc., China enjoys overwhelming military superiority given its higher missile inventory, arms imports and ability to spend more on acquiring advanced platforms. Specifically, China's defence budget has increased at constant double-digit figures in the last one-and-a-half decades, with more money spent on power projection forces like rapid response units, air force, navy, missiles and anti-satellite programmes. China's official defence budget (about $ 77 billion – but other estimates of the Pentagon and RAND Corp. indicate to about $150 billion) is more than twice that of the Indian defence budget.

Second, China's defence strategy transited recently into "local war under informationised conditions" with one of the main scenarios visualising conflict based on unresolved territorial disputes. Under this strategy, the PLA is to fight quick battles of resolution by pressing into service rapid response units, pre-emptive strikes against the adversary's strategic assets and cripple the will to fight. Given the "no first use" nuclear strategy (which is gradually changing recently into "conditional" "no first use") the PLA is likely to employ counter-strikes against the adversary's missile and strategic assets through conventional payloads. India and Bhutan are the only two countries with whom China has not resolved land territorial disputes. Although, both India and China have signed a "no-war" pact through the 1993 Peace and Tranquillity Agreement (PTA) and 1996 Confidence Building Measures (CBMs) agreement in the military field, increase in unbridled and intentional transgressions by the patrols on the undefined Line of Actual Control (LAC) could trigger skirmishes between the two countries.[41] Although the current

---

[41] It was reported that in the last 1 year there were as many as 270 such transgressions by the Chinese patrols. See "Chinese incursions into Indian Territory Rose Sharply in 2008," *Times of India* June 9, 2009 at <http://timesofindia.indiatimes.com/articleshow/4632640.cms>.

India-China security situation is generally termed as constituting "low level threat", the elevation of the situation to medium or even high levels of threat are visible in the 1962 war, 1967 skirmishes at Nathu La (in Sikkim), Samdurong Chu in 1987 and the late 2000 incident near Daulat Beg Oldi. Pointers towards possible friction between the two sides can be seen in the following situations:

- The PLA established a company at Besa in Arunchal Pradesh in 1987 after marching 11 km inside India.
- No major demobilisations of military personnel on both sides of the LAC.
- New areas of "additional difference" on the border dispute arose with Chinese patrolling activity seen at Chumar, an important area in Ladakh in the western sector and a gateway to Himachal Pradesh.
- Information about simulation centre at Huangyangtan in western China with Aksai Chin/Ladakh as the focus of military operations.
- Deployment of Su-27 fighters to Chengdu MR and airborne troop training in these areas.
- New airfields construction in Tibet.
- Military logistics improvements in Tibet.[42]
- Investments in the road and railway building activities in Pakistan Occupied Kashmir.[43]

Besides these, the Chinese side in the last one year has escalated its rhetoric on the eastern sector of the border in Arunachal Pradesh, although the 1957 and 1980 emphasis of the Chinese leaders were on the western sector of the border. Thus, after the then Chinese Ambassador Sun Yuxi's statement on Arunchal Pradesh as a disputed area on the eve of Chinese President Hu Jintao visit to Delhi in November 2006, an Indian administrative service officer from Arunachal Pradesh was denied a visa in mid-2007 to visit China. In addition, the new Chinese Foreign Minister, Yang Jiezhi, reportedly told his Indian counterpart that the April 2005 agreement between the two premiers (that populated areas will not be part of the possible border resolution effort) is no longer valid – have raised concerns in India. Subsequently, Sikkim – an area of no dispute hitherto – became problematic after the Chinese forces moved closer to the "finger point". All these were viewed as further strengthening of

---

[42] These points were raised by the Government of India, Ministry of Defence in its Annual Reports.
[43] For instance, the construction of 750 km railway line from Havellian and the 4730-meter-high Khunjerab crossing over Mansehra district and the Karakoram Highway.

the PLA's position in the decision-making processes of China and detrimental to Indian interests.

Third, related to the above, border consolidation and domination efforts and improvements in military logistics in Tibet pose security challenges to India. Tibet today has more than 22,000 km of roads, a railway line of 1118 km between Golmud and Lhasa (being extended up to Xigaze and plans to further extend up to Kathmandu in Nepal) and three airfields, in addition to fibre optic networks that enhances Chinese military logistics. From 1951 to 1995, the PLA built about 100 highways in Tibet. 4 main highways criss-cross Tibet with the Golmud to Lhasa Central Highway garnering nearly 80 per cent of people/goods entering into Tibet. Effectively, these facilities have been able to boost logistics up to township/airfield levels in Tibet. The Tibet railway can carry about 1,000 tonnes per day, including troops and material. Different estimates were made, with one pointing that the PLA can now mobilise swiftly about 12 divisions in 30 days by utilising the railways. Tibet railway can also mobilise short-range missiles to the war front, if necessary. The PLA general logistics department's role in the transportation of materials as a part of Tsunami relief operations in 2005–06 in the affected Indian Ocean states have indicated that the Chinese urge to extend logistics towards this region, although such capabilities are currently limited. The PLA navy's sorties at the Gulf of Aden definitely are poised to improve its performance in the Indian Ocean. The PLA air force interception rates across the border areas have increased over a period of time with its Tupolov Tu-154 M aircraft and other intelligence-gathering assets. With the joint use agreement in 2006 of an Il-76 modified A-50I AEW between China and Pakistan, such interception ratios are expected to increase further. Cumulatively, these exert pressures on India to improve infrastructure in the border areas. Consequently, the Indian government has announced building of nearly 11 strategic roads – with a majority of them planned in Arunachal Pradesh alone.

Fourth, India is concerned with Chinese missile deployments in Delinga, Da Qaidam and Xiao Qaidam in greater Tibet and Kunming military districts and the possibility of the nearly 800 short-range ballistic missiles shifted from Fujian and Zhejiang provinces to western areas in the event of Taiwan issue resolution. Although China refused to sign a "no first use" agreement with India, as it does not recognise Indian nuclear weapon status, the PLA general staff department reportedly had contingency plans for targeting several Indian cities and strategic hubs with its nuclear warheads based in Tibet and other places. This was said to be in the light of Indian missile capabilities, which could have reached the PLA units positioned in Chengdu or Lanzhou MRs or other strategic assets. In this context, Indian Ministry of Defence (IMD) in its annual report considered Chinese missiles in greater Tibet as posing a threat to its security.[44] In addition, the Indian Ministry of External Affairs (IMEA) annual reports refer to "reliable and widespread" information about China's transfer of weapons of mass destruction to Pakistan.[45] Nevertheless, no de-targeting or non-targeting agreements exist between India and China, nor are escalation control procedures in place, despite 3 rounds of talks on such issues between the two sides, besides initiating 3 strategic dialogues.[46] A related aspect is the Chinese anti-satellite test of January 11, 2007, which indicated that if such a capability were targeted against the one and only Indian military satellite in space, then Indian military networks, on which its command and control functions are dependent, would be jeopardised. Indian defence officials have indeed mentioned that GPS, navigation and military applications would be affected in such a case. The Defence Research

---

[44] For instance, Ministry of Defence Annual Report of 2002–03 (p. 5) stated:

> ... every major Indian city is within reach of Chinese missiles and this capability is being further augmented to include Submarine Launched Ballistic Missiles (SLBMs). The asymmetry in terms of nuclear forces is pronouncedly in favour of China and is likely to get further accentuated as China responds to counter the US missile defence programme. China's close defence relationship with Pakistan takes a particular edge in view of the latter's known belligerence and hostility to India and its acquisition of nuclear assets.

[45] In the strategic spheres, China's transfers to Pakistan include 5,000 ring magnets, nuclear weapon designs, ballistic missiles and launchers of 34 M-11/DF-11 missiles (to Pakistan's Sargodha Air Force Base near Lahore) delivered in November 1992; M-11 transporter-erector-launchers (1991); HY-1 and 2, FL-1 and 2 cruise missiles; possible assistance to indigenous Pakistani missile programmes of Hatf-1 and 2 series of ballistic missiles and Anza surface-to-air missile. China has also transferred 10 tonnes of ammonium percolate rocket fuel; missile guidance systems including gyroscopes, accelerometers and on-board computers and has assisted Pakistan in the missile production factory at Fatehgarh (Fatehgunj) near Islamabad. See "China's Missile Exports and Assistance to Pakistan" at <http://www.nti.org/db/china/mpakpos.htm> accessed on January 6, 2005. While China had exhibited reluctance for the smooth passage of the waivers for India at the International Atomic Energy Agency and Nuclear Suppliers Group (IAEA and NSG) meetings on civilian nuclear technology transfers, Beijing was quick to argue that it has a right to supply additional nuclear plants to Islamabad, without the NSG clearances.

[46] After India expressed interest in possible import of Patriot Advanced Combat systems-II from the US and Arrow missile systems from Israel in order to counter ballistic missile launches from Pakistan, Chinese official papers have criticised the Indian moves. They, nevertheless, do not mention about the destabilisation in the region caused by the Chinese missiles/technologies transfers to Pakistan or the continuing co-operation with Chinese scientists at Fatehgunj near Rawalpindi.

and Development Organisation of India (DRDO) chief said that the test is a "matter of concern" but India is unlikely to test its own Anti-Satellite Test (ASAT) for the moment. However, an arms race in space is likely between the two countries in the longer run. The announcement by the then Indian Air Force (IAF) chief on establishing an aerospace command can be seen as a move in this direction.

Finally, as a part of its hedging strategy of supporting those southern Asian countries who exhibited adversarial relations with India, China has supplied military equipments to Pakistan, Bangladesh, Nepal, Myanmar and Sri Lanka. Although India has codified these, during the talks with China as a part of the recent diplomatic normalisation process, as its "security concerns", little, if any, progress is achieved in this regard. Not only did China enhance its security and military relations with the Indian neighbourhood, but also initiated a programme of selling advanced weapons to these countries. The license manufacturing agreement with Pakistan on JF-17 aircraft (with Russian-supplied turbofan engines), transfer of 4 F-22P frigates (by 2012), joint use of Chinese airborne early warning aircraft with Pakistan (from November 2006), 2002 defence co-operation agreement with Bangladesh to further "institutionalise" such ties, enhancing military potential of these countries through defence industrial co-operation, establishing dual-use facilities in these countries (like Gwadhar port, Mandalay and Pegu airfields expansion, Great Coco, Hyangyi and Mergui, in Myanmar, container depot at Chittagong, Hambantota in Sri Lanka), are noted with concern in India, specifically in the light of "arc of destabilisation" trends in these countries. Besides, the PLA's interactions with Pakistan, Bangladesh, Nepal, Myanmar and Sri Lanka in the last decade indicate to an overwhelming numerical bias against India. China's "string of pearls" strategy of building quasi-naval bases in the Indian Ocean opens an additional front for India. Ever since Chinese ships made port calls at Karachi, Colombo and Chittagong in 1986 and the former Director of PLA General Logistics Department, Gen. Zhao Nanqi's outburst of 1993 on Indian Ocean not being India's ocean, Chinese naval challenges to Indian security have increased. The 2008–09 Chinese efforts to send contingents to the Gulf of Aden were indicative of the intentions of China. In the emerging group 2 (US and China) equations in the post-financial crisis world, the Chinese suggestion of co-sharing the Pacific and Indian Oceans with the US could marginalise Indian influence in the region. In the light of these developments, in late 2000, the Indian military establishment reportedly refused to consider the tender offered by military-related China

Harbour Engineering Company for dredging of a channel at the Mumbai Port Trust. In addition, India reportedly expressed its unwillingness to allow Chinese companies to build hydroelectric projects in Himachal Pradesh and other "sensitive" areas. Additionally, India has conducted multilateral naval exercises periodically with several countries to create stakes in the region.

Overall, the PLA modernisation and its efforts of co-operating with Indian neighbourhood are viewed in India either as a part of "strategic encirclement" or "marginalisation". Specifically, any Chinese military activation or domination of the border areas opens the possibility of a 2-theatre front for Indian forces. Indeed, in Indian wars with Pakistan in 1965, 1971 and 1999, the Chinese side sent subtle or even brazen threats of mobilising troops near the border areas. In such a scenario, the Indian military adopted a strategy of "deterring Pakistan and dissuading China". With Chinese missile threat and missile transfers to Pakistan increasing, India appears to be on the course of graduating from the above strategy to that of "deterring Pakistan and deterring China". This implies not only enhancing nuclear stockpile and developing and deploying Agni III missiles of 3,000 km and above range but also configuring long-range aircraft for nuclear missions and efforts to build second-strike nuclear capability. All these also imply that the Indian defence budgets are expected to be increased to meet the Chinese challenges. This indicates to the arms race between the two countries in the years to come. Another arena for arms race is the naval construction activity at Sanya (Yulin) in the southern province of Hainan. India has indicated its intention to respond to these plans with its own plans to construct a similar base at Rambilli. Indian naval demands for acquiring 2nd-strike capabilities are expected to increase in the coming years citing Chinese challenges.

Part II

China's Foreign Policy

5

China in the Asia-Pacific and Indian Ocean Region

A State of Flux

Ashok Kapur

China's strength alone will not be sufficient, and we shall also have to rely on the support of international forces...this adds to China's tasks in international propaganda and diplomacy

– *Selected Military Writings of Mao Tse-Tung*, p. 214.

Deliberately creating misconceptions for the enemy and then springing surprise attacks upon him are two ways - indeed two important means - of achieving superiority and seizing the initiative

– *Selected Military Writings of Mao Tse-Tung*, p. 239.

Adopt a sober perspective; maintain a stable posture; be composed; conserve your strength and conceal your resources; don't aspire to be the head; do something eventually

– Deng Xiaoping's statement, June 1989, cited in D.M. Lampton, *The Three Faces of Chinese Power*, p. 16.

China's record as a citizen of the world is strikingly threadbare

– *Economist*, March 21, 2009, p. 13.

This chapter examines the character and scope of changes in China's approach to Asia-Pacific since the late 1990s. The theme is that China's policies towards the region, and the pattern of power and relationships in the region are in a flux; they are not in disarray but they are unsettled and changing constantly. Has China abandoned it strategy (long term tactics) to divide and demoralise its rivals in its declared policy of a peaceful rise? Has it abandoned its strategic aim to form a China-centric hub and to form a structure of dominant-subordinate relationships in Asia? Has China's economic and military ascendancy, and the pattern of engagement between China and her neighbours and the major powers, thrown up dilemmas and a build-up of internal and external pressures for China? Or does a comparison between Maoist and post-Maoist China reveal a growing sophistication and a new style of diplomatic operation that emphasises the role of soft diplomatic and cultural power and an ongoing build-up of hard military power for future use? Do the quotations above represent the three sides of contemporary China that brings together the Maoist and the post-Maoist approach to external affairs of China? Finally, the implications of Chinese actions in the region for India are discussed.

The Expanding Boundaries of the Asia-Pacific Region and Growing Complexity of Issues

This chapter argues that an indicator of the growing importance of China in Asia-Pacific is that its power and influence since the 1990s, defined either as a pole of attraction or as a pole of opposition, shapes the strategic environment of Asia-Pacific as well as the Indian Ocean area. China's neighbours and the major powers are tied to her strategic and economic actions. The major and the minor powers in the Asia-Pacific/Indian Ocean area are now tied together. During the Cold War, East Asia, South Asia, Southeast Asia, the Pacific and Indian Oceans, and the Persian Gulf were treated by official and academic practitioners as distinct regions because inter-regional boundary crossing activity was limited. Now boundary-crossing activities relating to commerce, diplomacy, military activity, cultural exchanges, intelligence operations, tourism and the internet are entrenched. Because of the stickiness of international and regional security issues such as terrorism/counter-terrorism, nuclear and missile proliferation, maritime security, border and territorial conflicts, disagreements about the international status of Asian powers, and so on, de-coupling is unlikely.

Several examples can be given to support this approach. Maintaining its position and its legitimacy in Tibet is a core issue for Beijing for several reasons. Historically, Tibet was a field of power politics involving British India, imperial Russia and Manchu China. Beijing's takeover of Tibet in 1950 by military action was justified as a national defence issue, and one meant to curb "anti-imperialist" activities of Anglo-Americans and India; and a side element was to force USSR's retreat from the Xinjiang area. China calls Tibet an internal affair but it is also a core domestic, strategic and a diplomatic issue. It is a domestic issue because it is part of a policy to secure the internal parts of China such as Tibet, Taiwan, Hong Kong and Macau. It is a strategic issue because Tibet's location makes it a potential field of great powers" politics and penetration or a threat to China's southern zone and border defences. It is a diplomatic issue because China seeks to liberate "southern Tibet" (now India's Arunachal Pradesh) from Indian rule and influence, and consolidation of China's position in the Himalayan-Tibetan area is a prerequisite to pursue its boundary dispute with India. Tied to the legality of China's sovereignty in Tibet and the Uighur (Xinjiang) area is that China's rule has aroused Tibetan (Buddhist) and Muslim opposition. Without local consent, China's policies lack international legitimacy and leave it open to international pressure in terms of its human rights record and its governance practices. In addition, the Taiwanese people and government are not likely to embrace China's professions of a glorious future of nationalities in the light of the Tibetan/Uighur experiences.

The second example concerns Beijing's belief in the utility of naval power to deter power projection by USA, India and Japan in the Pacific/Indian Ocean area, and to project its naval power and its soft power. It needs naval power to guard its commercial interests and to support its search for resources in South America, Southeast Asia and Africa. Its decision to deploy its ships off the Somali coast to check piracy and to protect Chinese commerce is a step in this direction; such a deployment erodes the distinction between the Pacific and the Indian Oceans for China's naval planners. Its commercial and strategic interests in the Middle East and Africa explain its policy to build links with Pakistan and Myanmar as channels for the flow of Chinese commercial and political presence, and to gain vital basing rights in the Indian Ocean area.

The third example concerns Japan's evolving views of the Asian environment. Japan has diluted the constitutional ban against a military build-up. It now possesses a capacity to project its military power into the Pacific and Indian Oceans. It does this as a junior partner of the US through the instrumentality of the military guidelines of co-operation between the two powers. Japanese current diplomacy seeks to achieve a normal position in the international sphere and to put behind it the history of Japanese aggression in Asia. It actively pursues its territorial disputes with Moscow regarding the northern islands and with China in the Taiwan straits. During the Cold War, Japan developed strong investment and commercial ties in Southeast Asia and its economic clout enabled it to acquire the status of an honorary white in its dealings with the Apartheid regime in South Africa. Since the 1990s, Japan has rebalanced its approach to diplomatic and military affairs. Commercial activism is now balanced by a confidence to play a role as a permanent member of the UN Security Council and to project its military power and political influence into the Asia Pacific-Indian Ocean area. It plays an important role as a UN peacekeeper, it has acquired naval power to protect its commerce and resources chain, it seeks security against North Korean missiles and nuclear weapons, and it watches China's military build-up which could affect its strategic position. Challenges to Japan's security are growing as is its capacity to deal with them. The expansion of the geographical sphere of Japan's diplomatic and military operations, the robust character of its commercial presence in important parts of Asia, and the hidden strategic rivalry between China and Japan, point to a growing interactivity between Japan and its traditional and non-traditional allies in the Asia-Pacific and Indian Ocean sphere.

The fourth example concerns India. Since the late 1990s, India's external policies have been based on a geo-political approach. Under Nehru and the Nehruvians (1940s to 1990s) India had a non-nuclear weapons policy, it ignored the importance of sea power, its diplomatic activity centred mainly on China, Pakistan, Russia, Europe and USA, it advocated nuclear disarmament and it set itself up as a moral and peaceful-oriented country. This approach failed to satisfy Indian national interests. India's military development gained traction after its defeat by China in 1962. The 1998 nuclear tests and the announcement that India was a nuclear weapon state established a dynamic link between its nuclear weapons and foreign policy. By adopting economic liberalisation and globalisation, India joined the economic mainstream as well. A pattern of development of regional and international partnerships with traditional (e.g. France and Russia) and non-traditional (e.g. Israel, USA, Japan and Australia) allies emerged alongside the old rivalries with her regional neighbours – Pakistan and China. Two drivers – increasing complexity of a difficult regional neighbourhood, and the challenges and opportunities of a dynamic international strategic and economic environment – led Indian practitioners to shed Nehruvian idealism and pacifism, and to conduct India's affairs as a major power. The shift in attitude and policy reflected an awareness that the proper development of Indian national interests required a widened sphere of diplomatic and military operations and a widened strategic landscape that extended from Central Asia and Tibet in the north, to Israel and Iran in the west, to the Indian Ocean and South Africa in the south, and to the South China seas and Southeast Asia in the east. China closely follows Indian developments while outwardly pretending to be disdainful of Indian actions. India and China are tied because of traditional animosities and the willingness of the two to develop their escalatory potential and to stay in the strategic game. Geo-political and economic imperatives led India to pay attention to Central Asian affairs, and Iranian affairs, while the build-up of the needs to diversify the sources of defence supplies and modern military technology led India to abandon its traditional fixation with the Arab world and the Arab vote at the UN, and to seek links with Israel on the one hand, and Iran on the other. At the same time, the rivalry with China required a development of naval capacity to counter Chinese naval activity in the Bay of Bengal and submarine building in Hainan in the South China seas, to build its strategic weapons capacity to check pressures from Pakistan and China.

Changing Patterns of Relations: No Change in Balance of Power or Single Nation Hegemony in Asia

Diplomatic, military and economic developments in Asia reflect a growth in the number of players and issues that have made the Asia Pacific-Indian Ocean region a centre of gravity of international security and change. But a stable balance of power has not emerged; the prospect of the rise of a single power is not imminent.

Still, the PRC is the catalyst in the region in two ways. Its impressive economic growth makes it a point of attraction as a market, but it is also a point of opposition among its rivals who fear that China's rise may not remain peaceful as it completes its military modernisation. The rapid change in China's economic and military position has been accompanied by a softening of its diplomatic language and style. China no longer claims to be a revolutionary power but it is unclear if its new posture is a ploy to lull the opposition.

To assess the scope and nature of change in China's diplomatic stance, the chapter argues that a mixture of traditional-geopolitically and historically conditioned worldviews and post-Mao policies define China's approach to Asia.

Despite its massive economic and military strength, Beijing is preoccupied with its traditional concern about its frontier security and sovereignty in Tibet and Xinjiang where significant opposition exists to its policies. Taiwan is an unsettled core issue for China that intersects with the policies of the USA, Japan and Taiwan. Earlier, Beijing had concerns about developments in Manchuria and Mongolia. Massive migration of Han people into the frontier areas was, and remains, China's method to deal with the nationalities issue. China's view of its place in history and its sense of Han unity and Han geopolitics shaped its policy of demographic engineering. The issue of Chinese (Han) identity and a belief in Chinese civilisational or cultural superiority is historically the driver of China's "nationalities" policies. China's internal debate about "Han chauvinism" and "local chauvinism" has been an issue in China's politics since the 1950s; it is still not settled as uprisings in Tibet and Xinjiang in 2008 revealed.[1]

China's international orientation has changed but what does it mean? Its first generation ideology had stressed the importance of China as the revolutionary power in a new world order but post-Mao leaders replaced the old view by a diplomatic language that stresses China's peaceful rise, and its interest in normalisation and stability in a multi-polar world. Mao Tse-tung and Chou en-Lai, China's two prime first generation ideologues, stressed a strategy to build anti-imperial fronts, to change the world system.[2] This chapter

---

[1] Victor Louis, *The Coming Decline of the Chinese Empire*, (New York: Times Book, 1979), is a provocative work by an alleged KGB operative. It provides a useful commentary on China's actions to integrate Manchuria, Mongolia, Tibet, Xinjiang and Turkestan by the use of coercion and massive Han migration. For China's view of its nationalities policy and the problem with "Han" majority chauvinism and "local chauvinism", see Chou Enlai, "Questions Relating to Our Policies Towards China's Nationalities," August 4, 1957 statement, *Selected Works of Zhou Enlai*, vol. 2, (Beijing: Foreign Languages Press, 1989), pp. 253–78.

[2] For example see: "China's Revolution and the Struggle Against Colonialism," *People's China*, 16 February 1950, pp. 4–5 argued that China's policy was meant "to oppose the colonial rulers and their running dogs". For extract see Alan Lawrance, 1975, *China's Foreign Relations Since 1949*, (London: Routledge and Kegan Paul), p. 155; *Peking Review*, 25 October 1963 urged the "further development of the struggle against imperialism, old and new colonialism", and the "primary and the most urgent task" cited in Lawrance, *China's Foreign Relations*, p. 168; John Gittings, *The World and China, 1922–1972*, (London: Eyre Methuen, 1974) pp. 260–64, notes that China's strategy was to build its strength, gain US respect and build the third world front against the superpowers and to fight imperialism.

argues that the first generation's ideological approach has been amended, not abandoned, in the following ways. First, China needs a period of peace for its four internal modernisations to take effect; this includes military modernisation along with economic and social reconstruction. China claims that it is committed to a "peaceful rise". But there is a debate within China itself about the meaning of "peaceful rise";[3] PRC's neighbours (i.e. India, Japan, Australia, Singapore) as well as the USA have not bought into this theory, hence their wariness about PRC's future strategic intentions. Their approach is to build their defences against China as a precaution and to increase PRC's interdependency with the world economy and world politics. This pattern of diplomatic engagement and military build-ups among China's neighbours is ongoing.

In addition, China has applied its traditional united front strategy by building international triangularities to enhance its international and regional position. There are important examples of this pattern of strategic behaviour that is not advertised by Chinese practitioners but it is being studied by scholars and official practitioners. Since the early 1960s, the PRC formed a PRC-Pakistan strategic and diplomatic front against India.[4] The growth of Indian economic and military power and international alignments checks China's ambitions in the Himalayan and South Asian areas. The bilateral Sino-Indian dialogue gives the triangle a sense of normalcy but this front retains its importance for China as a line of diplomatic and military pressure against India since the early 1960s.

Another major example of China's interest in triangular diplomacy was the formation of the PRC-USA versus USSR triangle in the early 1970s. President Nixon, Henry Kissinger and Mao-Zhou had a common interest to contain Soviet Union. The reliance on triangular diplomacy is consistent with the Maoist view (quoted above) about China's dependence on international support to pursue its interests; it cannot gain advantage alone and requires foreign help to advance its international position.[5]

---

[3] David M. Lampton. *The Three Faces of Chinese Power* (Berkeley: University of California Press, 2008), p. 33, outlines the debate between four views. 1. In Chinese language "rise" means "thrusting up" which creates bad optics; 2. Peaceful rise is anti-historical, no power rose peacefully; 3. If the emphasis is on peacefulness, it reduces Beijing's ability to deal with the Taiwan question by force; 4. Peaceful rise could disadvantage the PLA in China's internal and bureaucratic politics. If the aim is peaceful, why spend massive amounts of money on military modernisation? This debate started in 2003, and it is still unresolved.

[4] Yaacov Vertzberger, *The Enduring Entente, Sino-Pakistani Relations*, 1960–1980, Washington Papers/95, New York, 1983. Praeger is a nuanced account of the scope and character of this unique relationship and its geopolitical context for Chinese and Pakistani practitioners.

[5] Hongqian Zhu, "China and the Triangular Relationship," Chapter 2 in Yufan Hao and Guocang Huan, *The Chinese View of the World* (New York: Pantheon Books, 1989).

PRC is not alone in adopting a united front strategy. The US-Japan-Australia military alliance was initially geared to deal with the Soviet threat during the Cold War. This alliance stems from America's diplomatic tradition which has been to have superior military capacity to defeat an enemy but to fight with the support of an alliance, albeit a temporary one, as in the two World Wars and in regional military campaigns in recent years. The US-led alliance setup in Asia-Pacific was a continuation of this historical tradition in American statecraft. Following the end of the Cold War in Asia, the retention and expansion of the alliance network implies its use vis-à-vis China. Other countries have embraced this approach vis-à-vis China. The formation of a US-India strategic partnership during the last decade is implicitly tied to the Indian and American assessments of China's future strategic orientation just as the Indo-Soviet alignment since the late 1950s was driven by a common concern to check PRC's ambitions in the Himalayan and South Asian region. China describes such activities as "encirclement" or containment of China but there is no indication that it is willing to abandon the practice of forming triangular fronts against its rivals. Therefore, the chapter argues that PRC's diplomatic and leadership style has changed (comparing the first generation leaders with their successors), the aim of making China a revolutionary world power has changed, but the method of using strategic triangles and united fronts, has been expanded to parts of Asia-Pacific and the Indian Ocean area. Consequently, China's neighbours and its international rivals have also adopted an alliance strategy that is tied to China's growing power. Because China continues to participate in united front strategy despite its peaceful professions and a declared desire to normalise and stabilise regional and international relations, its rivals too have joined this game.

How should the perspective of "China and Asia-Pacific in transition" be framed and validated? There are several angles to consider. One, post-Mao PRC is both a pole of attraction and revulsion as noted above. Second, its major international competitor in the region, USA, is also a pole of attraction and revulsion. China objects to American actions concerning Tibet and Taiwan and the challenge they pose to its "core interests" and "core values", but at the same time seek US co-operation and recognition of its status.[6] Neither, however, is pre-eminent in material or moral terms in the region. Both must work hard to maintain and expand their relationships and influence. For

---

[6] The idea of repulsion and attraction among countries is borrowed from Owen Lattimore, *The Situation in Asia* (Boston: Little Brown, 1949), pp. 89–90.

the PRC, this requires it to build its position vis-à-vis the USA, Russia and its geographical and strategic neighbours; for the USA this requires it to maintain its position vis-à-vis its traditional allies in the region (Japan, Australia, Taiwan, South Korea and in parts of Southeast Asia) and to develop non-traditional alignments (i.e. India). Third, without a commonly accepted security architecture in Asia-Pacific, a significant part of the transitional process is that China's neighbours, and US allies have both gained diplomatic and economic space and ability to negotiate and manoeuvre with China and the US. PRC's coercive and economic capacity is growing, but a similar process is underway among its neighbours and consequently, China does not have a significant balance of decisive advantage. As Chinese power grows, the wariness among its neighbours also persists, and as the neighbours demonstrate a capacity to check Chinese ambitions, Chinese practitioners must deal with policy dilemmas or face friction with neighbours. Because its front building strategy and triangular diplomacy has reached its limits, Beijing must now learn to struggle with its principles and to find compromises.[7] "In transition" means that China and members of the Asia-Pacific and Indian Ocean community must deal with a framework with two parameters: one, a formal balance of power system does not exist in the region because of the volatility within the region and as a result of internal changes in the politics and policies of China and her neighbours; two, Asians do not accept the notion of China or the USA as a balancer in the region or either as a dominant power. These parameters provide diplomatic and economic space to the major and minor power holders in the region, and they give them room to manoeuvre with China and the USA.

Tendencies in Asia-Pacific

1. *The tendency towards great power-hegemony by China and the USA is challenged by others in the region.*

The characterisation of Asia-Pacific and China "in transition" implies the rise of a few marked tendencies and several uncertainties. Consider the following. Because strategic and economic triangularities have emerged in the region, multi-polarity, not bilateralism, is the frame of reference in the conduct of Asia-Pacific countries. China favours multi-polarity, it rejects

---

[7] Struggling with compromises and building fronts is a theme that follows the analysis by D.S. Rajan, "China: An Internal Account of Startling inside Story of Sino-Indian Border Talks," C3S paper no 168, Chennai Centre of China Studies, June 10, 2008.

American unipolarity. Recent Chinese writings toy with the idea of "non-polarity" but the preferred frame of reference is big power triangularity that involves China and other big powers.[8] However, "great powers" hegemony or clubbing as avenues to promote their interests, which China favours, is not practical in Asia-Pacific because of the rise of secondary players like North and South Korea and Association of Southeast Asian Nations (ASEAN) countries, and the growth of regionalism and multilaterism. Many Asian countries rely on sub-regional groups such as ASEAN, Shanghai Cooperation group and the East Asian economic community.

Regionalism has different uses for Asian countries depending on their international position and interests. China's use of regionalism fits the pattern of using regionalism to suit the country's national interests and the views of its bureaucracy. Asian states have adopted a mix of unilateral, regional and international measures during the past 50 years. An isolated and insecure state such as North Korea acted unilaterally to build its nuclear and missile power and then it sought international recognition of its status and interests by joining a regional six nations dialogue. Iran has also adopted the North Korean approach with similar interests and results. Most Southeast Asian nations belong to the ASEAN where the principles of decision-making by consensus, peaceful negotiations rather than military force and war, quest for good neighbourly relations and the growth of a multilateral trade system are the established norms. However, territorial disputes exist in the ASEAN and the South China Seas which, for the most part involve China, and China's neighbours are wary about China's peaceful intentions given its massive military modernisation program.[9] Such evidence indicates that these countries rely on unilateralism to build their respective military capacity and to form alignments with extra-regional powers to manage their threats even as their public diplomacy is cast in terms of ASEAN political values.

---

[8] For a general outline of multi-polarity in Asia Pacific see Hao and Huan, *The Chinese View of the World*, pp. 5–7. For a discussion of the importance of triangularity relating to China see pp. 45–47. For the link between peaceful co-existence and China's strategy to build an anti-colonial and an anti-imperialist front see the discussion in pp. 230–31. The last point is crucial; it indicates that peaceful co-existence is not a standalone policy for China because it is tied to China's front building activity against the Russians and the Americans; it also indicates the opportunistic use of third world countries in her diplomatic campaign which was guided by leadership perceptions of China's interests. Currently, there is also a debate within China between multi-polarity and non-polarity. See Huang Zhengji, "Multi-Polarity or Non-polarity", *International Strategic Studies*, China Institute for International Strategic Studies, Beijing, no. 4, October 2008, serial no. 9, pp. 13–16.

[9] Kathrin Hille and Time Johnson, "SE Asia Arms Purchases Fuel Fear of Clashes", *Financial Times*, FT.com, March 14, 2010.

Thus, regionalism is used to promote peace-oriented values and the trading system on a multilateral basis while unilateralism and military activity is used to build checks and balances along lines of balance of power theory; the two approaches are not mutually exclusive. East Asian nations too, follow the combination of peace-oriented values, military modernisation, regionalism and multilateralism to promote their interests and the views of their bureaucracies. By present signs the mix of peace-oriented, trade-oriented diplomacy of a majority of Asian countries, and on the other hand, realpolitik driven military modernisation and alliance building activity in the Asia-Pacific and Indian Ocean region does not have a discernable point of equilibrium because the external and domestic contexts of decision-makers in Asian countries are evolving and are in a state of flux.

China too actively participates in Asian regional organisations in Southeast Asia, East Asia, Central Asia and South Asia along the aforesaid lines. "China's Foreign Affairs, 2008" the official publication of the Department of Policy Planning, Ministry of Foreign Affairs (MOFA) of China records PRC's participation in at least 15 Asia-specific regional groupings.[10] The focus of China's participation varies and the messages are meant to promote Chinese interests in different regions. In the Asia Pacific Economic Co-operation, China pushes economic co-operation with a "practical and non-binding approach" based on "volunteerism and consensus".[11] A non-binding approach favours complacency and bureaucratic politics, and consensus building among nations also protects the national interest of China as it is defined by her political and bureaucratic leaders. With the Shanghai Co-operation Organisation the focus is on co-operation in political, security, economic and cultural fields. Good neighbourliness, mutual trust and co-operation are the main norms. The broader scope reflects China's concerns with terrorism, separatism and extremism in its southern frontier areas as well as its interest to guard against the extension of Russian and American influences in Central Asia and the Himalayan areas.[12] With ASEAN, China values trade links, political co-operation and trust, mutual economic benefit and peaceful development. The approach to the Asian Regional Forum (ARF) reveals China's concerns. To quote:

> Under the influence of the Cold War mentality, there was a trend towards building up bilateral military alliances to gain absolute military superiority.

---

[10] *China's Foreign Affairs*, MOFA, World Affairs Press, 2008, pp. 358–77.

[11] Ibid., p. 358.

[12] Ibid., p. 363.

This undermined efforts to build political mutual trust and caused uncertainty to regional security

China urges its audience to "respect diversity, strengthen co-ordination, put differences in proper perspective and avoid confrontation" while seeking common ground through consultation. The official view is that

Countries in the Asia-Pacific have abandoned the old thinking on and (sic) logic of security based on mutual suspicion, raw power and imposing one's own values and ideologies on others[13]

This set of Chinese expectations does not match the reality that China's neighbours are wary about China's military development and they are engaged in their respective military build-ups in relation to China's growing strength. The lack of transparency about China's military strength and intentions is compounded by the fact that MOFA, which issues the public statements in regional organisations is a state organ while the PLA, is not formally a part of the state apparatus. Since its organisation as the military arm of the Chinese communist party, it has remained outside the state apparatus, and its deliberations in war/peace questions and its relationships to MOFA on policy issues are not well-known. There are several instances where MOFA has taken a harmony-oriented approach while the PLA has adopted an aggressive view of Chinese sovereignty issues such as the South China seas, Tibet, Xinjiang and Chinese territorial disputes with India and other neighbours. Given the difference between the soft and the hard lines of Beijing practitioners, the soft line taken by MOFA in regional organisations tends to be discounted. The speculation is that the PRC's approach to regional organisations reveals two different motives. First, it is to project China's soft power by a posture of diplomatic reasonableness and peace-oriented rhetoric. Second, to promote regionalism in a way that suits its strategic interests in its frontier zone in the Himalayas and Central Asia, and in Southeast and South Asia where it seeks to become a political and an economic hub. On the other hand, however, China is not fully committed to regionalism or to peaceful settlement of disputes. It reserves the right to use force if necessary to incorporate Taiwan into China. It reserves the right to settle the boundary dispute with India by force if necessary. It has developed a strong military stance in the South China seas

---

[13] Ibid., pp. 370–71; also pp. 364–66.

where many territorial disputes exist between China and South East Asian countries. Its policy to teach Vietnam a military lesson in 1979 ended in failure but it revealed an inclination to use force unilaterally without reference to the UN Security Council of which China is a permanent member. This forum is committed to the principles of consensus building and multilateralism as a basis to settle world problems by diplomatic or military means, an approach which China advocates in relation to the Iran nuclear issue.

China's approach to regionalism is a calculated way to build its external links and to promote multi-polarity. However, the approach has a hidden agenda. It has not come to terms with the reality of Japan and India as rising economic and military powers that need to be brought into the global multi-polar mainstream at the UN Security Council along with other rising powers – Brazil and South Africa. China's multi-polarity advocacy sounds good but it is not inclusive. China's approach may be tested against two paradigms suggests current international relations theory. The first seeks globalisation and economic multi-polarity to organise trading and financial arrangements. The second seeks a courtly system with an inner court of great powers to manage international security affairs, and an outer court of secondary powers. China's push for a G-2 (US/China) and P-5 (UN Security Council permanent members) managed international security system are examples of China's preference of the courtly system with an inner court. Regional organisation at best belong to the outer court – so organised to keep the modern "barbarians" in check.[14]

Chinese international diplomacy highlights the central place of its internal economic modernisation, its economic importance for the US economy and its position as a stakeholder in international security affairs. But there is another reality which undermines China's case to be recognised as the leading power in Asia; geopolitics is also in command in Asian affairs. China still has a difficult territorial dispute with India that does not lend itself to a peaceful or a military resolution easily under current projections. China and India have been rivals since the late 1940s in the view of the Chinese leaders. Its frontier politics are troubled in Tibet and Uighur region; hence Tibetan Buddhism and Islamist Uighurs (earlier this was Turkmenistan) along with the spread of Christianity in China, are bringing religion into play in China's internal politics. The Taiwan

---

[14] Martin Jacques, *When China Rules the World* (London: Penguin, 2009), p. 242 provides the classic Chinese view of the world.

question also has multilateral dimensions because it involves the interests and influences of USA and Japan in Taiwan, and the issue cannot be resolved simply by declarations that there is a single China and Taiwan is its inalienable part. Few of China's neighbours pose a territorial threat to China but the threat perceptions among China's neighbours about its "peaceful rise" are stimulating military build-ups by China's neighbours in Southeast Asia and East Asia.

These tendencies suggest the emergence of polarities in the Asia Pacific region where China (an emerging giant) and America (a superpower under challenge) are both poles of attraction and revulsion in the view of countries who must deal with them in strategic and economic affairs. The polarity at the international level indicates a proliferation of major and minor players (statist and non-statist) and the rise of issues which can no longer be dealt with by the UN Security Council. The rise of regional mechanisms to deal with specific problems is a response to the failure of international institutions to solve them. For example, ASEAN members have adopted an informal, consensual style of action which has an Asian character and which differs from the UN-method of resolutions, sanctions and moral judgment against the offending party. The six nations' talks are meant to deal with the particular problem of North Korean nuclear and missile proliferation and the general issue of stability in the Korean peninsula. The Shanghai co-operation meetings are meant to promote strategic and economic dialogue among the concerned countries in Central Asia. The Obama administration now seeks to develop a regional dialogue involving Iran, Afghanistan, Pakistan, India, Russia and USA, to check the Taliban. These examples indicate that the UN Security Council is not seen by the participants as the central agency of action in regional security. China has a dilemma. On the one hand, it prefers the great powers' co-operative approach to international security but, on the other hand, the power to decide Asian affairs has passed out of the hands of the great powers club; alternatively the growth of regional groupings that are meant to address specific regional issues requires the involvement of the relevant countries where the power that counts is the present power of the involved parties rather than the position of a country on the UN Security Council.

2. *China's diplomatic style and tactics have gained sophistication since the 1990s but the changes are still dominated by traditional Chinese interests and a preoccupation with its newly won international status.*

China's changing diplomatic tactics may be explained by one central element, i.e. its need to manoeuvre itself in a difficult international environment and to increase its tools and skills set. Its diplomacy is in continuous motion;

it studies changes in its external environment, it tries to exploit external contradictions and build pro-China fronts, it struggles with internal policy compromises when compelled, and it makes international deals which serve its interests. Chinese communist diplomacy since the 1940s reveals a high degree of international activism and volatility. Before its victory in 1949, Mao made an overture to Washington to make a deal, arguing that Chinese were nationalists. Mao was rebuffed by the US government and then Mao turned to Moscow for a friendship treaty (1949).[15] The shift towards Moscow was tactical. It was meant to minimise Beijing's international isolation and it showed a concern with the danger of US/Western containment of China. Moscow too had an interest to keep China on its side.[16] China embraced the theory of peaceful co-existence with India and Indonesia in the mid-1950s. This theory gave it manoeuvrability in the third world and it was meant to manage its international isolation. During the 1960s, Mao, Zhou En lai, Lin Piao and Chen Yi, China's senior leaders were forceful advocates of the theory of revolution in world affairs in opposition to the policies of Washington and Moscow. However, the principles of peaceful co-existence and armed struggle were used by Chinese leaders in a pragmatic way. The danger of US containment of China was recognised but the goal of making a strategic deal with the USA was not abandoned. Mao's view was that there was no rush to join the UN or to secure US recognition because the longer the delay, the better was the likely bargain with Washington. The Mao-Zhou tactics was to wait for the USA to come to Beijing and to propose a deal that recognised its international importance.[17] Meanwhile, despite the prominence of revolutionary theory in Chinese propaganda, Beijing

---

[15] Mao made two requests for US support, in 1944–46 and again in 1949. These attempts show a leadership orientation to make a deal with the USA rather than to build an ideological opposition to it even though by any measure the USA would qualify as the "arch imperialist". The details of the early attempts at deal making with the US are in Donald S. Zagoria, "Choices in the Post-war World (2): Containment and China", in Charles Gati, ed., *Caging the Bear* (New York: Bobbs Merrill Co, 1974).

[16] "Stalin knew from many sources… [that] Zhou Enlai had been enthusiastic about the prospect of balancing Soviet influence in China with an American presence".
See Valdislav Zubok, "To Hell with Yalta! - Stalin Opts for a New Status Quo", *The Cold War in Asia*, p. 25, Cold War International History Project, Woodrow Wilson International Centre for Scholars, Washington D.C., 1995/96.

[17] In 1957 Mao argued for a delay in establishing diplomatic relations with the USA. He felt that "the longer you drag on [these issues], the more debt you [USA] will owe us". Speech, Mao on "Sino-American and Sino-Soviet Relations", January 27, 1957 in *The Cold War in Asia*, p. 152.

opened up with Pakistan in the early 1960s as a line of strategic pressure against India. The theory was that "the enemy of my enemy is my friend," a theory which Pakistan shared with China. China's interest in Pakistan had two motives: the use of force against India in 1962 failed to end the rivalry with India, and secondly, the Pakistan link formed a cultural and a strategic bridge between Communist China and the Muslim world in the Middle East. In addition, Beijing got a foothold in Southeast Asian affairs by its support of the Vietnamese struggle, by its diplomacy in the Indo-China conferences, and its low cost arms aid and moral support to the Vietnamese countered American as well as Soviet activities in China's underbelly. All these actions developed Chinese *manoeuvrability* beyond its borders. It engaged Chinese diplomacy with that of the major and minor powers in the region. At the same time, the *theory of peaceful co-existence* as the basis of China's attitude vis-à-vis its smaller neighbours like Burma and Pakistan and in Southeast Asia, showed the use of *soft power*. But soft power had its limits. It was abandoned in the fight with India in 1962 because of the view that India was acting in collaboration with Western imperialists and India stood in the way of China's expansion in the Himalayan zone and in the third world. For China, India's push for China's admission into the UN was a trap because it would require China to follow international norms, and the discipline was likely to reduce Chinese manoeuvrability and eliminate the value of the idea of victimhood of China at the hands of foreign imperialists.[18]

China's quest to manoeuvre itself towards a strategic deal with the big power that counted, USA, bore fruit in the early 1970s when Henry Kissinger and President Richard Nixon made their famous journeys to Beijing. This marked the formation of an international strategic triangle based on the common enmity of Washington and Beijing against Moscow. But just as the Chinese leaders expanded their international space and manoeuvrability by the Nixon/Kissinger visit, the American leaders used the opportunity to convince the Chinese leaders that the US-Japan alliance was also in China's interest as a check to the development of Japanese neutralism which could attract other foreign influences into Japanese affairs, or foster Japanese

---

[18] According to B.N. Mullik, Nehru's Director of Intelligence (1950–65) Beijing felt that it would lose "a great deal of freedom of action which she was exercising then [if she joined the UN]. Moreover, she felt she had not suffered at all internationally by being kept out of the world body. China felt that efforts by Japan, India and the UK were meant to drag China into the UN to restrict her development". See B.N. Mullik, *My Years with Nehru* (New Delhi: Allied Publishers, 1971), pp. 288–89.

militarism without the discipline of the US alliance with Japan. This was an interesting side development given that Chinese military and diplomatic history is preoccupied by the problem for China of Japanese militarism since the 1930s in Manchuria and in China (Nanking incident). Declassified US government documents reveal that in the US assessment, Chinese leaders feared the Japanese along with the Russians (the latter were hated and feared but the Japanese were only feared).[19] To the extent that Beijing's leaders bought into the US argument, Washington emerged as a balancing pole in two strategic triangles: US-China-USSR; and US-China-Japan during the 1970s and the 1980s.

Chinese policy has been to build the economic and coercive capacities of China as well as its soft power. It requires coercive capacity to deter Taiwanese independence, to keep USA and China's neighbours in check, it requires economic capacity to enhance its appeal as a major international player and to use its economic leverage to bargain for Western restraint respecting China's policies relating to Tibet and Taiwan, and about human rights and democracy.[20] Within this framework its aims and strategies have shifted in response to changing domestic and international situations and the growth of Chinese economic and military strength.

Chinese aims are constant in three areas: to build its internal economic and military strength and domestic opinion to support its policies; to build the area of manoeuvrability in international and regional relations by adopting a process of shifting alignments and shifting enmities; and to consolidate its position in its southern frontiers (Tibet and Eastern Turkistan or the Uighur area) and to gain Taiwan as a part of China. These constant elements are fixed markers in Chinese foreign affairs; these are the drivers. The strategies or diplomatic tactics have shifted from time to time. In the 1950s it tilted

---

[19] These points are based on official records of conversations of Nixon, Kissinger, Mao and Chou Enlai in F. S. Aijazuddin, ed., *The White House and Pakistan*, Oxford: Oxford University Press, pp. 526–39 and 168.

[20] Lampton, *The Three Faces of Chinese Power* discusses the three aspects of China's rising power – coercive, economic and persuasive (soft). The preoccupation with big power-ism was evident in Mao's three worlds theory which he announced in 1974. USSR and USA formed the first world; Europe was the second world; and the developing countries formed the third world. The theory defined Beijing's relations with third world countries in terms of their Soviet connections which highlighted its major concern with Moscow and showed its fixation with the primacy of the social imperialism over Western imperialism in China's ideological and strategic thought. This way China set itself up as a hub, which opposed Soviet imperialism and, as a point of attraction and accommodation between China and USA, because both had a common enemy in USSR. See also Hao and Huan, *The Chinese View of the World*, pp. 235–37.

towards Moscow to break out of its diplomatic isolation imposed by the West and to protect its political and military interests in the Far East from the danger the Korean War posed to China's physical security. Bipolarity was the structure of international relations during the 1950s; to counter this, China's leaders propagated the theory of an intermediate zone, which was similar to Nehru's third force but there was a difference. Nehru sought a peaceful change under the leadership of third world moderates like Nasser and Tito; Mao and Zhou sought revolutionary change that elevated China's leadership and international position vis-à-vis the Big Two. Later as the Sino-Soviet controversies (border and ideological) erupted, and as Chinese power and confidence increased, Beijing sought to reduce its dependence on Moscow's aid and advice and the change paved the way for a Sino-US dialogue (initially through Warsaw ambassadorial talks) in the 1960s that culminated in the 1972 Shanghai communiqué. This institutionalised and legitimised the formation of the US-PRC versus USSR strategic triangle and it brought to fruition Mao's dream of the 1940s to make a deal with America.

China's approach and history of its diplomatic record since 1949 suggests that its "principles" are a form of strategic propaganda rather than a guide to Chinese diplomatic actions; the principles are negotiable or they can be set aside. The principle of peaceful co-existence was propagated by Zhou Enlai along with India's Nehru and Indonesia's Sukarno but it was set aside by the decision to go to war with India in 1962 and by the build-up of the Indonesian communist party with a loyalty to China and revolutionary change. The first action breached the peaceful resolution principle, and the second one breached the principle of non-interference in internal affairs. The Chinese actions also breached another principle of communism. One would expect a revolutionary power to build a united front of communists worldwide. China it seems wanted to protect its interests rather than that of other communist parties. For instance, India and Indonesia had legal communist parties but the 1962 war discredited the Indian communists because of their support of China's actions. China's leaders supported communism in Indonesia knowing that the Indonesian military would fight the threat to their position by Indonesian Communists. Mao deliberately acted along these lines to remove the threat of independent third world communist parties that could pose a challenge to his authority as the foremost Asian communist and to China as the sole Asian communist power. In other words, the Chinese approach in these instances was neither ideological nor simplistic, it was not governed by its advertised revolutionary strategy (see Mao and Lin Piao statements); its drivers were to maintain its manoeuvrability in relation to the Big Powers and to elevate its position as a great power vis-à-vis third world states and the major powers. The contention is that the role of ideology has obviously declined in the hands of Mao's successors, and economics is in command as noted by Hua and Huan[21] but the key drivers in Chinese actions all along were/are the Beijing's dominant view of geopolitics, the international situation and its implication for China's regional and international position. China's rhetoric about revolutionary change and armed struggle has changed, having been replaced by the theory of "rising China" which itself was replaced by the idea of a "peaceful rise".[22] The 2008 Chinese Defence Paper projects an optimism about an active and a forward defence that can challenge China's neighbours and the USA.[23] In other words, China's rhetoric is subject to change as its power and confidence grows.

3. *From 1982 onwards China's diplomacy represents a mix of new as well as old characteristics; consequently domestic debates about strategic issues have grown within China.*

In 1982, China announced a *new "independent policy of peace"*. This was a change in its diplomatic propaganda. The change was significant because earlier China had sought international change as a revolutionary power centre. The acknowledgement of the importance of international and regional stability to facilitate her internal modernisation drive was a major shift in Chinese leadership thinking. The focus on modernisation, stability in regional affairs and global pluralism is the current phase in Chinese foreign affairs. The changed Chinese stance reflected the influence of international changes on China. Consider the evolution in Beijing's thinking. From 1949 China's public discourse showed an anti-US, anti-imperialist fixation in its public discourse but, as explained earlier, this was a shallow phenomenon. It was a ploy to arrange the terms of a US-China settlement that was based on an American recognition of China's international position and Chinese recognition of the value of regional and international stability.

---

[21] Hao and Huan, *Chinese View of the World*, pp. 16–17.

[22] Lampton, *The Three Faces of Chinese Power.*

[23] For an overview of China's evolving military doctrine, see Bhaskar Roy, "China's Defence White Paper 2008 – An Indian Perspective", Chennai Centre for China Studies, February 11, 2009; also Ching Yi Lin, "China's 2008 Defence White Paper: The View from Taiwan," *China Brief,* 9.3, February 5, 2009; and Willy Lam, "China flaunts growing naval capabilities," *China Brief,* 9.1, January 12, 2009. For an assessment of the strategic analysis by Professor Paul Dibbs, Australia's top expert of Asian affairs, see Subhash Kapila, "East Asia Strategic Calculus: The Australia Factor," Chennai Centre for China Study, paper no. 182, July 3, 2008.

However, China's strategic interests in a volatile international environment cannot be served simply by making a deal with the USA. China's ascendancy on the world stage since 1982 is obvious but so are the challenges to China's core interests in Asia. There is no assurance that point(s) of equilibrium can be established in the long term should China's politics and economy falter and increase internal political and social tensions, or should the hard and soft power of China's neighbours continue to grow in ways that deny China the prospect of asymmetrical gain for itself. For example, China's physical control over Tibet and Uighur areas is not a point of equilibrium in internal Chinese affairs because Beijing's leaders are relying on brute force to enforce its rule in these areas and the signs indicate growing dissent against its policies among its minorities and in the world community. The unstable situation in Afghanistan and Pakistan, the extension of US military power from Europe to Central Asia to the Afghanistan-Pakistan sector, and Moscow's push to reassert its strategic and economic presence in Central Asia, requires Chinese diplomatic and military attention. The Himalayan area is a front for China in terms of its policies in Tibet, Nepal and India. The first two are meant to secure its frontier zone in the Himalayas, the second is meant to manage its rivalry with India in Asia and the Indian Ocean area. China's northern zone in Asia Pacific is comparatively stable because the distribution of military and economic power is predictable, and regional alliance arrangements function as pathways for inter-state actions; the rules of engagement among North Asian players provide limits against dangerous escalations even in the absence of a peace treaty in the Korean peninsula. But the rules of engagement in China's southern zone are still unclear.

Despite the manageable instability in northeast Asia, China's leaders face long-term uncertainties. The North Korean nuclear question and the lack of a peace settlement between the two Koreas leaves the Korean peninsula open as a field of great powers' (American, Chinese, Russian and Japanese) politics. Beijing must grapple with the danger that the North Korean regime is unstable and it could become a swing factor: it is unpredictable in its military actions, and it has a declared interest to make a direct deal with America that could reduce China's influence in North Korea. Currently, Washington and Pyongang are using Beijing as a stepping-stone to facilitate their deal making that promotes their respective interests. China has a dilemma: on the one hand, it is in the bilateral diplomatic front line to maintain North Korea's engagement in the Six Nations talks and to maintain China's credibility as an international stakeholder in the critical non-proliferation issue; on the other hand, the extension of USA and other Western commercial and military activities in the two Koreas would mean the development of a long-term presence in China's northern areas.

Japan's diplomatic and military orientation is also changing as the US-Japan military guidelines pave the way for Japan to play a bigger military role in the Pacific area including Taiwan; and the evolving internal debate within Japanese party politics indicates an incremental reduction in the commitments in Article 9 of the Japanese constitution. Uncertainties exist as well with respect to Southeast Asia where countries like Singapore have not accepted the peaceful rise of China theory, and the Beijing push of its commercial and military presence into Myanmar has alerted the Asian players to the danger of creating a channel for the flow of Chinese influence and power through the old World War II Burma-China road to the Bay of Bengal. In South Asia the unsettled Sino-Indian border indicates the lack of a political settlement between the two Asian rivals. The increase in naval activities in the Indian Ocean area in recent years widens the scope of contention at land and at sea and brings into play a number of players – USA, Australia, Japan, Singapore and India in the Indian Ocean even as all sides continue to trade with each other and develop the economic and political links with China. Last but not the least, Pakistan, China's all-weather friend in South Asia, is under internal stress because of the rise of Taliban activity in Pakistan's northwest and in Afghanistan and as a result of the failure to develop strong political institutions within Pakistan.

Is China's diplomacy in the region moving into a stalemated position? If not, then what is Beijing's unfinished business to achieve its goals? China's options with three issues – Taiwan, military modernisation and naval development, the internal debate about China's peaceful rise and the 2008 Defence Paper illustrate the discussion.

China's Growth: Forming a Strategic Stalemate in the Region?

China's evolving strategic thoughts and actions suggest the existence of unfinished business for China and her neighbours. Chinese practitioners emphasise the positive effects of the growth of China's power and its growing diplomatic importance in regional security affairs in Asia. Qian Qichen, China's foreign minister from 1988 to 1998 projected USA and China as two "world powers" and noted that the USA was over-extended in the world and it needed China. He took a big power view of international relations, giving the UN Security Council the importance to "decide world problems" and stressed China's importance because it had "strategic status on the international stage." Friendly relations with neighbouring countries were deemed necessary for internal development. At the same time the strategic aim was to "divide and demoralise the anti-China forces." Japan was viewed as a "weak link in the united front of western countries" and it needed to be dealt with accordingly. Taiwan and Tibet were internal questions. The role of religion received the minister's attention as an issue of growing importance but its implications for the future of Christianity, Buddhism and Islam in Chinese politics, especially in its frontier politics was not addressed.[24]

These views help us understand China's frame of reference, its self-image and image of others and they exude a sense of growing self-confidence about China's growing importance. But there were several interesting slipups or revelations which make the views incomplete and a source of uncertainty for China's neighbours. One, dividing the opposition is an accurate description of Chinese tactics but this method was the preferred method of Western imperialists and the Roman Empire builders. The implication is that Chinese opposition to Western imperialism concerned the ill-effects on China's society and political status and not per se with imperialism or with the divide and rule method. Second, the search for friendly relations with other countries was tied to the importance of internal development that included military modernisation. Does that imply that the value of friendly relations could diminish with the growth of Chinese economic and military power and self-confidence? Could the meaning of "peaceful rise" change as China's power grows? Thirdly, is the Chinese view of Japan as the weak link in the Western front wrong and counter-productive in Sino-Japanese relations? Surely Japanese practitioners would want to alter Chinese perceptions by increasing Japan's military capacity and its alliance arrangements with the Western and other Asian powers? Fourth, could religion become a complicating element in Chinese politics as a result of rising religious sentiment among the Chinese people in a difficult economic and social environment? Fifth, the Qichen view did not assign any importance to Japan as a strong power in Asia, and Beijing's view of multi-polarity rests on a view of the UN Security

---

[24] Qian Qichen. *Ten Episodes in China's Diplomacy*, (New York: Harper Collins, 2005), pp. 319, 335, 305–06, 291, 156, 150, 296–97 and 30.

Council as the deciding forum for world problems. This is a narrow view of multi-polarity which explains China's reluctance to expand the UN Security Council by bringing in Japan and India into a reformed UN structure.

The Qichen views and the questions posed above suggest that Beijing has unfinished business in Asia Pacific-Indian Ocean areas and China's neighbours have new business as a result of a rising China. As a result of changes in Chinese policies after 1982, the strategic environment in Asia-Pacific has changed from a period of high tension, conflict and war in the Sino-Soviet, Sino-Indian, Sino-Japanese and Sino-Taiwan relationships into a pattern of a relaxed strategic competition and political dialogue(s) among the major and minor players. Conflicts and controversies still exist but they are managed by the formation of institutionalised process(es) of dialogue among the parties concerned; and this process is occurring outside the framework of the UN Security Council.

The build-up of this dual pattern is significant in the context of the rise of Asia in the development of global political and economic relations. The Asia-Pacific and Indian Ocean areas (not Europe, Middle East, Africa and the Americas) are the centre of gravity with a significant rate and scope of change – measured in terms of the changing distribution of world's economic and military power and patterns of alignments. This region is now the main field of international power politics because the strategic interests of USA, PRC, Japan, Russia, India, Australia and the two Koreas and Taiwan are engaged on a continuous and intense basis. The region today is different from its historical past. Asia has been a field of power politics in world history – as a trading magnet and as an arena for European and Asian rivalries and imperial expansions. In the past, China was an object, not a catalyst of external actions. In the past, international politics were big powers' politics; conflict and war often yielded a power structure that produced some stability and predictability in the region's international arrangements. For example, during the nineteenth century, Britain was the premier commercial and naval power in the region (Pacific and the Indian Oceans) but competition with the USA led to its subordination in the Far East. With extended lines of military and political communications, Britain has had to concede strategic ground to American commercial and military pressures. The rise of Japan as Asia's first modern industrial and military power at the turn of the century led to Japanese invasion into Manchuria, which paved the way for the fight between America and Japan during the Second World War. Japan destroyed Britain's military position in Southeast Asia that was symbolised by the fall of Singapore and the push towards the Indian frontier. Following Japan's surrender to USA in 1945, a new power structure emerged in the Far East. Note that Japan surrendered to the US power because the Japanese conservatives had an interest to make a deal with America to gain its protection and to preserve the position of the Emperor and the Conservative elements in the Japanese society and politics; this bargain was made and it has endured, and it remains an important contextual element in the history of US-Japan relations. The lesson of the past is that Japanese conservatives, who have ruled Japan for the most part since the early 1950s, do not see Japan as a defeated country; its surrender on the other hand was dictated by circumstances and practical considerations. It may be viewed as a tactical compromise rather than a permanent acknowledgment of a defeated country status. A country that does not see itself as a defeated power is no one's permanent ally, as Owen Lattimore wisely noted in his brilliant analysis of the Asian situation.[25] In this perspective, Beijing's effort to divide and demoralise Japan and the Western alliance in the Far East is doomed to fail. Significant adjustments have taken place in Japanese defence thinking and strategic planning. The changes represent a growing challenge to the Chinese power and interests.

Pursing unfinished business is the theme for China and her neighbours in Asia but this should be viewed as an ongoing process rather than an activity with a defined end condition.. Two tendencies are in play in the evolving policies. On the one hand, there is a thaw in the security relations among the major players and there is a commitment to build security dialogues among them; on the other hand, there is an active process to secure high technology oriented military modernisation that reveals growth in capacity to conduct electronic warfare by China and her neighbours. Frequent displays of power projection capabilities are evident in the naval and space arenas.

The Taiwan issue also shows the complexity in the interplay between the two tendencies and the dilemma they create for the practitioners. On the one hand, China maintains that Taiwan is an internal matter that does not brook foreign interference but, on the other hand, the US-Japan military guidelines and US-Taiwan relations have placed the Taiwan issue in a multilateral context. China remains hopeful that as the US power weakens, Taiwan will fall to China under the "one country, two system" formula which was successfully applied to the restoration of Hong Kong to Chinese

---

[25] Owen Lattimore, *The Situation in Asia*, chapter 6 titled "Japan is Nobody's Ally".

sovereignty. But this is not a given in the foreseeable future. China has developed and flaunted its naval capabilities along with its capacity to destroy space based satellite and communications systems, and these developments have caught the attention of strategic planners worldwide.

Chinese writings have begun to recognise the difficulties. The 2008 China Defence White Paper sets the theme: China is "still confronted with long-term, complicated, and diverse security threats and challenges" although "China's security situation has improved."

The challenges include "separatist forces" in Taiwan, East Turkistan and Tibet which threaten China's unity and security.[26] For Tibet and East Turkistan (Xinjiang, Uighur areas) Beijing employs the authoritarian model which has not gained the consent of the local population; in the two instances Buddhism and Islam are in play which indicate the presence of religion as a durable element in China's internal politics. Whether military force, patriotic education and Han migration into these areas can solve Beijing's problem, is open to question, and the issue could come to the foreground should Beijing's internal political authority and legitimacy weaken as a result of a possible economic and social unrest within China. Beijing's template for dealing with its external strategic environment in Asia Pacific is now based on a new military doctrine of "active defence". This represents a shift from the Maoist emphasis on a mass based large army for national self-defence. The new emphasis is to be adept in electronic warfare and it involves acquisition of naval power projection capacity to deal with traditional inter-state war situations as well as non-traditional situation such as piracy management in the Arabian Sea.

China's activism in recent years involves the development of its economic, military and diplomatic machinery, and the skilled use of its growing capacities. Since the early 1980s, China has been on a path to develop its economic position in the global economy. Since 1989, it has been on the path of military modernisation taking into account the lessons of the 1991 Gulf war that became a basis of the revolution in military technology and electronics in modern warfare. Since early 1980s, Beijing has been active in normalising relations with its neighbours – USSR, Japan, Indonesia and India, among others; it has built bridges to the Middle East and Africa, and it successfully secured the return of Hong Kong and Macau to Chinese sovereignty and control. Taiwan, however, remains a point of struggle with the Taiwanese

[26] China's Defence White Paper, *China Brief*, 9.3 (February 5, 2009).

government and its people and in China's relations with USA and Japan. India too is a point of contention in Beijing's actions. It opened up a trade relationship with India, it formally accepted the principle of tranquillity in the Sino-Indian border arrangements (1993 and 1996) and it agreed to continue talks to settle the boundary issue. In accepting Sino-Indian border trade, Beijing accepted Sikkim as the Indian side of border trade. But China's view on Sikkim is ambiguous, it is open to interpretation and change in the future if and when "the conditions are ripe," (this was also Beijing's formula to avoid settlement of the boundary question in the 1950s whenever the issue was raised by India). It is, therefore, unclear if Beijing actually accepts Sikkim as a part of India, and that it is willing to acknowledge the change through publication of a new map or by way of a Gazette notification. In a related matter, Beijing recognises that Arunachal Pradesh exists beyond the line of actual control but it does not recognise India's sovereignty over it, claiming it as a part of China or "southern Tibet". In other words, the existence of significant points of territorial contention in the geopolitically charged Himalayan region divide India and China. Moreover, the development of a diplomatic dialogue with India was parallel to the provision of Chinese and North Korean nuclear and missile aid to Pakistan. It is significant that the decision to transfer sensitive nuclear aid to Pakistan was reached at the highest level by Deng Hsiao Ping in 1982.[27] In other words, Beijing formed a strategy of dual activism in the Subcontinent – of active military defence to build an anti-India military and a nuclear front, and the use of active diplomacy to make Beijing the hub of diplomatic activity vis-à-vis India as well as India's neighbours.

Chinese activism in the South Asian region was reinforced by its activism at the international level. This has implications for Asian countries including India. Beijing has constantly, since the 1990s, projected a view about the importance of G-2 (USA and China) rather than a G-4 (USA, China, Japan and India) or a G-5 (including Russia) in directing international relations. The adoption of a narrow and an opportunistic view of big powers-dominated UN Security Council reveals China's intentions towards the countries which are excluded from the big power listing. China values its seat at the high table but it does not have a good track record as a global citizen.

---

[27] Thomas C. Reed, "The Chinese Nuclear Tests, 1964–1996," *Physics Today*, September 2008 notes that in "1982 China's premier Deng Xiaping began the transfer of nuclear weapons technology to Pakistan, and in time, to other third world countries". Reed, a former nuclear weaponeer, was Secretary of the US Air Force, 1976–77.

The discussion turns on whether this pattern of Chinese activism in military and diplomatic affairs, and the obvious growth in its economic capacity, has produced asymmetrical gain for China in relation to her points of comparison: USA, Russia, Japan and India.[28] If China is already the second world power after USA, or the leading Asian power, or expects to become one in the foreseeable future, then the comparison should be between the USA and China. The reality is that talk about a G-2 system to deal with world problems is an aspiration that bumps against the reality of a G-5 plus (USA, PRC, Japan, Russia and India) structure of Asian multi-polarity. China's adoption of a G-5 comparison set, the wariness about China's "peaceful rise" among China's neighbours, and China's internal debate about her foreign policy options suggest a lack of asymmetrical gain for China in the recent past and the forseeable future.

In addition, the 2008 Defence White Paper and other Chinese writings indicate that the challenges before China are long term and complicated. Consider the frame of reference in recent Chinese analyses. Discussions in a recent issue of "International Strategic Studies" published by China's leading strategic think tank, the China Institute for International Strategic Studies (CIISS), make points which help our argument:

1. The Japan-US alliance is a problem for China. Japan is seen to bid for "dominance" in East Asia and to check China through its alliance with USA; this is a challenge to China.
2. The US-Japan alliance prevents the peaceful reunification of Taiwan. The Law Concerning Measures the Peace and Security of Japan in situations in Areas Surrounding Japan (1999) expanded the co-operation area to include the South China seas and the Taiwan straits. Furthermore, Japan's statements in 2004 view the Korean peninsula and the Taiwan straits as sources of "obscurity and uncertainty", and stability in the Taiwan straits is a "common strategic objective" and a part of the US-Japan security arrangements. This is a "serious challenge" to Chinese efforts to solve the Taiwan issue.
3. China sees itself as a part of a triangle with USA and Japan in these areas.[29]

---

[28] See Lampton, *The Three Faces of Chinese Power.*, Table 1, pp. 22–23.
[29] Yang Yang, 2008. "The Adjustment of Japan-US Alliance and the Strategic Options for Chinese Foreign Policy," pp. 34–38, *International Strategic Studies, CIISS*, Beijing, 4, 2008. Revised April 28, 2010

These comments by high-level Chinese commentators indicate an awareness of the rise of a robust US-Japan military relationship that centres on the situations in the Korean peninsula, the Taiwan straits and the South China Sea, and that require a continuous triangular engagement between China, Japan and USA in the military and diplomatic sphere. Our presumption is that such engagement is likely to be long term because the issue of North Korean nuclear and missile proliferation is not likely to resolve soon. With Japan's military build-up and its ongoing security debate, and the military build-up among China's neighbours, there is opposition to the rise of China as a regional power. Many countries in Asia, Middle East and Africa, and the major powers of the West, seek maritime security in the Pacific and the Indian Ocean sea lanes to assure movement of commerce including oil imports from the Persian Gulf. Beijing makes a valid claim about its "indispensible" role to facilitate regional security and stability but this is an assertion about its right to participate in regional security situations in its geographical proximity and its responsibility as a UN Security Council member to act as a responsible stakeholder in Asia Pacific and Indian Ocean affairs. However, these claims are not the basis of a prediction that China's peaceful rise implies recognition of its pre-eminent position in Asia.

Our judgment is that a comparison between Chinese statements in the recent past and the present (2008–10) suggest an erosion of China's international position. Recall that Qian Qichen (cited earlier) saw the PRC and USA as two world powers. Recent analysis by CIISS however, suggest the rise of major challenges as a result of developments in the US-Japan military arrangements and the changing orientation in internal Japanese thinking and defence policy. In other words, a world of two world powers with the prospect of accommodation and clubbing together by the two is now replaced at least by the reality of a triangular US-China-Japan strategic relationship that impacts the Asia Pacific sphere. In the past, the Chinese strategy was to divide and demoralise the anti-China front; this was Qian Qichen's view. The presumption was that Japan was the weak link in the anti-China front. Now the strategy and the presumption are questionable as a result of developments in the region in recent years. The conclusion is that Beijing has failed to demoralise Japan and to prevent the formation of the US-PRC-Japan strategic triangle. As long as China's neighbours to its north and south are able to maintain their military modernisation in relation to Chinese military developments, a strategic stalemate is likely to endure rather than produce asymmetrical gain for China.

Implications for India

The chapter argues that the PRC currently employs a two-track approach to Asia-Pacific affairs. Diplomatically it seeks normalisation and regional stability; militarily it seeks modernisation and development of power projection capabilities. The "peaceful rise" of China is an ambiguous formula because it could produce an extended period of no war in China's relations with its neighbours but the possibility of Chinese aggressiveness cannot be ruled out. China is still a dissatisfied power in the region, there are outstanding territorial questions involving Japan, India, Vietnam and other countries, and the prospect of peaceful reunification of Taiwan with China remains an unsettled issue. Faced with entangling alliances (e.g. US-Japan, US-Australia) and alliance-like linkages (e.g. US-India, US-Singapore and other Southeast Asian countries) China may continue on its peaceful rise but this assumes that her neighbours are able to create situations to force China to deal with her dilemmas through a process of compromise of its core goals. Note that China's neighbours have formed triangular strategic alignments involving the US and Japan in North Asia and a similar alignment, albeit on an informal level, involving USA, India and US allies in South Asia and Southeast Asia; such alignments complicate China's strategic options. The operative theory is that one must get close to Beijing precisely because it is not trusted; that is, one must be close to one's friends and closer to one's rivals for this reason. Implicit in the approach is a desire to keep China tied to entangling commitments about regional security and stability and to expose China to a critical mass of external issues that require it to promote domestic consensus-building and tradeoffs among competing policy demands. This implies a growth of internal debates within China that cannot be managed by patriotic education.

The approach of China's neighbours has two discernable long-term aims: to ensure that China does not secure asymmetrical gain in any way, and to create policy boundaries that require China's officials and scholars to debate the issues and methods internally and rationally. The theory is simple. By widening the issues in the strategic basket, it becomes necessary to expand the list of participants, and this process is likely to yield dilemmas and internal debates. Consider the following examples.

1. Should Beijing adopt a bellicose stance against Japanese militarism and the past history of Sino-Japanese relations or should it make diplomatic overtures to normalise relations with Japan? The former approach could hasten Japan's

militarisation and deepen her military ties with USA. The latter approach could produce a triangular relationship where China has some input into Japanese and American decision-making.

2. Should Beijing adopt an anti-US position in the Korean peninsula and tilt clearly towards Pyongang (as it did in the Korean war) or should it tilt towards the goal of regional security and stability, and accept South Korean and American approaches to North Korea? The former approach would align the interests of authoritarian Chinese and North Korean models; the latter opens North Korea to Western and Japanese commercial and strategic influences; in addition, it widens the potential influence of Christianity in North Korea that reflects the impact of past missionary activity in North Korean society.

3. Should China maintain its deep military links and political support for Pakistan's government or should it adopt a semi-neutral stance in issues of importance to USA and India i.e. counter-Islamist terrorism, scale back on transfer of nuclear and missile aid to Pakistan, take the back seat on the Kashmir issue, and discourage Pakistani military adventurism in the region?

Our theory about the value of encouraging the formation of policy dilemmas for a rival power is premised in the belief that entangling dilemmas and entangling triangular relationships are a form of conflict management and possibly of conflict resolution in the future. The delay in the peaceful re-unification of Taiwan with the Chinese mainland, and the prolonged negotiations about the future of the Sino-Indian border are desirable in the sense that they stimulate internal debates among the practitioners on all sides, they increase the size of the decision-making pool as more voices come to the policy table, and they reduce the danger of poor decision-making if the set of decision makers is small and the process is secretive. Indian practitioners can develop their diplomatic and military skills-set by studying the pattern of interactions in the US-Japan-China strategic triangle (and other sub-regional triangles) and the dilemmas it creates for China. Indian practitioners and scholars can discover the importance of triangular diplomacy and statecraft and its calming effect on regional enemies or rivals. This theory requires continuous and controlled military and economic development of members of a strategic triangle so that the anti-status quo power is not in a position to end the game by defeating its rival and/or a member of the triangle does not self-destruct and lose the game.

Finally, Indian practitioners and scholars need to assess the destructive results of Chinese activities in the Tibet-Himalayan-Pakistan zone. Despite massive Chinese aid to Pakistan and diplomatic support for its rivalry with India, Pakistan is a failing or a failed state and the question now is not if but when Pakistan will self-destruct in a balkanised set of smaller states that represent its various regional ethnic nationalities (i.e. Sindhis, Balooch, Pushtoon, Punjabi and Kashmiri). This possibility cannot be ruled out in this decade. Chinese aid to Pakistan has taken Pakistan on the road to self-destruction and also harmed the prospect of building strong democratic institutions and civil society within Pakistan, and to develop peace oriented relations with India and Afghanistan. In comparison, Bangladesh has emerged as a viable entity despite its troubled history of military rule. Bangladesh has been in the nation-building business for a short span. It did not receive lavish aid from the West and China as Pakistan did, and it has slowly learnt the importance of building its political institutions on a democratic basis that is grounded in Bangladeshi nationalism. China's brutal suppression of Tibetans, the use of massive Han migration to alter the Tibetan personality, its attack on the Tibetan demand for autonomy, and its refusal to allow the world's press to report on Tibetan developments, is another prominent example of destructive effect of China's policy in the Himalayan region. China's approach to Nepal and the Sino-Indian boundary question is tied in the Chinese mind to the Tibet issue because the flow of Tibetan refugees from Tibet to India through Nepal embarrasses the Chinese authorities. Consequently, the Himalayan-Tibetan area remains a point of contention between communist China, Buddhist Tibet, Maoist Nepal and democratic India. The last example of Chinese destructive action lies in continuing efforts to subvert the local population on the Indian side south of the McMahon Line, which is the de facto line of control and tranquillity in Sino-Indian agreements of the 1990s. These efforts have mostly failed in Arunachal Pradesh including the highly symbolic Tawang Monastery which China claims. That such attempts to subvert the local population and local politicians continue, implies a belief in Maoist propaganda practices, and the use of deception about regional stability and security in inter-governmental communiqués. The lesson for Indian practitioners and scholars is that China's policies in the area are driven less by consideration of ethics, good governance and reason and more by a desire to divide and demoralise China's rivals in the area. The implication is that China is likely to be reasonable when all other methods fail, which means that ways have to be found to orchestrate Chinese failures and to advertise them because Beijing does not like to lose face in front of international audiences.

Indians should learn from the Asia-Pacific experiences because as China's neighbours they have been able to avoid the destructive effects of Chinese policies following the rise of Communist China and the Korean War. In the Far East, the diplomatic and military experiences have relied on the formation of anti-China fronts which have induced Beijing to negotiate on that basis. In comparison, Indian practitioners of the Nehruvian vintage (1947–90s) thought that bilateral and peace diplomacy was sufficient to secure Chinese restraint; it is not.

6

China and the United States

Jostling Begins

Arthur Waldron

W HAT will be the implications for the United States (US) and the rest of the world of a China on the threshold of great power status? Beijing as much as announced that she sought such a position when in December 2006 state television aired a twelve-part series titled "*The Rise of the Great Powers.*" [*Daguo jueqi* 大國崛起] This explained to viewers how the Portuguese, Spanish, British, German, Japanese, Soviets and others, concluding with the US, had attained great power status by combining territorial expansion, domestic dynamism, economic acumen and military power.[1]

As China has seemed to draw near to this goal, contrary views have been heard. Some see this expected development as fundamentally a source of problems: a good example in Chicago's John J. Mearsheimer who stresses that "China's rise" will not be peaceful.[2] Others see a strong and capable China as the potential solution to world disorder. Joined with the US in a refashioned "Chinamerican G-2" of Harvard's Niall Ferguson sees this new China as a potential source for order in a chaotic world.[3]

---

[1] The entire series is widely available on Chinese DVDs; it may also be viewed online at http://www. youku.com/playlist_show/id_5976.html; accessed May 24, 2009.

[2] John J. Mearsheimer, "China's Unpeaceful Rise," *Current History* 105.690 (April 2006), pp. 160–62.

[3] Quoted in Pankaj Mishra, "The War of the Worlds," *Financial Times,* June 6–7, 2009 p. 13.

Chinese and American Traditional Views

China has nearly always seen herself as by rights if not in reality, "top country" sitting at the top of an international hierarchy over which she exercises ultimate authority, directly or indirectly. No reason exists to imagine that this fundamental conviction has changed.[4] The US, by contrast, has tended for a century, to see China as fundamentally a benign international force, lacking external ambitions and preoccupied with her internal situation. Washington has long expected the imminent and welcome arrival of a new Chinese power on the international scene, with numerous beneficial results. This idea guided the new diplomacy of the 1970s, conceived by American President Richard Nixon. This was premised on the indefinite existence of a powerful Soviet Union hostile to China. It envisioned Beijing and Washington co-operating closely to balance the power of the then Soviet Union and enjoyed some success during the roughly two decades following, during which the Soviet Union continued to exist. That such a friendship would usher in a new era of co-operation, and with that a new, stable and peaceful world order has a history extending, as will be seen below, to the end of the nineteenth century.

The problem is that China has never shared this American vision and nor does it do so now. China's idea of what she will be and what role she will play when and if restored to dominant status differs fundamentally from what Americans have so long imagined. According to official Chinese reports on April 26, 2010,

> The United States is the greatest perceived threat to the People's Liberation Army (PLA), a top military strategist told *China Daily* on Sunday, confirming remarks made last week to a group of visiting senior US officials. As the US was the only country capable of threatening China's national security interests in an all-round way, the US, as the experts convened at the reported meeting confirmed.

Beijing saw Washington not as an ultimate friend, partner and collaborator, but rather as her most dangerous and capable adversary.[5]

---

[4] T. F. Tsiang "China and European Expansionism" *Politica* 2.5 (1936): 1–18. John K. Fairbank and S. Y. Teng, "On the Ch'ing Tributary System" *Harvard Journal of Asiatic Studies* 6.2 (1942): 135–246. John K. Fairbank,ed *The Chinese World Order* (Cambridge, Mass.: Harvard University Press, 1968). (author has repeated no) "Historical Notes on the Chinese World Order" in *The Chinese World Order*, ed. Fairbank, pp. 20–33.

[5] "US biggest perceived threat to PLA: Strategist" *People's Daily Online,* April 26, 2010. http://english.peopledaily.com.cn/90001/90776/90883/6962455.html; accessed on April 26, 2010.

The years ahead are therefore likely to witness two sets of collisions. We may expect a certain degree of friction between the two powers, perhaps even conflict – the report just cited added that

> (frictions over) the cross-Straits relationship was the most likely to provoke a Sino-US nuclear war.[6]

Equally importantly, we will witness a painful recalibration of views, particularly by the US, as she realises that China is not set to play the role assigned to her, and also by her neighbours as they realise that her intentions are not benign. Particularly challenging will be how China (and the US) as well as other countries deal with what can only be a challenge to the dense web of international security relations with the US. For Europe and Japan, for example, American power is explicitly the defensive force of first and last resort. But many other countries, not having formal security relations with the US, have nevertheless assumed that in case of crisis, the US would come to the rescue, and have configured their strategies and forces accordingly.

China's Recent Situation

A China seeking to disrupt this web, by deterring American intervention, denying area access to American forces, and so forth, will necessarily force a global rethinking of security policy. To be sure, even today American ability to carry out even the explicit tasks she has guaranteed by treaty (e.g. defend Japan) may be doubted. Washington is grievously overstretched and by the standard of commitments, implicit or explicit, lacking in resources. That much was realised in the Nixon administration and is precisely why Washington then sought an alliance of sorts with China. Now China is emerging, with a wealthy government and powerful military, and without the restraint formerly imposed by the Soviet Union to the north, able to pursue her own agenda – an agenda that is turning out not to complement those of the US and many other countries, but be firmly at odds with them.

China shares borders with more countries than does any other state. Any change in her international behaviour therefore will almost inevitably lead to significant consequences, for we live in a highly non-permissive international environment. Effectively no territories are without claimants and the various countries of the world as well as international organisations are vigilant about

---

[6] *China Daily* cited in note 5.

violations, which means that unlike the middle of the nineteenth century, the present is a very difficult time to create new empires or even spheres of influence. Nevertheless, speculation is rife, both in China and abroad, that Beijing has some such project in mind. "Lost territories" – in reality bits of the old Manchu Qing [青] empire (1644–1912) – such as Mongolia and Taiwan, as well as portions of today's Russia, have not been forgotten. Seaward ambitions exist as well: speaking of the numerous reefs and islets that dot the South China Sea and that have been claimed by many of the surrounding countries, the former Chinese Foreign Minister Huang Hua [黃華] told this author, "we will gradually pick them up one by one"[7] – as Beijing has in fact been doing, e.g. by establishing a military base on Mischief Reef in 1994, just 130 miles away from the Philippine island of Palawan.[8] As Beijing's ambitions for territory and power have begun to dawn on the world and the US, speculation has begun about just how big a sphere China will carve out for herself. A recent issue of *Foreign Affairs* suggests one incorporating eastern Russia, Southeast Asia as well as portions of South Asia, with only Japan and India expected to resist.[9]

The current borders of the People's Republic of China include, with the exception of now-formally-independent Mongolia and Taiwan, which remains autonomous and beyond Beijing's reach, effectively all the territory conquered or ruled by the non-Chinese Manchu Qing. Twice as extensive as its predecessor, the ethnically Chinese Ming [明] (1368–1644), the People's Republic is territorially the third largest state in the world (after Russia and Canada). From northeast to southeast, her land border touches North Korea, Mongolia, Russia, Kazakhstan, Kyrgyzstan, Tajikistan, Afghanistan, Pakistan, India, Nepal, Bhutan, Myanmar, Laos, and Vietnam, 14 in all. To the east, her coast faces South Korea, Japan, Taiwan and the Philippines. If we include the waters of the South China Sea, which China looks set to claim as territorial, then she also borders Cambodia, Malaysia, Singapore, Brunei and Indonesia.[10] China's are among the farthest flung borders of any country.

Like it or not, therefore, China cannot escape a global role. She is a major player everywhere she has a border, and beyond. Her ships regularly penetrate Japanese waters around the Senkaku Islands [尖閣諸島] called by the

---

[7] In Beijing, 1994.

[8] See Wikipedia, s.v. http://en.wikipedia.org/wiki/Mischief_Reef; accessed on April 26, 2010.

[9] Robert D. Kaplan, "The Geography of Chinese Power," *Foreign Affairs* 89.3 (May/June 2010): 22–41, map is at page 27.

[10] For background see James R. Holmes and Toshi Yoshihara "China's "Caribbean" in the South China Sea" *SAIS Review* 26.1 (Winter-Spring 2006) pp. 79–92.

Chinese the Diaoyutai Islands 釣魚台群島].[11] Her navy excludes Vietnamese ships from the traditional fishing grounds that China claims.[12] Russian naval gunfire and the sinking of a Chinese merchant ship at Vladivostok in February 2009 serves to remind that tension with her powerful northern neighbour is always present just under the surface.[13] The recent conclusion of the Sri Lankan war against Tamil separatists was paid for by China who will receive port facilities at "the once sleepy fishing town of Hambantota." These will have the potential to pin British and American forces at Diego Garcia, as well as Indian interests.[14] This port can be added to a growing list that also includes Sittwe in Myanmar, Chittagong in Bangladesh and Gwadiar in Pakistan.[15] So East, South and Southeast Asia are, to an extent, already well in play.

China is active in the Middle East and a major patron of and seller of arms to Iran.[16] "Frictions and disputes', according to official Chinese media, characterised relations with Europe in 2008.[17] Her presence in Africa has recently begun to attract attention.[18] She already has access to Port Sudan, south of the Suez Canal. If, to this is added ports on the east and west coasts of that continent, which seem only a matter of time, China will have a strong position in the Indian Ocean as well as the ability to operate in the South Atlantic and north to Gibraltar.[19] President Hugo Chavez of Venezuela has called himself a "Maoist" (one wonders what the Chinese made of that!).[20] The crews of the Chinese aircraft carriers currently being built will train, for now,

---

[11] See Wikipedia http://en.wikipedia.org/wiki/Senkaku_Islands; accessed on June 13, 2009. The author was thoroughly briefed on such incursions by the Japan Self Defense Agency during a visit in December 2007.

[12] "FM: South China Sea Fishing Ban "Indisputable," *Xinhua* June 9, 2009. http://news.xinhuanet.com/english/2009–06/09/content_11515539.htm; accessed on June 13, 2009.

[13] "China Says Russia's Attitude on Cargo Ship Incident "Unacceptable" *Xinhua* February 20, 2009.

[14] See Vijay Sakhuja, "Sri Lanka: Beijing's Growing Foothold in the Indian Ocean" *China Brief* IX.12 (June 12, 2009), pp. 7–9. Also "Chinese billions in Sri Lanka fund battle against Tamil Tigers" London *Times Online* May 2, 2009 http://www.timesonline.co.uk/tol/news/world/asia/article; accessed on June 13, 2009.

[15] "Chinese billions" cited above.

[16] See John W. Garver, *China and Iran: Ancient Partners in a Post-Imperial World* (Seattle: University of Washington Press, 2006).

[17] "A final glance at Sino-European Relations 2008" *Xinhua* December 19, 2009 http://english.peopledaily.com.cn/90001/90780/91343/6557963.html; accessed on June 13, 2009.

[18] Arthur Waldron, ed. *China In Africa* (Washington, D.C.: The Jamestown Foundation, 2008, 2009).

[19] Arthur Waldron "Africa in China's Grand Strategy" talk presented at Jamestown Foundation Conference, May 20, 2009, Proceedings now in press.

[20] See Wikipedia http://en.wikipedia.org/wiki/Foreign_policy_of_Hugo_Chávez; accessed on June 13, 2009.

with the Brazilians.[21] The thought of the great American strategist Alfred Thayer Mahan is all the rage.[22]

International Developments

These developments bring us to the conspicuous increase in Chinese harassment of American naval vessels and other military assets.[23] On June 11, 2009, near Subic Bay in the Philippines, a Chinese submarine collided with the sonar array being towed by the destroyer John McCain.[24] In other incidents Chinese vessels harassed an unarmed US navy craft gathering intelligence in international waters. A good example is that of the navy ship *Impeccable* which was confronted by Chinese "fishing vessels" in March 2009.[25] This was only one of a series of dangerous events prompted, in part, by an American desire to know more about the huge underground naval base that China has constructed at Hainan Island, her southernmost substantial territory.[26] They are only the most recent of a steady stream of relatively minor incidents.[27] In November 2007, for reasons still murky, China, at the last moment, refused entry into Hong Kong to the US aircraft carrier *Kitty Hawk* for a long-planned Thanksgiving holiday. By the time the Chinese had changed their minds, the carrier was already sailing up the Taiwan Strait, pursued, according to some reports, by a Chinese submarine and surface vessel.[28] In April 2001, a Chinese fighter collided with an American PC-3 in international air space, causing the death of the Chinese pilot and the crash landing of the American aircraft.[29]

---

[21] "PLAN Officers to Train on Brazilian Aircraft Carrier" *China Brief* IX.12 (June 12, 2009), pp. 1–2.

[22] AS "Banyan" notes in the London *Economist*: "Chasing Ghosts: The Notion that Geography is Power is Making an Unwelcome Comeback in Asia," June 11, 2009 http://www.economist.com/world/asia/PrinterFriendly.cfm?story_id=13825154; accessed on June 13, 2009.

[23] Willy Lam, "China Flaunts Growing Naval Capabilities" *China Brief* 9.1 (2009) http://www.jamestown.org/single/?no_cache=1&tx_ttnews%5Btt_news%5D=34334; accessed on June 13, 2009.

[24] CNN.com http://printthis.clickability.com/pt/cpt?action=cpt&title=Sub+co...2009%FUS%2FO6%22F12%2Fchina.submarine%2Findex.html&partnered=212106; accessed on June 13, 2009.

[25] CNN March 9, 2009 http://www.cnn.com/2009/POLITICS/03/09/us.navy.china/; accessed on June 6, 2009,

[26] Thomas Harding, "Chinese Nuclear Submarine Base: China Has Secretly built a Major Underground Nuclear Submarine Base that Could Threaten Asian Countries and Challenge American Power in the Region, it Can be Disclosed," London *Daily Telegraph* May 1, 2008 http://www.telegraph.co.uk/news/worldnews/asia/china/1917167/Chinese-nuclear-submarine-base.html; accessed on May 06, 2009.

[27] http://en.wikipedia.org/wiki/Hainan_Island_incident; accessed on April 5, 2009.

[28] Andrei Chang, "Behind the Kitty Hawk Spat" UPI December 3, 2007.

[29] 2001http://edition.cnn.com/2001/US/04/01/us.china.plane.06/; accessed on February 28, 2011.

All of these ominous incidents are suggestive of a new Chinese self-confidence and assertiveness. The question is why China is choosing the international arena for assertion, rather than, for example, devoting the funds and efforts to improving the lot of the hundreds of millions of Chinese farmers who live in abject poverty? Such international assertion is also dangerous to China, for a genuine conflict at any of the more than a dozen potential flashpoints just enumerated, from Russia to Vietnam or beyond, would pull China into a war in which she would be outgunned, geographically overextended, and almost certainly humiliated. As pursuit of national interest, Beijing's current forward policy makes no sense, at least not as the *griff nach der Weltmacht* [lit. "grasp for world power," referring to German policies in the period leading to World War I] that it may seem.

A good way to understand the danger is to think of the role played by tiny Belgium (11,787 square miles, smaller than Taiwan) in World War I. In all their scenario-building, the German general staff never considered that Belgium might put up more than just a symbolic resistance. When she did fight, she tied up and slowed down enough German troops to deny them victory at the Battle of the Marne in September 1914. Germany was of course immensely bigger and more powerful than Belgium. The lesson, as repeatedly taught in war, is that small or seemingly negligible obstacles can stymie mighty powers. Every one of the countries surrounding China, we may assume, is working on a military strategy designed to do just that.

Nor is it persuasive to argue that China is driven primarily by the desire to secure natural resources and trade routes. China is a breathtakingly wasteful user of energy. One standard unit there produces an output value of US $ 0.36 as compared to $ 0.72 for India, $ 3.24 for France and $ 5.58 for Japan. Clearly, what is needed is not oil fields in Latin America and Africa, mines in Australia, with a blue-water navy and ports to secure trade, but rather simply conservation at home.[30] Probably the best explanations for Beijing's behaviour are found in domestic politics of nationalism as will be discussed below.

Like Russia, as described by Moltke the Elder, China is not, and never has been, either as important or unimportant, as strong or as weak, as either she

---

[30] Li Xiangyang *Shei lai wei 21 shiji Zhongguo jiayou?* [Li Xiangyang *Who will "fill up" 21ˢᵗ century China with oil?* 李 向阳 谁来为 21 世纪中国加油] (Beijing: Zhongguo shehui kexue chubanshe, 2005), p. 278. For views that stress energy and resources *as* rationales, see Gabriel B. Collins, Andrew S. Erickson, Lyle J. Goldstein, and William S. Murray, eds. *China's Energy Strategy: The Impact on Beijing's Maritime Policies* (Annapolis, MD: Naval Institute Press, 2008) and Robert I. Rotberg, ed. *China Into Africa: Trade, Aid, And Influence* (Washington, D.C.: The Brookings Institution Press, 2008) esp. pp. 1–20.

herself, or those who spin international orders based upon her imagine. The vast extent of her territory alone is a sufficient strategic headache. She must always reckon with the likelihood of multi-front war, the strategists" nemesis, and this without adding the foreign hostages to fortune represented by the overseas Chinese bases enumerated above. Surely China would be better served by maintaining a military sufficient for self-defence and a policy of friendship with neighbours. The pursuit of territorial claims that cannot be realised without massive use of force (e.g. with respect to India, Taiwan and Japan) makes no sense at all. Nevertheless those who see China emerging as a global adversary are likely to be disappointed. The problem is that even without the motivation of global ambitions, which we will argue below, Beijing lacks space for manoeuvre, in today's interlinked and non-permissive security environments, her policies, even if locally directed, may nevertheless prove sufficiently provocative to the system as whole as to lead to war.

Interpretations

So how do we account for China's new global assertiveness? The chief concern of whoever rules China has always been to keep the territory stable and maintain that rule intact – a domestic concern. Foreign matters impinge only in as much as they affect that goal. The domestic unity and mobilisation that would make the state a great power has, moreover, regularly been sacrificed to the desire of the ruling group to keep its specific grip on the control of the nation. As Peter Lorge (b. 1967) explains, with great insight:

> Successive Chinese dynasties used the military *to keep the empire separated into small enough groups that no one of them could threaten the throne*…Chinese dynasts built their empires *by destroying regional powers and accommodating local ones*. The empire was not a homogenised nation tightly connected by shared local or cultural ties. Elite culture was shared, drawing from a canon of philosophical, literary and historical texts, but most of the population spoke mutually unintelligible dialects, had no contact with anyone beyond perhaps the nearest market town, and practiced only vaguely similar cultures.[31]

This observation is as true of the People's Republic of China today as it was of the earlier dynasties. China has regularly been shaken by massive uprisings such as the military mutiny of An Lushan [安祿山] (ca 703–757) that fatally undermined perhaps the greatest of all dynasties, the Tang [唐] or

---

[31] Peter Lorge, *War, Politics and Society in Early Modern China 900–1795* (London and New York: Routledge, 2005) p. 177.

the Taiping Heavenly Kingdom [太平天國] (1850–64) that hastened the end of the Qing [清](1644–1912) or more recently, the astonishing Chinese civil war (1945–49) that saw the initially far more numerous, experienced, and better trained armies of the Nationalist or Kuomintang [國民黨] government of Chiang Kaishek [蔣介石] 1887–1975) overthrown by Mao Zedong's [毛澤東] rural insurgency – or just 20 years ago the peaceful democratic movement of 1989 that swept up the whole country, to be crushed only with brutal force at the Tiananmen Massacre [天安門大屠殺]. Foreign influences played a role in all of these: An Lushan was not Chinese but perhaps Sogdian; the founder of the Taipings was a heterodox Christian; the Communists had Soviet support.

The democracy movement is more complex. To be sure, it demonstrated a popular embrace of ideas having resonances in the Chinese classics but that in their foreign form had been part of the Chinese intellectual landscape since at least the May Fourth Movement [五四運動] of 1919. Some of the leadership saw it as promoted by outside agitators. During the debate about how to react, Deng Xiaoping [鄧小平] scarcely stopped to consider how indigenous grievances might have stirred up unrest: he moved immediately to blaming it all on Taiwan agents and the CIA.[32]

The reality was in fact more frightening. Foreign influence played only a minor role in the democracy movement. Rather, highly placed Chinese were sympathetic at the time. After the massacre they became radicalised to the extent that they risked terrible punishment by helping Zhao Ziyang [趙 紫陽] the prime minister who resigned just before the shooting began, to compile and publish his memoirs abroad (and in Hong Kong). Du Daozheng [杜 導 正] former chief of the General Administration of Press and Publications, effectively Censor-in-chief during the 1980s, assisted with the recording and transcription of Zhao's interviews, which took place under the noses of those supposed to be watching him.[33] The release of the book in time for the twentieth anniversary of the massacre, in spite of every party effort to stifle it, demonstrates just how much the Chinese government has to fear from ostensibly loyal high officials.

To its leadership, then, even without any foreign relations at all, the existing Chinese state, still a Leninist dictatorship following the governmental

---

[32] Liang Zhang, Andrew J. Nathan, Perry Link, and Orville Schell *The Tiananmen Papers: The Chinese Leadership's Decision to Use Force Against Their Own People – In Their Own Words* (New York: Public Affairs, 2001).

[33] *Prisoner of the State: The Secret Journal of Premier Zhao Ziyang* by Zhao Ziyang, ed. Bao Pu, Renee Chiang, Adi Ignatius (New York: Simon & Schuster, 2009).

model of the Soviet Union, is terrifyingly unpredictable, uncontrollable and potentially unstable. Maintenance of party rule, whatever the cost, is the guiding principle. Today's Chinese government, like that of the former USSR, understands how fragile is its hold on power and out of fear of destabilisation, whether internally or externally caused, leads it to seek real or imaginary enemies in order to direct popular hostility abroad, while at the same time attempting to create a zone in which it can live more or less autarkically, without taking the risks entailed by opening to the world.

Keeping the communist party in power at home is the single overriding concern of the government in Beijing today. A good parallel is the Soviet Union in 1947 when George F. Kennan explained the domestic sources of its drive to occupy and place under communist control the great swaths of adjoining territory.[34] The need to maintain a precarious peace and stable political control at home is the driver of Chinese foreign policies that may, to those on the receiving end, appear to be aggressive or imperialistic. Motivation does not excuse international misbehaviour. Understanding the sources of that misbehaviour, however, makes it easier to counter. A state configured as just described will necessarily be weak both with respect to internal and external challenges. It will take an interest in foreign matters only insofar as they affect that goal.

With this perspective in mind, let us consider the increasing military friction between China, her neighbours and the US. China's security activities now range far beyond her immediate neighbourhood, as we have seen. China's pace of military modernisation is becoming impossible to ignore. She commands an impressive range of technologies that operate in outer space, beneath the sea and everywhere in between. Chinese military and strategic targeting of the US has become very clear. As Chairman of the US Joint Chiefs of Staff, Admiral Mike Mullen observed in May, 2009:

> They are developing capabilities that are very maritime focused, maritime and air focused, and in many ways, very much focused on us.[35]

China would appear to be trying to ease the US out of her position in East Asia. If successful, this will put in jeopardy security arrangements with Japan, Korea, Taiwan, Australia and other countries. But the trend is evident – and it is in keeping with the fundamental Chinese strategic dictum to "attack alliances" [*fa jiao* 伐j交].[36]

---

[34] X. "The Sources of Soviet Conduct." *Foreign Affairs* 25, no. 4 (1947): 66–582.

[35] "China military build-up seems U.S.-focused: Mullen" Reuters UK May 4, 2009.

[36] See Victor H. Mair, tr, *The Art of War: Sun Zi's Military Methods* (New York: Columbia University Press, 2007), p. 84.

This obvious conclusion – that for whatever reason China is targeting the US military presence in Asia with the goal of forcing it out – is extremely difficult for Americans to accept.

The American Approach

For more than a century the US has imagined that an emerging China would be an international leader; indeed a keystone of international order broadly aligned with the US. This was what US President Richard Nixon had in mind when he met Chinese leader Mao Zedong in 1972. Nixon thought of Mao as a man of great wisdom concerning international affairs, with whom he would discuss every sort of issue, leading to a meeting of minds and – this is suggested by patterns of redaction in declassified documents – the substitution of China for Japan as Washington's primary Asian ally.

Thus on February 21, 1972 the American opened his talk with Prime Minister Zhou Enlai [周恩來] as follows:

> [...] I hope to talk with the Prime Minister and later with the Chairman about issues like Taiwan, Vietnam, and Korea.
>
> I also want to talk about – and this is very sensitive – the future of Japan, the future of the subcontinent, and what India's role will be; and on the broader world scene, the future of US-Soviet relations. Because only if we see the whole picture of the world and the great forces that move the world will we be able to make the right decisions about the immediate and urgent problems that always completely dominate our vision.

Nixon was disappointed when Mao responded: "All those troublesome problems I don't want to get into very much."[37] Mao did not share Nixon's eagerness for China to step out onto the world stage, arm in arm with the US. The chairman and his colleagues knew that China was weak, impoverished and chaotic in the aftermath of the Great Proletarian Cultural Revolution, which had reached its destructive climax in the second half of the 1960s. What they wanted from the US above all were concessions, e.g. on Taiwan, that would reduce pressure on the regime and assistance in recovering while keeping party rule stable. They were also quite happy to use the American counterweight against the Soviet Union, which was menacing at that time. Nixon loved international relations: his domestic policies by and large fared

---

[37] William Burr, ed. *The Kissinger Transcripts: The Top Secret Talks with Beijing and Moscow* (New York: New Press, 1998), p. 62.

poorly but he made his mark abroad. Mao, by contrast, saw the outside world as a source of "troublesome problems" to be kept at bay.

That China might use military means to keep those troublesome problems at bay has also been a very difficult notion for leading American analysts of foreign policy to accept.

During the Clinton administration (1993–2001), Professor Joseph S. Nye who helped to codify security policy with respect to Asia, neatly sidestepped possible internal sources of Chinese behaviour concentrating instead on the effects of American policy. He describes how he thought that administration should behave:

> We knew that the hawks who called for containment of China would not be able to rally other countries to the cause. *We also knew that if we treated China as an enemy, we were ensuring future enmity.* While we could not be sure how China would evolve, it made no sense to foreclose the prospect of a better future.[38]

A variant of this idea was the belief that China simply wanted to join the international system and be treated as an equal member, which is associated chiefly with Robert Zoellick, who in a speech in New York on September 21, 2005 proposed that "the United States step up efforts to make China a "responsible stakeholder" in the international system."[39]

Being a stakeholder would mean that China would accept the international political and economic system as it exists today, because she realised that doing so was in her own best interest; that China would more likely face a prosperous and peaceful future if she co-operated with the existing economic and political powers, followed international law and trade practices such as they are – in effect, cast her lot with the *status quo*.

Views like those of Nixon, Nye and Zoellick have dominated most foreign assessments of China since the 1970s. They are the foundation of the current highly tolerant trade and diplomatic regime, indeed of the whole policy called "engagement." Zoellick is almost certainly correct that co-operation with this

---

[38] Joseph S. Nye, "Assessing China's Power" *Boston Globe* April 19, 2006. http://www.boston.com/news/globe/editorial_opinion/oped/articles/2006/04/19/assessing_chinas_power/; accessed on May 24, 2009

[39] "Zoellick: 'Stakeholder' concept offers new direction for U.S.-China relations" *Xinhua* January 25, 2006 at http://english.peopledaily.com.cn/200601/25/eng20060125_238050.html; accessed on March 6, 2009.

approach would be China's best choice. What is not clear – as will be seen in more detail below – is whether China sees the situation in the same way.

These views fundamentally misread the sources of Chinese behaviour. She does not seek an active international role for its own sake but rather to keep her communist regime in power. What the party sees as necessary and therefore understandable defensive actions, the rest of the world, by the same token, may find them as threatening and at times baffling. The two countries misunderstand one another, as the citations above indicate. They have done so, moreover, for a very long time.

For China, the US is both the most worrying potential source of instability from abroad while at the same time, owing to the particular view that country takes of China, also if properly manipulated, potentially, the most effective foreign shield against such dangers – indeed, enabler of Chinese goals.

The US has long taken the view that when China finally emerges as a power, she will somehow be the ideal partner for Washington. Repeatedly Washington has proven willing to deliver on what it might contribute to such a relationship in the absence of its actual existence, hoping thereby to make it a reality faster. This process, in turn, has allowed China to use the US and the international system to help fend off the threats she so fears. Expectation of friendship with China has been an enduring aspect of American foreign policy. This expectation has a structure. Its premise is that China has not reached her full potential as a state nor taken her destined place in the world order. The reasons for these failures are considered to be defects in her domestic system combined with misunderstanding and mishandling of her by other powers. At the time of writing, it is believed that this situation is about to change. Renewed vigour within China is seen as bringing about a close and genuinely cordial relationship with the US above all other powers. The consequence of this, so the recurring argument has it, will be a fundamental transformation of global politics. Let us examine some instances.

In 1910, the American author, explorer and missionary William Edgar Geil revisited China after a five–year absence. Most historians would see 1905–1910 as years during which the Qing monarchy gradually lost its grip, to be overthrown in 1911. Not so Geil. He proclaimed that

> The change which has taken place in China during the last five years is unique in world history. Never has so vast a population undergone so great an intellectual revolution in so short a time.

Contrasting what he had just seen with what he remembered from five years before, when he explored the Great Wall, Geil bubbled with enthusiasm:

> Idols stood in every Taoist or Buddhist temple. Beggars filled the streets. Convicts wearing heavy wooden yokes begged for food along the highways. Educated Chinamen looked on all physical work as a disgrace...

Now:

> The government has erected model alms-houses and public schools in which are taught mathematics, chemistry and other western sciences. Beggars have been banished from the streets. Convicts dressed in red and white trousers are mending the roads...Highly educated Chinamen...are taking vigorous exercise daily in national gymnasiums...[40]

What we read here is the account of China that, with variations, has endured right up to our own time. The story line is that until a few years before the case is being made – before the end of the dynasty, the rise of the Kuomintang, the coming to power of the Communists, the end of the Cultural Revolution, take your choice – China was indeed benighted and backward. A remarkable change has overtaken her recently, however; one that is transformative, laden with implications for China, the US and the world and the world's systems.

In 1911, another American missionary Joseph King Goodrich published *The Coming China*, an account of how the constitutional system announced by the Qing monarchy in 1909 would utterly transform the situation:

> [C]hanges of the most stupendous import, and almost cataclysmic in their effects, are manifestly to take place in China before long; the changes which the past ten years have wrought were radical, it cannot be denied, yet they were but suggestions of what is likely to be.[41]

In 1915, the future American Minister John Van Antwerp MacMurray wrote to his mentor, Woodrow Wilson then President of the US, of his own strong feelings:

> [F]rankly sympathetic with the Chinese character...and with Chinese national aspirations, and jealous of this people's right to develop into a nation.[42]

---

[40] "China's Awakening Shown Throughout The Country," *New York Times* September 4, 1910 Sunday Magazine p. 11.
[41] Joseph King Goodrich, *The Coming China* (Chicago: A.C. McLurg & Co., 1911), p. 138.
[42] April 15, 1915 Seeley Mudd Library, Princeton University.

When in the late 1920s the Kuomintang took power, another such wave of enthusiasm followed. The party had been founded by Sun Yat-sen [孫逸仙]; after his death it fought its way to power under his deputy Chiang Kai-shek. Most observers, like Herbert Hoover's Secretary of State Henry Stimson, believed that the new party in power "represented the beginning of a permanent change in the Chinese government and character".[43]

Chiang's rule was viewed as very progressive. He was featured ten times on the cover of *Time* Magazine.[44]

China's heroic resistance to invasion by Japan in World War II lifted Chiang's prestige higher. Franklin Roosevelt believed Chiang's China would be a keystone of the post-War world order. He insisted on meeting Chiang, with Winston Churchill at Cairo in November 22–26, 1943, much to Churchill's disgust. This approach was promoted within the State Department by the then highly influential Stanley K. Hornbeck.

Of the sceptics, the group around General Joseph Stilwell proved most influential. Stilwell dismissed Chiang as "the peanut': useless either militarily or politically. Perhaps the late Princeton professor Marius B. Jansen best captured the full dimensions of the visceral dislike some had for Chiang. It was not simply that they felt Chiang was not doing a good job, Jansen observed. Rather, the crux of the matter was that by occupying the top position in China, Chiang was preventing someone much better from being in charge; someone who, unlike Chiang, would succeed in making the country blossom and flourish as American expectations required.[45]

The feeling of disappointment with China, almost betrayal, became acute as the Japanese punished the two hundred divisions fielded half by Chiang and half by independent forces loosely co-operating. The US cheered China on but did very little by way of actually assisting her military effort: Washington's eyes were firmly on continental Europe and the islands, but not the mainland of Asia. When in 1944 the Japanese launched the Ichigo [一号作戦] offensive, which came very close to capturing Chongqing [重慶], the wartime capital,

---

[43] Quoted in Akira Iriye, *After Imperialism: The Search for a New Order in the Far East, 1921–1931* (Cambridge, Mass: Harvard University Press, 1965) p. 258.

[44] Haygood, Daniel. "Saving Face: An Analysis of Ten Time Magazine Front Covers Featuring Chiang Kai-shek" Paper presented at the annual meeting of the International Communication Association, New Orleans Sheraton, New Orleans, LA, May 27, 2004 <http://www.allacademic.com/meta/p113298_index.html

[45] Author's conversation with Marius Jansen ca. 1990.

and defeating Chiang, Stilwell was angry that the Chinese had not been able to supply more troops to his operations in Burma.[46]

As this disaster of Chinese collapse seemed to loom, Washington panicked and began to pay attention to the view of the Chinese communists as the true leaders of resistance that had been popularised by such sympathisers as Edgar Snow whose *Red Star over China* appeared in 1937 and Freda Utley whose *China at War* was published in 1938, by no less than Faber & Faber in London, and John Day in New York, the press owned by Richard Walsh, the second husband of Pearl Buck which put out many left-wing accounts of China. This led a somewhat desperate Washington to send the American Army Observation Group (more commonly known as the "Dixie mission') to the Communist capital at Yan'an on 22 July, 1944 (It would remain until 1947). Although the Communists did little to fight the Japanese – the textbook used in the Chinese military academy lists only thirteen battles between 1937 and 1945 during which the war raged – they nevertheless won great admiration for what were claimed to be their innovative and highly effective yet irregular tactics, and the sense grew, in elite American circles, that Mao would be far better than Chiang as the leader of post-War China.[47]

As war with Japan transformed almost without pause into a civil war disastrous for Chiang and the Kuomintang, which put power into the hands of the Chinese Communists as Cold War ensued, writers influenced by the Stilwell version of events, Barbara Tuchman most notably, began to develop a counter-factual version of history in which China and the US would have been friends and allies, if only Washington had been more sympathetic to the Communists and receptive of their initiatives. Tuchman published a study of Stilwell most importantly; also a long essay in which she constructed a bright post-war world "If Mao Had Come to Washington: An Essay in Alternatives."[48]

Advocates of this view came to be known as the "lost chance in China" school. Like the parallel approaches we have mentioned, it took for granted that China's attitude towards the US depended primarily on how Washington treated her. Had the US supported the left and the Communists, abandoned the hapless Nationalists, and welcomed Mao at war's end, that would have

---

[46] See Wikipedia, s.v. http://en.wikipedia.org/wiki/Operation_Ichi-Go; accessed on 06 June, 2009.

[47] *Battles of The People's Liberation Army* [Textbook used in military academies: Zhongguo renmin jiefangjun zhanyi zhanli xuanbian 中国人民解放军战役战例选编 (Peking People's Liberation Army Political University Publishing House, 1984). Vol. 1, pp. 113–213.

[48] *Foreign Affairs* 51.1 (October 1972): 44–64 http://www.foreignaffairs.com/articles/24374/barbara-w-tuchman/if-mao-had-come-to-washington-an-essay-in-alternatives consulted 06 May, 2009.

led to a better outcome, preventing not only the Chinese Civil War, but also the Korean and Vietnam wars among others. Of course, such a view denies all control over her own actions to the Chinese by seeing them as reactive than active – a condescencing view that has been thoroughly discredited in any case.[49] Indeed a Chinese variant of the theory is today emerging, which blames Peking for mishandling American overtures.[50]

Nevertheless from roughly the 1950s until Nixon's trip to China in 1972, the period during which the US recognised and maintained a formal military alliance with Chiang's refugee government in Taiwan, a positive view of the "New China" that Mao Zedong was thought to be building, and that was solving at the root such problems as poverty and medical care, and of the potentialities of an American relationship with that country prevailed, with a few exceptions, within the American intellectual and foreign policy elites. Information about just how repressive and destructive was Mao's regime was available during all of this period, but discounted. Thus, knowledge of the terrible famine that followed the Great Leap Forward [*da yue jin* 大躍進] of 1958–61 was available at the time from a variety of sources, but the reality of the famine was acknowledged by the China – watching establishment only after the Chinese government allowed it to become known – by supplying the Princeton demographer Ansley J. Coale with demographic data that permitted him to "discover" the catastrophe, as the Chinese intended.[51]

The "lost chance" school, however, powerfully affected the new China policy introduced in the 1970s by Richard Nixon and Henry Kissinger. Kissinger told Zhou Enlai and Mao Zedong how he had come to understand the state they had created was a genuinely indigenous Chinese product in which Communism had not been imposed by a conqueror, as in eastern Europe. Like their predecessors, the American President and his national security adviser had expectations for China and the US. They believed they were, at long last, undoing the mistakes of the 1950s, when the US had continued to recognise (until 1979) as government of all of China the refugee Kuomintang administration on the island of Taiwan. Ending that anomaly would clear the

---

[49] Chen Jian, *Mao's China and the Cold War* (Chapel Hill: University of North Carolina Press, 2001).

[50] A military airlift that affected China's future [yingxiang Zhongguo qiantu he mingyun de yici zhanlue kongyun 影响中国前途和命运的一次战略空运] Manuscript by Professor Niu Dayong, Peking University, Department of History （北京大学历史学系教授 牛大勇 MS 2008）.

[51] Ansley J. Coale, *Rapid Population Change in China, 1952-1982*. (Washington, D.C.: National Academy Press, 1984).

way, so they thought, for shared concern about the USSR, and perhaps some inherent sympathy, to draw the two countries closer together, almost into an alliance.

The Chinese Approach

But if, as suggested already, the future of China and the US is not, for deep internal reasons, one of international partnership – as Washington perennially hopes and Beijing regularly denies[52] – then what is it? We may take China's denials seriously, moreover, in that they suggest a lack of the sort of ideological interest in places having no immediate economic or security importance that was characteristic of the Soviet Union. What must be understood is that the Chinese communist regime feels itself threatened by the world in general and the US in particular. She will, therefore, take actions to secure herself: actions that will prove threatening to others, destabilising to the international system, and ultimately subversive of the very interests Beijing seeks to further.

As we have already mentioned above, ideas of freedom and democracy greatly frighten the Chinese regime. The great communist world is gone, having disappeared between 1989–91 in a series of developments that profoundly shook Beijing's confidence. Of the once mighty Communist world, she is left with a few remnants of little use, like Cuba and now perhaps Venezuela and Bolivia. Meanwhile, countries that formerly were counted as her allies are evidently making plans for self-defence. Vietnam with its long history of resistance to Chinese domination as well, reputedly, has a clandestine nuclear weapons program[53] and North Korea will soon be able to mount a nuclear strike against Beijing if in fact she cannot do so now. Beyond that, the trends of opinion and political alignment are not good. Africa, for example, is now far freer than China. China is making large political and economic investments in Africa, but Africa may not prove to behave as Beijing hopes. According to Freedom House; 10 sub-Saharan African countries are free, 23 are partly free and 15 are not free. More precisely, only 31 per cent of sub-Saharan Africa is not free according to Freedom House,

---

[52] For a denial, see: "Wen rejects allegation of China, US monopolizing world affairs in future" *China Daily* May 21, 2009 http://www.chinadaily.com.cn/china/2009–05/21/content_7920906. htm; accessed on 06 April, 2009.

[53] Author's personal information.

which classifies all of China as not free.[54] The idea of African democracy subverting Chinese authoritarianism may seem far fetched, but odd as it sounds on first hearing "the world is band-wagoning with America" – which is to say, most countries are turning out to be more interested in being like the US than like China (which was not always the case) – creating a world community in which prevail the sorts of values the Chinese communists fear most. (The phrase about band-wagoning with America I owe to a high official of the Ministry of Foreign Affairs in Tokyo, whom I met in December 2007). Others may marvel at China's ability to silence overseas critics and mobilise economic leverage for political ends, but viewed from Beijing, the international environment has a certain menace. Too much political change is being talked about and taking place. Rulers are not keeping the lid on their populations as they should nor are the great powers keeping the lesser powers in line, as they should. The imperative, therefore, is for China to change the world in ways more favourable to the survival of her regime and, as will be seen, to create a self-sufficient parallel international order within which she can safely locate herself.

As Professor Edward Friedman puts it:

> The CCP imagines a chaotic and war-prone world disorder of American-led democracy – promotion being replaced by a beneficent Chinese world order of authoritarian growth with stability. There may be far less of a challenge to China from democracy than there is a challenge to democracy from China.[55]

Countering this trend:

> China is a superpower probing, pushing and pulling the world in its authoritarian direction. ... For Confucian China, China is the core, apex and leader of an Asian community. The CCP intends for authoritarian China to establish itself as a global pole.[56]

Surrounded by the larger international system, then, but not as a part of it, China seeks to establish another international community, large enough to stand alone if necessary, congenial to itself. China seeks to make herself economically and militarily invulnerable to the actions of other states. She is seeking friends where she can find them: many in Africa but not only there.

---

[54] http://www.freedomhouse.org/uploads/fiw09/MOF09_SSAfrica_FINAL.pdf consulted 06 April 09.
[55] Edward Friedman, "China: A Threat or Threatened by Democracy?" *Dissent* 56 (Winter 2008), pp. 7–12. At 12.
[56] Friedman, P. 11.

She is securing resources worldwide, not least in Africa, to insulate against breaks in the flow of energy or minerals that might endanger her economy. By the same token, she is developing a powerful military and a series of bases for it, ranging from Hainan to Burma to Sri Lanka to Pakistan and beyond, probably to Africa, with which she hopes to protect these resource flows. Otherwise, the survival of the government will be hostage to the constantly changing international economic picture. Far from wishing to join the international system, then, China is seeking to opt out of it as much as possible by creating a set of institutions and constituencies that will assure the survival of her regime, come what may. Doing this does not require dominating the world. It does, however, require setting up limited but sufficient China-specific orders in politics, economics and security.

The area in which this order obtains need not be large. My own view is that China will seek to include within it all of her neighbouring countries, with Russia, India and Japan being in her view potential problems. No need exists for China to contend with other powers such as the US for world power nor does she desire to do that. America has long proven a reliable enabler of Chinese policies, attempting to sacrifice Taiwan, keeping Japan from becoming self-sufficient militarily, promulgating rosy views of a China, lobbying for rapidly modernising and liberalising, to be granted full trade and economic privileges when her own currency is still not convertible, and so forth. Both those who see China as a possible partner in a "Chinamerican" world condominium as some fashionable commentators suggest and those who fear China as a power having boundless ambitions are likely to be disappointed. What China wants is a pond of her own. In this perspective, most of the world is relatively unimportant unless resource rich or strategically located. As a result, the policies even of a rather strong China are likely to be focused on her neighbourhood, which is to say Asia.

China's policies will be designed to cushion her regime; to buffer it; to make it independent of anything outside its borders, and, in particular, invulnerable to any sort of external pressure. Achieving that goal does not require global hegemony – which would probably in fact undermine it. Nor is it easy given the degree of Chinese dependence upon, e.g. American markets and financial markets. But it does require that certain policies be pursued internationally to protect the regime.

Such an analysis, which sees China as using the world to protect herself against the world, makes sense of current behaviour. China does not want to be a partner, as Nixon imagined, for a real and open friendship with

Washington, is a poisoned chalice for the communist regime, as Beijing well understands. China moreover has no interest in whether the US or anyone else labels her an enemy. She knows her enemies already: concepts such as freedom and international law, and countries strong enough to bring pressure on her economy and regime. Beijing likewise has no desire for stakeholdership in an international system that, if taken seriously, would penalise her economy for its mercantilism and stigmatise her regime as oppressive. She is not interested in developing an efficient economy so much as in being sure that living standards rise enough to keep the party in power, whatever the cost in forfeited optimalities. She wants to be strong enough militarily to keep any major power from intruding on her or coming too near her borders.

Therefore we see China seeking friendship not with great powers like Russia or India or Japan, but with the weaker and more numerous states of Africa, Latin America and the Indian periphery. We see her turning for oil supplies not to the Saudis, who are too closely identified with the current great powers, but rather to Nigeria, Venezuela, Angola, Sudan and other middle level countries. Militarily we see her working to ease the US out of Asia, neutralise Taiwan and Japan and pin India, while developing her own group of strategically-placed special friends: Iran, Pakistan and perhaps North Korea. Naval bases in friendly African countries will complete this effort. What we are seeing is a policy not of engagement with the world, but of parallel development with the rest of the world, while remaining as independent of it as possible. The question is just how dangerous it is going to be to make the world safe for China in her current political form.

The answer, I fear, is that the safer China becomes in her own eyes, the more dangerous she is for the world. Let us examine this first as it affects existing states and alliance systems.

By investing massively in South Asia and Africa, while developing a strategic presence in those places, China has sought to create a "string of pearls" – a chain of military bases that will support her blue water navy, which in turn will safely convoy the raw materials from and the exports to a growing array of captive markets. This reassuring vision, however, should be worrying. For the string of pearls is really an array of hostages, mostly in places that have no instinctive rapport with China. Furthermore, by establishing bases in places where they have rarely been seen before, the Chinese invite reactions not in their favour.

South Asians, for example, personally tend to have very little use for Chinese, though they will happily accept money, like the Indians, and port facilities like the Bangladeshis, and weapons and ports like the Sri Lankans, and nuclear weapons and missiles like the Pakistanis. China has staked a great deal on this set of relationships and its westernmost outpost, Iran. Can China really be assured, however, that the Hindu, Buddhist and Islamic peoples with whom she is dealing, most of whom live in politically more sophisticated if poorer states, will be her instinctive allies? A whole host of reasons from economics to politics to religion suggest that China's attempts to render South Asia unthreatening have infact opened up new and great dangers, from nuclear missile races to Islamic insurgency.

Furthermore, how is China to deal with long-standing and growing American activities in the region? The US is deeply involved in Afghanistan and Pakistan, both bordering countries, involvement which, moreover, gives both countries somewhere else to turn internationally, even as it stirs up Islamic feelings to which China, given her mistreatment of East Turkestan and her own Muslims, is most sensitive. It is difficult to imagine a genuinely co-operative relationship between Washington and Beijing in that part of the world, which means, unfortunately, friction.

What about India, non-aligned, democratic and free, economically smaller than China but having a more rational system, alarmed by China's military occupation of the former buffer state of Tibet, by her nuclear arming of Pakistan, and by her all-too-transparent attempt to tie India down by feeding a circle of local disputes, from Nepal and Sikkim east and west and then south to Sri Lanka? India will be a problem for China unless Beijing abruptly reverses these policies. Even more, Indian-American relations are in flux. At times, as in the Nixon audience mentioned above, the US has seemed willing, indeed eager, to divide such world power as she has with another country – China being the regular nominee, for example of Professor Ferguson mentioned above. China may have come to believe that she can infact scotch the growing *entente cordiale* [lit. cordial understanding, referring to the alignment between Britain and France concluded in 1904] between Delhi and Washington, but facts do not support that. The attempt by China to intimidate and immobilise India through proxies has frightened that country, leading her to take measures for her own defence and to seek powerful friends. In recent years, Chinese pressure on Arunachal Pradesh has steadily grown, culminating with the recent announcement that China plans to dam the headwaters of the

Brahmaputra river.[57] India will have no choice but to react. The result will be a situation more, not less, worrying to China, and one possessing the possibility for global repercussions of exactly the sort China fears.

We see the same sort of pattern with respect to Australia. In recent years, the country has sought close relations with China. Her trade is massive. But the most recent defence review recommended not neutralisation and acceptance of a de facto Chinese sphere of influence, but rather substantial increases in Australian military spending and force structure. The alliance between the US and Australia is being stimulated, not stymied, by Chinese actions.[58] A strong Australia, in turn, is a keystone to the stability of Southeast Asia.

Most importantly the crucial countries of Northeast Asia are following a similar pattern. Japan remains non-nuclear, but spurred by the "North Korean" (read "Chinese') threat she is greatly upgrading her forces and intelligence gathering capabilities. The infrastructure of anti-missile defence is creating a seamless linkage between American and Japanese forces of a sort that has never existed before. South Korea will look with more favour on the US too, now that North Korea has the ability to strike with nuclear weapons. Recently a large Chinese naval task force sailed, initially undetected, very close to the Japanese island of Okinawa and a Chinese helicopter buzzed a Japanese frigate. This can only be called a foolhardy and counterproductive display of force by China, for Japan, the almost-superpower of Northeast Asia took the incident very badly, and created a high-powered defence and intelligence institute to monitor Chinese activities. The Japanese are far better soldiers, engineers and technologists than the Chinese. At present, the US-Japanese alliance is in flux. Chinese provocation is likely to have only one outcome – the emergence on her northeast flank of a true military superpower, precisely the opposite of her interest.[59]

Russia enjoys complex relations with China, not least as a major arms supplier. But the long term threat that China poses to Russia's Far East is obvious. The recent Chinese acquisition of maritime rights at the North Korean

---

[57] "China Admits to Brahmaputra Project," *Times of India* April 27, 2010. http://timesofindia.indiatimes.com/india/China-admits-to-Brahmaputra-project/articleshow/5841348.cms; accessed on 26 April 2010.

[58] John Garnaut and Jonathan Pearlman, "Rudd accused of fuelling new arms race," *The Canberra Times,* April 5, 2009 http://www.canberratimes.com.au/news/national/national/general/rudd-accused-of-fuelling-new-arms-race/1503271.aspx; accessed on June 6, 2009.

[59] "Chinese Navy expanding role/Government to closely monitor activities in areas around Japan," *Daily Yomiuri* April 15, 2010 http://www.yomiuri.co.jp/dy/national/20100415TDY02T03.htm; accessed on April 26, 2010.

port of Rajin, just at the Russian border and not far south of Vladivostok, is bound to worry longer-term thinkers in the Kremlin.[60] Even Taiwan, which is widely seen as turning, under President Ma Yingjeou [馬英九] toward China, is likely to bump up against the real military and political limits China places on that relationship, and maintain close ties with the US.

Finally, the constant ramping up of China's direct military challenges to the US must be mentioned. The friction involving US reconnaissance ships has already been discussed. More important is the rapid growth of the Chinese military, both qualitatively and quantitatively, and the way that build up clearly targets the US – its space assets and carrier groups in particular. We are already seeing signs of American reactions to these threats. As opinion shifts in Washington from complacency about China's power and greed with respect to her wealth, back to an understanding that real American interests are at stake, we may expect the US to adopt a China policy somewhat different from that described above.

At Bottom Conflict?

Such is the paradox that flows from the two situations we have described. First, China is without doubt becoming stronger and more influential, a development that the US professes to welcome as it has done for a century. From the Chinese governmental point of view, the foreign policy aspects of the rise are purely matters of justice, such as restoring alienated territories (Taiwan) or designed to create a safer immediate environment for the continuation of the Communist party dictatorship. Yet, that very rise increases rather than diminishes tension in areas long formally or informally associated with the US, along an arc from West Asia to Northeast Asia. This is because for China to be successful, she must neutralise or sever security connections among her foreign neighbours and with the US that have existed, in many cases, since the end of World War II. That cannot be done without destabilising the entire world order. Given a real crisis, in none of these places is the US likely to abandon an old friend or even a new interest to China. As China grows stronger, the formal and informal free world alliance systems based on the US are strained in the short run. But in the longer run they grow stronger. China could avoid this problem by changing her system and joining the world and

---

[60] Michael Mazza, "China and the Lost Pearls," *The American*, April 23, 2010. http://www.american.com/archive/2010/april/china-and-the-lost-pearls; accessed on April 26, 2010.

she may do so. But one cannot count on that, as the old American policy of "engagement" sometimes seemed to.

Our last concern must be with the possibility of actual conflict. We know that China has already intentionally interfered with US Navy freedom of navigation operations in international waters near China; a rogue pilot, without any clearance, nine years ago, brought down an American reconnaissance aircraft and lost his life in the process. The states of Asia, and not just China alone, possess vast quantities of weapons – enough for mutually assured destruction, probably many times over. So too does the US. Any actual conflict would be a disaster for all involved. Yet as this chapter has made clear, the trend in the Asian region, driven by the Chinese communist party's need for security in office, has been towards increasing rather than decreasing tensions. That means, if anything, a greater likelihood of conflict. The student of international relations and of wars is always cautious about sparks. That China's predicted rise (she could equally well fall victim to internal crisis) will be characterised by friction and clouds of sparks is really beyond doubt. The question is what, if anything, those sparks might ignite. The sad answer is that plenty of powder and dry kindling is to be found in the region.

In considering conclusions, one must constantly bear in mind that China is riddled with internal weaknesses and may be paralysed by crisis, internal conflict, or undergo a change of regime. Such events are just as possible as the continued economic and military rise that has been posited to make the argument of this paper. If the hypothesis of continued rise proves correct, however, then we may be certain that it will elicit responses not favourable to China's interests, or indeed to the interests of her regime, some of which we have already discussed or alluded to.

A good example is North Korea where a client state that was a long thorn in the side of South Korea and her Western allies and thus, seemingly, a plus for China, has become a threat and a liability. Nuclear North Korea – and her nuclear capability is unlikely ever to disappear – may not yet be able to target the continental US with one of her Hiroshima-sized bombs, but Beijing is only a bit over five hundred miles from Pyongyang, and could be obliterated easily, now – by the first of China's former tribute states to go nuclear.[61] This is a vulnerability that the Chinese find unacceptable, almost unimaginable,

[61] Willy Lam, "Beijing Mulling Tougher Tactics Against Pyongyang" and John J. Tkacik, Jr. "Sea of Blood, Year of Friendship: China–North Korean Relations in 2009" both in *China Brief* IX.12 (June 12, 2009) pp. 2–3 and 4–6 respectively.

and to deal with which they are at a complete loss. China is furthermore torn between actually dealing with the problem in a multilateral way, or continuing clandestine support for Pyongyang. Her choice will affect how other nations see her.

Other states likely to react to China's build up include Russia, South Korea, Japan, Taiwan, Australia and India, as well as Mongolia, and states in Central and Southeast Asia. Some, like India, have already become nuclear powers in order to deter China. This author was told by former Indian Defence Minister George Fernandes that his country's nuclear and thermonuclear tests in 1998 were "directed against China, not Pakistan" making clear that the Prime Minister had authorised this statement to him and other foreign visitors. Japan is already a virtual nuclear power; Taiwan would require "a year" to deploy a nuclear capability, according to an authoritative source; Australia retains the ability to become a nuclear power though how quickly is debated; even Vietnam, as mentioned, is reported to have started a nuclear weapons program.[62] These and other countries would see possession of nuclear weapons, as North Korea does (correctly) as a powerful deterrent against attack and a card to play in international politics, as well, of course, as a weapon.

For purely deterrent purposes, however, nuclear weapons may not be needed. At least one of the countries mentioned has opted for non-nuclear thermobaric devices as an equally destructive alternative to nuclear capability. Another possibility, and for once one that is encouraging, is that precision guided munitions, targeted correctly and used in sufficient numbers, could paralyse an adversary and destroy war-making capability with every bit as much effectiveness as nuclear bombs, without grievous casualties among innocent civilians. The question is whether psychologically the prospect of such effective technical immobilisation will have the same awe-inspiring deterrent effect of a great fireball and mushroom cloud. Rationally it should, but human beings are not rational creatures.

Given China's geographical extent, each and every country on her periphery or near waters she claims is likely to develop some countervailing military capability. Singapore, for example, is extravagant in her proclaimed friendship with China – but she maintains a potent military, which one doubts is directed entirely against Malaysia and Indonesia, and has constructed berthing facilities for American aircraft carriers. In some cases one country alone (Japan, a united Korea) would have the capability to stalemate China

---

[62] Author's personal information.

in conflict. Certainly the sum of the defensive capabilities of all those now feeling a wind blowing from Beijing is more than enough to balance China. Whether China understands this is, however, another question.

So from a military point of view, China's rise is likely to do no more than raise the general level of military spending and capability across Asia and elsewhere in the world, without in fact gaining any advantage for Beijing. Equilibrium will be maintained, if we are fortunate, at a higher and more costly level. If war should break out – and the more flashpoints the more likely that is – then the catastrophe for the world would be total. One hopes that all involved understand this fact

Finally, it is important to remember that any rise of China will affect not only that country's neighbours but also that country herself. The Chinese state that is growing wealthier and more assertive is attempting to keep control over a population that is similarly enjoying improvements in living standards and education, as well as real but limited increases in freedom of speech and publication, in universities in particular. Numerous grievances are felt, over corruption, arbitrary government, grossly unequal distribution of income and so forth. Violent incidents between people and authorities are increasing. This situation, recall, is taken in this paper as the root cause for military build-up and increasing stress on nationalism. It is a situation, however, that is likely to come under ever greater stress if China continues to become stronger, wealthier and more assertive.

The implications of a rising China for her neighbours and for the US are extremely important and potentially worrying, as this chapter has argued. In America, as some of the material cited above suggests, a strategic rethinking about China appears already to be under way. This is a very important development. But it may be that the most important implications of China's putative rise to great power status will be for China herself – for her polity, for her governance and for her domestic order.

7

China's Resource Diplomacy

India Struggles to Catch-up

D. S. Rajan

I T is natural for all countries in the world to depend on resources for their economic development, but the case of the People's Republic of China (PRC) is special, considering its rapidly rising economy and increasing global profile; what will be the international impact from the rise of China as a resource-backed economic giant and what should be the responses to the same, have become key questions for rest of the nations in the world.

The existing energy situation in the PRC needs to be addressed first. By all indications, it appears not promising, prompting the government to urgently revamp its energy policies. Notwithstanding the impressive economic achievements made since the launching of reforms in 1978, there is still no visible improvement in China's access to energy domestically. The country continues to lack adequate oil and other energy resources at home, essential for sustaining its growth; there is a deep mismatch within China between its energy production level and the total domestic energy consumption. High consumption has been due to the government's stress so far on exports and investing in the capital-intensive manufacturing sector, for which a remedy has been sought through the 11th Five Year Plan (2006–10). Also, the PRC's efforts to exploit the potentials of new sources in the western and southern provinces of Xinjiang and Tibet are yet to maximise and its offshore production activities are being hampered by the competing claims of neighbouring nations on maritime borders.

The PRC has only 5 billion tonnes of oil resources, less than 7 per cent of the global average. China became a net oil importer in 1993, as it came under compulsion to accelerate its oil import for maintaining its economic growth. It is now the world's second largest oil consumer after the United States (US);[1] China is estimated to have surparssed the US as the world's largest oil consumer in 2010.[2] Between 1993 and 2006, China's oil consumption nearly doubled, from 2.9 million barrels per day to 7 million barrels per day, representing an annualised growth rate of 7 per cent.[3] By 2015, the consumption may rise to 11.2 million barrels per day.[4] In 2010, the percentage of China's oil consumption grew by more than 50 per cent.[5] In 2009, oil imports were more than 200 million tonnes with about 50 per cent foreign dependence rate. China's foreign oil dependence rations reached 55 per cent in 2010.[6] Sea-borne imports which cannot be reduced by overland pipelines, constitute more than 80 per cent of this total.[7] Importantly, the increasing energy demand from China is contributing to high oil prices in the world market.

The 2007 Government White Paper[8] titled "China's Energy Conditions and Policies", the first such document to be issued in the country, is noteworthy for its directions concerning the country's future energy policy. It firmly declared that "China did not, does not, and will not pose any threat to the world's energy security," indicated that from now on, priority tasks in the country would include promotion of renewable energy and assured that Beijing will behave responsibly as an "irreplaceable component of the world energy market and as a player in maintaining global energy security."

It added that China would pursue energy imports and exports, and improve policies for fair trade in accordance with its commitments to the World Trade Organisation (WTO) and the WTO rules. China will, step-by-step, change the current situation of relying too heavily on spot trading of crude oil,

---

[1] *China Daily*, March 2, 2009.

[2] China Business News Report, published from Beijing, 12 January 2011.

[3] EIA's "International Energy Outlook", 2005 and EIU report 2006.

[4] Annual Report on the Military Power of the People's Republic of China, US Department of Defence, March 2009.

[5] *The Hindu*, January 6, 2011 quoting a senior official of National Development of Reforms Commission.

[6] "China records a milestone in off shore oil, gas output." *The Hindu*, January 6, 2011 quoting a senior official of China National Off shore Oil Corporation, Fu Cheng Yu.

[7] Andrew S. Erickson, "Pipe Dream: China Seeks Land and Sea Energy Security", *Jane's Intelligence Review*, Issue No.21/8, August 2009.

[8] China's White Paper on Energy Conditions and Policies, the PRC State Council Information Office, Beijing, December 2007. (Details of the paper carried by www.china.org.cn on February 26, 2008.)

encourage the signing of long-term supply contracts with foreign companies and promote the diversification of trading channels.

In a nutshell, the prevailing gap between the energy supply and demand at home, poses a serious challenge to China's economic growth, which is, in turn, crucial for the country's political stability. Policy statements from Beijing have reflected the leadership's awareness of the gravity of the problems; also most significant has been the inclusion of two leaders (He Guoqiang and Zhou Yonggang) with a background in the petroleum industry in the top policy making body, Politburo Standing committee, during the Chinese Communist Party Congress in October 2007, showing the importance China is giving to future energy security. Right now, as per policy, the state is taking measures to augment the domestic capacity with focus on renewable energy. It is especially accelerating gas pipeline projects in the country, for example the West-East pipeline project to cover 15 regions with a capacity to carry 30 billion cubic meters of natural gas.[9] Externally, it is increasing the country's reliance on energy imports, primarily metals and fossil fuels and making investments in energy resources abroad. The fact that Beijing has chosen a course of "resource diplomacy" to facilitate the latter, should not come as a surprise.

Notable has been the reinforcement of "resource diplomacy" in an official paper,[10] which declared that energy security is the centrepiece of China's foreign policy. Observing that oil price fluctuations are not beneficial to both producers and consumers from a long-term perspective and that the current high oil demands have put enormous strain on global energy security with grave implications for the global economy, security and political stability, it wanted international co-operation to achieve the guarantee of energy security. In the main, it has conveyed an important message – China's foreign policy from now on will be driven more and more by the need for resources – oil and natural gas, industrial and construction materials, foreign capital and technology.

With clear foreign policy goals on energy security, the PRC is encouraging its state-owned companies to reach exploration and supply agreements with resource-producing nations throughout the world. Simultaneously, Beijing is

---

[9] *Xinhua*, "Eastern Segment of Second Gas Pipeline Breaks Ground", February 8, 2009.

[10] Russel Xiao, "Energy Security is the Centerpiece of China's Foreign Policy", Report on Foreign Relations in 2008, 18 July 2008, *China Brief* No. 8/16, the Jamestown Foundation, August 5, 2008, quoting Wen Weipo of Hongkong.

acting at state levels to influence such nations, which are getting manifested in four ways – conducting high level diplomatic exchanges, promoting bilateral trade, extending economic aid especially for infrastructure building and providing military assistance. Financially helping its energy firms operating overseas is another means being devised by Beijing to help them acquire resources from abroad. As part of the PRC's National Energy Administration's three-year plan for the oil and gas industry, the government is considering setting up a fund to support such firms in their pursuit of foreign mergers and acquisitions, on the basis of deliberations at the National Work Conference on Energy held in Beijing in early February 2009.[11]

Given below is a region-wise account of China's reach for resources.

Middle East

Since China became an oil importer in 1993, Beijing's diplomatic priority has been to forge strong links with the governments in the oil-producing Middle East nations, especially Iran and Saudi Arabia. In 2004, China imported roughly 2 million barrels of oil per day, with half of it coming from the Middle East[12]. This may rise to 10 million barrels per day within a quarter-century.

Let's take the case of Iran. It is the third largest oil exporter to China, behind Angola and Saudi Arabia (as of January to June 2006).[13] Iran currently provides 11.3 per cent of China's oil needs.[14] Chinese investment in Iran's energy sector began in 2001 as part of the PRC's "Go-Out" strategy. A momentum in this regard is being seen since 2004. China's Petrochemical Corporation (SINOPEC) International Company signed a 25-year contract with Iran in late 2004, providing for production and export of Liquefied Natural Gas (LNG) to China. In 2006, China National Offshore Oil Corporation (CNOOC) signed a US $ 16 billion deal with Iran covering the development of the latter's northern Pars gas field and the construction of LNG plant for export of gas to China.[15] Subsequently, a US $ 2 billion agreement was signed by China with Iran on December 9, 2007 providing for Chinese investment in a project to develop Iran's Yadavaran oil

---

[11] "Oil Firms Set to Cash in on Forex Surplus", *China Daily*, February 21, 2009.

[12] China Country Analysis Brief, US Department of Energy, Energy Information Administration, July 2004.

[13] "Saudi Arabia, Angola, Iran remain Top Three Oil Suppliers to China", *People's Daily Online* despath dated February 10, 2010.

[14] Ibid

[15] Sally Jones, "Iran and China's CNOOC sign US $ 16 billion gas deal", *Dow Jones* news wires, December 20, 2006.

field (50 per cent equity holding by China's SINOPEC International Company and 29 per cent equity holding by India's ONGC Videsh).[16] In January 2009, the PRC's China National Petroleum Corporation (CNPC) and the National Iran Oil Corporation (NIOC) signed a US $ 1.7 billion deal for the development of Iran's North Azadegan oil field, which has estimated reserves of 6 billion barrels of oil. In the following March, a consortium of three Chinese companies and the NIOC signed a US $ 3.3 billion deal to produce LNG in the Iranian South Pars gas field.[17] Overall, however, China's presence in Iran's energy sector so far remains limited, as Tehran does not allow wholesale takeover of its energy market and infrastructure by foreign companies.[18]

Beijing's diplomatic, aid and trade initiatives, along with military assistance, are backing China's energy quest in Iran. Recent high-level exchanges of visits between the two nations included one made by Iranian President Mahmoud Ahmadinejad (Beijing, September 6, 2008). On trade, China is already among Iran's major partners and the trade volume between the two countries is estimated at US $ 29 billion in 2008, as against US $ 400 million in 1994, marking an annual increase of 40 per cent.[19] On the military side, despite Beijing's denials, it is felt that China's arms sales to Iran since the 1980s have bolstered the Iranian military and weapon production capabilities considerably, with long-term and far-reaching consequences on the balance of power in the Middle East.[20] China's military assistance to Iran is also believed to have covered missiles and nuclear weapon technology.[21]

On the Iranian nuclear issue, China had always opposed sanctions against Tehran. However, since 2006, it is adopting a pragmatic position towards Iran, as part of its new course towards all those nations labelled by the West as "rogue" states, e.g. the Democratic People's Republic of Korea (DPRK), Sudan and Myanmar; evidence in this regard has been China's support in March 2008 to the third round of United Nations (UN) sanctions against Iran. While doing so, Beijing continues with its position to back multilateral efforts to

---

[16] Paper submitted by Professor Ma Jia Li, China Institute of Contemporary International Relations, Beijing, at the conference on "India/China/USA triangle", convered by the Centre for National Renaissance, New Delhi, at Kochi, Kerala, India, January 21–23, 2008.

[17] Sally Jones, "Iran and China's CNOOC sign US $ 16 billion gas deal".

[18] Paper submitted by Professor Ma Jiali (see Note 16 above)

[19] Amar Toer, "Trading with Iran: A closer, Look at the Economics behind the Politics", www. al-majala.com, dated April 6, 2010.

[20] Parris Chang, "China's Policy towards Iran: Arms for oil", *China Brief*, No.8/21, the James Town Foundation, November 18, 2008.

[21] Ibid.

solve the issue. As per views being articulated by Chinese scholars[22], the PRC's strategic interests in Iran are influencing its position that the Iranian nuclear issue needs to be solved through peaceful means. They have said that China has only a limited influence on Iran, unlike in the case of Beijing-Pyongyang relations and that it cannot therefore take a lead in solving the Iranian nuclear tangle. In an overall sense, the Chinese intentions not to let down its energy partner, Iran, on the nuclear issue come out clear.

Energy requirements are pushing China to get closer to Saudi Arabia also. Saudi Arabia is the biggest oil exporter to China. The Saudi share of Chinese oil imports is already 17 per cent and is likely to grow further. The two sides signed a Strategic Oil Co-operation agreement in 1999. The PRC's SINOPEC reached agreements with its Saudi counterpart Aramco in 2004 on building two oil refineries in Saudi Arabia. Very recently, five landmark agreements including one on Makkah monorail project[23] were signed between the two sides during Chinese President Hu Jintao's visit to Riyadh (February 2009).

Saudi Arabia's opening its domestic market for Chinese investment has been reciprocated by Beijing through allowing participation of Saudi companies in China's downstream refining business. As part of its policy of linking energy with trade and diplomacy, China is speeding up its business relations with Saudi Arabia. The latter has become the largest trading partner of China in the region and in 2008, the value of trade exchange between the two countries exceeded $ 41.8 billion.[24] Diplomatically, Beijing has been successful in making use of the exchanges of high level visits between the two countries (King Abdullah to China in January 2006 and President Hu Jintao to Saudi Arabia in February 2009), to stress the importance it attaches to energy ties with Saudi Arabia.

China-Saudi Arabia energy ties need to be seen in the context of certain political convergence between the two sides. For instance, both are wary of the US tendency to criticise Beijing and Riyadh's human rights abuses. Also, Saudi Arabia recognises China's potentials to act as a counterweight to the US in the Arab-Israeli dispute. On the part of Beijing, it may like to leverage its relationship with Saudi Arabia (for that matter with the entire Middle East) to curb any external tendency supportive of the activities of Islamic

---

[22] Jia Qingguo, "Directions of China's Foreign and Security policy", School of International Studies, Beijing University, People's Daily online, May 14, 2009.

[23] Ghansanfar Ali Khan, "China to Bill Makkah Monorail", Gulf News, February 11, 2009.

[24] "China's President Arriver in Riyadh at Start of Trip of Friendship", *Xinhua* February 10, 2009.

extremists within China, like those belonging to the Eastern Turkestan Islamic Movement (ETIM).[25]

China's resource links with Iraq, Syria and Libya as well as the Gulf Co-operation Council, are also getting strengthened. China stands as the first country in the world to successfully bid on a major oil deal in the post-Saddam Iraq.[26] China has started getting oil from Syria.[27] Its energy relations with Libya may go up after the conclusion of their oil exploration and production sharing agreement in 2004. Also, Beijing is seeking to conclude a Free Trade Agreement (FTA) with the Gulf Co-operation Council (GCC).[28]

Central Asia

The main player in China's energy relation in Central Asia is Kazakhstan. China now controls 25 per cent of Kazakstan's crude oil production. In 2005, China acquired Petro Kazakhstan Oil Company. China's CNPC agreed in April 2009 with Kazakhstan State Oil Company KazMunaiGaZ to jointly purchase Kazakh oil company, JSC Mangistaumunaigas (MMG), for US $ 3.3 billion. The agreement is part of a US $ 5 billion "loan-for-oil" deal that China concluded with Kazakhstan early that month.[29] Beijing has so far signed three oil production-sharing agreements with Kazakhstan, along with a deal on a pipeline. Kazakhstan has become an important overseas market for CNPC.[30] China has given loans worth US $ 10 billion to Kazakhstan to enable the latter to buy oil fields from foreign stakeholders and expand domestic priority infrastructure projects.[31] The first leg of Kazakhstan-China oil pipeline, operational since 2006, supplied China with 4 million tonnes of oil in that year. The stated target is to raise it to 20 million tonnes in 2011.[32] When fully completed, the pipeline would enable Beijing to import some 200,000 barrels of crude per day.[33] Kazakhstan along with Uzbekistan and Turkmenistan, is

---

[25] Dan Bluementhal, "Providing Arms, China and the Middle East", *Middle East Quarterly*, Spring 2005.

[26] Sophie Reach, "Shell-China Joint Bid for Iraq Oil", Reuters, as reported in *China Digital Times*, April 14, 2009.

[27] Paper submitted by Ma Jialia, (see Note 16).

[28] *Xinhua*, "China to seek early FTA", February 12, 2009.

[29] "CNPC Buys Kazakh Oil Company", report of www.china.org.cn April 28, 2009.

[30] Xiao Wan, "CNPC Buys Kazakh Oil Company", *China Daily*, April 28, 2009.

[31] Isabel Gorst, "Kazhakastan plus anti China Sign Pipe line Deal", *China Digital Times*, May 19, 2009.

[32] Alestra, "Phase 2 China, – Kazhakastan Oil Pipe Line Starts Building", www.businesshighbeam. com. December 18, 2007.

[33] Paper Submitted by Ma Jiali, (see Note 16)

building a 2,000 kilometre pipeline to carry gas to China, having capacity of 30 billion cubic metres, with each of the three nations contributing one-third. This pipeline is slated to extend up to Karachaganak field. Russia is also showing interest in that field; a competition in this regard between the Chinese oil companies and Russia's Gazprom, is therefore likely.[34]

China-Kazakhstan energy ties are progressing in parallel with a movement forward in the bilateral diplomatic and trade relations. Chinese Premier Wen Jiabao was in Astana in October 2008, which was followed by the visits to Beijing by Kazakh President Nursultan Nazarbayev in April 2009 and February 2010, Bilateral trade volume between the two nations reached US $ 20.4 billion, marking 44.5 per cent increase from the figure for 2009.[35] In 2007, bilateral trade volume between the two nations reached US $ 13.87 billion, 66 per cent more than that of the previous year. China was the third biggest market for Kazakhstan's exports and second biggest exporter to Kazakhstan during the period from January to September 2008. Trade co-operation between the two countries has expanded from the traditional energy sector to many other sectors.[36]

China's energy relations with Turkmenistan and Uzbekistan are also getting closer. Under a China-Uzbekistan agreement reached in 2007, the latter agreed to export half of its gas to China and build a 330-mile long pipeline to China to transport the gas. Opening of a 1,833-km long gas pipeline on December 14, 2009 connecting the energy fields in Turkmenistan, Uzbekistan and Kazakhstan with Xinjiang, as part of the 7,000 km long East-West trunk route, has been a significant development, as half of China's gas consumption is expected to get covered under it.

China has two strategic objectives in Central Asia – tapping the oil and gas resources of the region in the interest of the country's energy security and countering the Uighur separatist movement in Xinjiang, with the help of bordering Central Asian states. Regarding the first, China would prefer getting energy supplies from countries like Kazakhstan, Uzbekistan and Turkmenistan in the region as well as Russia, so as to reduce its vulnerability to any turmoil in the Middle East.[37] To realise the other objective, China would

---

[34] http://www.stirringtroubleinternationally.com/, 17 November 2008.

[35] China-Kazakastan tightly connected by both friendship and strong strategic partnership, www.eurodialogue.org dated February 2009, quoting Chinese foreign minister Yang Sie Chi.

[36] *Xinhua*, October 29, 2008.

[37] Marshal J. Goldman, "Silk Road to Oil Road", Harvard University at conference mentioned at 6 above.

naturally like to rely on the Central Asian member nations of the Shanghai Co-operation Organisation. The proximity of the oil fields and relatively weak US presence in the region is an additional advantage to China for oil imports from Central Asia. For Kazakhstan, Uzbekistan and Turkmenistan, their gas pipelines to China could appear as a means to rely less on Russian oil pipelines; in turn, this may raise questions for Russia in the matter of its control over the region's energy resources, leading in the final count to a possible Russia-China misunderstanding.

Russia

Through energy ties with Russia, China intends to diversify its energy supply sources and reduce its dependence on sea-borne shipping for importing oil and gas. Discussions between the two nations on a package of oil deals started in 2001; negotiations in October 2008, February 2009 and April 2009 have led to concrete results. A prominent outcome is the signing of a long-term "loan for oil" pact signed by them providing for co-operation in oil exploration and building of pipelines.[38] Russia is to supply 300 million tonnes of crude to China from 2011 to 2030, in return for Chinese long-term loans to Russian oil firms to the tune of US $ 25 billion.[39] Regarding pipeline needed to transport oil, talks have been on between the two sides since as early as March 2003. Moscow has agreed to build a separate branch to China via the latter's border county of Mohe, of Russia's planned Taishet-Skovorodino-Nakhodka trunk line, leading up to Daqing in China's northeast; construction of the Chinese section of the pipeline started in May 2009.[40] Beijing has described the deals as marking "a major breakthrough in bilateral energy co-operation and reflecting efforts of two countries in coping with the sharp drop in oil trade caused by the global financial crisis."[41]

Russia-China trade has received a boost, along with their expanding energy ties. Bilateral trade volume stood at US $ 56.8 billion in 2008, an increase of 18 per cent over 2007.

---

[38] Wang Zhuoqiang, "China to Boost Russia Energy Links", *China Daily Dispatch*, March 6, 2009.

[39] David Winning, Shai Oster and Alex Wilson, "China–Russia Strike US $ 25 Billion Oil Pact", www.wsj.com. February 18, 2009.

[40] "Work Starts on Pipe to Russia Oil", www.china.org.cn, May 19, 2009.

[41] "China–Russia Make Major Breakthrough in Energy – Cooperation", *People's Daily Online*, March 6, 2009.

In January 2009, however, Russia's import from and export to China plunged 51 per cent and 27 per cent respectively year-on-year, the first declines in 10 years, in response to the global financial crisis hitting export sectors.[42]

Russia's attraction for China is not only due to energy factor, but is also because of the former's potential as an arms supplier. Weapons and technologies from Russia remain important for China. From 1990–2007, Russia sold China US $ 25 billion of arms.[43]

Africa

China's energy policy in Africa received an impetus at the China-Africa Co-operation Forum (Beijing, November 2006), attended by 48 delegations of African political and business leaders. China and African nations agreed at the forum to "nurture their international competitiveness and capability in economic globalisation as a means to elevate their status in international affairs".

Beijing specifically announced on the occasion that it would double its assistance to African countries by 2009, provide them with US $ 5 billion in concessional loans and credits, establish US $ 5 billion fund to encourage Chinese investment in Africa and cancel the interest-free debt owed by 33 African states. In general, the PRC's renewed interest in Africa stems from two requirements – diversifying its sources of energy supplies and identifying new areas for investment, so as to satisfy China's increasing demand for resources. Gaining support in Africa for its stand on Taiwan and Tibet issues is also an objective, though not as major as gaining energy access is, for China.[44]

Beijing's energy foray into Africa became prominent in 1999 when it became a part of the Greater Nile Petroleum Operating Company (GNPOC) in Sudan, with 40 per cent stake (rest of equity holders – Sudan government and the national oil companies of India and Malaysia). Since 2003, Beijing's drive to gain access to oil producing assets in Africa including Sudan, has been quick, perhaps learning lessons from the perceived Chinese difficulties in locating new energy supply sources [for example, the failure of China's CNOOC to gain control of the American company Union Oil Company of California

---

[42] "China and Russia Sign Oil-for-Loan Deal", www.eeo.com.cn, February 18, 2009.

[43] Stephen Blank, "Recent Trends in Russo-Chinese Military Relations", *China Brief*, The James Town Foundation, 9.2, January 22, 2009.

[44] Chinese Foreign Minister's Press Meet, March 11, 2009.

(UNOCAL)]. In the post-2003 period, the Petrodar Company in Sudan was included in China's consortium[45] and Sudan's the latter's oil exports to China went up (14 billion barrels of crude exports to China in 2006). Also, Sudan became the only country in Africa where Chinese companies produced oil.[46]

Taking Africa as a whole, China's efforts to secure energy supplies from the region seem to be paying good dividends ever since 2003. Exports from Africa to China are increasing, 50 per cent of which is oil. African oil-producing countries are now supplying about one-third of China's crude imports; in the latter the shares of the individual nations are as follows: Sudan (25 per cent), Angola (47 per cent), Congo (13 per cent), Equatorial Guinea (9 per cent) and Nigeria (3 per cent). Notably, in these very same countries, the Chinese Foreign Direct Investment (FDI) is getting concentrated. China is also benefitting from the non-oil resources of South Africa – iron ore, diamonds, platinum and aluminium, timber and cotton.[47]

China's resource demand in Africa is boosting its commercial ties with that region; China's trade with African nations was at the level of US $ 4 billion in 1995; it increased to US $ 55.5 billion in 2006 and is expected to reach US $ 100 billion by 2010.[48] Beijing is providing soft loans and adopting political means to increase its advantage in competing for natural resource assets in Africa. A "loan for oil" to the tune of US $ 1 billion, has been extended by China to Angola to help oil imports from the latter. A total sum of US $ 5 billion oil-backed Chinese loans was given to Angola for post-2002 war reconstruction.[49] Not surprisingly, China's development aid mainly goes to countries where Chinese companies invest in resource extraction or have other economic interests. High-level visits to Africa by China's top leaders since April 2000 and Beijing's organisation of annual conferences of the Forum on China-Africa co-operation, speak for China's intentions to use its diplomatic clout for influencing the resource-rich African nations.[50]

China's military presence in Africa has grown. Beijing's motivations are clear – need to protect the country's economic interests in the continent,

[45] Paper submitted by Ma Jiali, (see Note 16)
[46] Alex Vines, "China in Africa: A Mixed Blessing", *Current History*, May 2007.
[47] "China and South Africa", www.chinacomment.wordpress.com July 1, 2008.
[48] Ian Taylor, "China's oil diplomacy in Africa", *International Affairs Journal*, No.82/52,2006.
[49] "Angola Says Foreign Credit Growing, Dispatch of the Namibian", April 19, 2006.
[50] Jonathan Holsag, "China's New Security Strategy for Africa", Submitted at 6th Shanghai Workshop on Global Governance. 14–15 March 2008. www.carlysle.army.mial/usawc/parameters/articles/09

responsibility as a Security Council member to make contributions to UN peacekeeping missions and the necessity felt to counter US military presence in Africa. After the Cold War, China's arms sales have constituted a large part of China's trade with oil and mineral-rich but "repressive" African regimes such as Zimbabwe and Sudan. According to Peter Brookes of The Heritage Foundation, China sold Sudan $ 55 million worth of arms between 2003 and 2006.[51] Beijing has been opposing Western sanctions against Sudan on the Darfur issue in line with its policy of "non-intervention" which in reality subordinates human rights causes to economic interests. Since 2006, however, China seems to be taking note of the dent to its international image being caused by its stand on the Darfur issue; signals of some modification in its stand on the issue are appearing. In September that year, China urged the Sudanese government to accept a UN plan to solve the issue and in July 2007, supported stationing of UN forces in Sudan. In May 2009, China sent its special envoy to Sudan for holding discussions on how to solve the Darfur humanitarian crisis.

Latin America

The release of China's policy paper on Latin America and the Caribbean (November 2008) marked the importance that Beijing attaches to the region. It listed economic co-operation and trade for mutual benefit with Latin America as one of China's objectives and encouraged the Chinese companies to invest in energy fields in the region. Getting the support of Latin America to the PRC's "One-China" policy found a special mention in the paper.[52] Also figured in it was China's interest in procuring Latin America's raw material and foodstuff, ranging from oil and copper to soy beans, besides helping to develop Latin American infrastructure capable of producing and delivering these products.

Among Latin American countries, Venezuela, Brazil, Ecuador and Argentina occupy a prominent place in China's energy calculations. The CNPC is involved in Venezuela since 1997. Under a "loan for oil" agreement signed in November 2007, China was to pay US $ 4 billion, into a $ 6 billion fund to develop Venezuela's oil industry, in return for the rights to explore for oil in the latter's Orinoco region, potentially among the world's

---

[51] Tangkeh Joseph Fowale, "China's Military Presence in Africa", May 24, 2009.
[52] www.gov.cn/english/official/2008/11/05/content/1140347.htm.

richest deposits.[53] Venezuela's crude oil export to China has now reached 380,000 barrels per day (in 2005, it was 39000 barrels per day), about 2.3 per cent of China's total oil import; this is slated to rise to 1 million barrels per day. In April 2009, China negotiated deals to double the development aid to Venezuela to US $ 12 billion, lend Ecuador US $ 1 billion to build a hydroelectric plant, provide Argentina with a loan of US $ 10 billion in Chinese currency and lend Brazil's national oil company worth US $ 10 billion.[54] In February 2009, during the visit of Chinese Vice-President Xi Jinping to Venezuela, it was agreed to increase Venezuela's oil shipments to China to 1 million barrels a day.[55]

China is Latin America's second largest trading partner, after the US. China's trade with Latin America increased 10-fold over the decade through 2007, to US $ 102 billion. China has signed FTAs with Chile and Peru. Beijing also has new donor membership in the Inter-American Development Bank, in which the US is playing a predominant role.[56]

China's military links with Venezuela is developing. The latter is to get 18 Chinese K-8 trainer light attack aircrafts to combat drug related crimes, out of which 6 reached Venezuela in March 2010.[57] While Venezuela sees political significance to energy relations with China,[58] Beijing takes a practical view,[59] looking at the same as part of South-South co-operation.

Asia Pacific

For China, energy relations with Myanmar and the littorals of South China Sea and East China Sea have become important, because of the latter's rich oil and gas potentials; the ties are also sensitive to the PRC on the basis of its recognition of the prevailing linkage in the region between China's energy demand and the competing claims on maritime border.

---

[53] "Chinese Foreign Ministry Spokesperson Ma Zhaoxu's Regular Press Conference", May 26, 2009.
[54] Simon Tomero, "Deals Help China Expand Sway in Latin America", *The New York Times*, April 16, 2009.
[55] Alan Stoga, "Dollar Diplomacy in Style", *New York Times*, www.flymedia.com, February 23, 2009.
[56] William Ratcliff, "China's Latin America Tango", *Wall Street Journal*, November 27, 2008.
[57] "Venezuela Receives K8 Trainer Plans from China", English.cctv.com dated March 14, 2010.
[58] Sara Miller Llana and Peter Ford, "Chavez, China to Co-operate on Oil, butfor Different Reasons", *Christian Science Monitor*, January 3, 2008.
[59] Dr Jiang Shixue, Institute for Latin American Studies, Chinese Academy of Social Sciences, Beijing, *Christian Science Monitor*, January 3, 2008.

It is natural that Myanmar with proven oil and gas reserves has emerged as China's important target in terms of energy sources. Demonstrating the same has been the January 2007 agreement between the PRC's state-owned CNPC and the Myanmar Oil and Gas Enterprise (MOGE) providing for Chinese exploration of oil and gas at an area of approximately 10,000 square km off the Arakan coast. The PRC signed a contract with Myanmar worth US $ 2.5 billion in the same year on building a 2,000 km cross-border oil and gas pipeline, linking the latter's south-western port of Sittwe with Chongqing municipality in south-western China after passing through Ruili and Kunming (both in Yunnan) and Guizhou province. The political nature of the contract became clear, as it's signing closely followed the Chinese veto of a punitive resolution in the United Nations Security Council (UNSC) against Myanmar on the human rights issue.[60] The pipeline's construction was to start in the first half of 2009 as part of Yunnan's overall energy development plan for the year worth US $ 15.9 billion (72 billion Yuan). Once completed, it would strengthen China's access to Myanmar's rich energy reserves and more importantly, would reduce the level of China's dependence on the piracy-prone Malacca Straits, which also involves long distances, for energy transport. China is also to help in the development of hydroelectric projects in Myanmar.[61] A China-Myanmar-Bangladesh tri-nation road network is also being planned.[62] Beijing has a transport project in Myanmar, known as "Irrawaddy corridor" which envisages establishment of road links between China's Yunnan province with Myanmar and a railway connection between Kunming (China) and Lashio (Northern Myanmar). The corridor is expected to facilitate the economic development of the three south-western provinces of China – Sichuan, Guizhou and Yunnan, through achieving their connectivity with Myanmar.[63]

China's trade with Myanmar is on the rise concomitant with their deepening energy ties. According to Chinese official statistics, from January to December 2008, bilateral trade between the two nations stood at US $ 2.626 billion,

---

[60] Professor Zang Xuegang, "China's Energy Corridors in Southeast Asia, *China Brief*, the James Town Foundation, No.3/2008.

[61] Pau K. Lee and others, "China's Real Politic Engagement in Myanmar", *China Security Issue Journal* No. 13/2009 www.china security.vs/index/php?option.com

[62] "Myanmar Proposes Road Network with China and Bangladesh", Recuter Dispatch in *Bangladesh Economic News*, May 18, 2009.

[63] Testimony by John Garver, at US-China Economic and Security Review Commission, US, July 22, 2005.

a rise of 26.4 per cent from the corresponding period in 2007. China has become the number 4 foreign investor in Myanmar as against its number 6 rank in the past.[64]

Regarding China's energy deals with South China Sea littorals, one arrived at during the meeting between the prime ministers of China and Vietnam (Beijing, October 25, 2008) has been notable. It provided for beginning of joint surveys in disputed waters beyond the mouth of Beibu Bay (Gulf of Tonkin) at an early date and jointly exploiting the demarcated zones for their fisheries and oil and gas potential.[65] Also signed in the same period was a strategic co-operation pact between the PRC's state-run CNOOC and its Vietnamese counterpart, Petro-Vietnam. The joint statement issued after the meeting mentioned that China and Vietnam have agreed to find a "fundamental and long-term" and "mutually acceptable" solution to the South China Sea maritime boundary issue, in accordance with the 1982 United Nations Convention on the Law of the Sea (UNCLOS). It added that the two nations would, in the meanwhile, observe the Code of Conduct and refrain from any action that would complicate or escalate disputes.

On issues existing between China and East China littorals, the "principled consensus'[66] reached between Beijing and Tokyo in June 2008 to conduct joint oil exploration in areas where sovereignty is under dispute, has been significant. According to it, the two countries will be permitted to jointly explore a 2,700 sq-km area near the median line (south of the Asunaro gas field, called Longjing by China). It also paved the way for investment by Japanese corporations to develop the Chinese-operated Chunxiao (called Shirakaba by Japan) gas field, also near the median line. Nevertheless, Sino-Japanese tensions continue due to Tokyo's strong objections (January 2009) over Beijing's "unilateral" exploration in some disputed areas (Tiwanwaitian for China, Kashi for Japan). In response to the charge, Beijing is asserting that these areas are Chinese territory and the PRC has therefore sovereign rights to explore.[67] Till such time the maritime borders are settled, such irritants in Sino-Japanese relations are bound to persist.

---

[64] Statement of New Chinese Ambassador to Myanmar, *Xinhua*, Yanggon, Feb 26, 2009.
[65] "China and Vietnam Pledge to settle Disputed Border and Bolster Border Trade", Agency France Presse (AFP) Dispatch, October 26, 2008.
[66] PRC Foreign Minister Yang Jiechi's press meet, Beijing, March 11, 2009.
[67] Wu Dawei, Chinese Vice-Foreign Minister, "Chunxiao Oil Field's Sovereignty Rights Belong to China", www.china.org.cn, international news, June 20, 2008.

Notwithstanding its rivalry with Japan on maritime border claims, China has actively promoted its trade relations with Japan. In 2008, their trade grew by 12.5 per cent year-on-year, to US $ 266.40 billion. However, the trade volume would shrink in 2009 for the first time in 11 years due to the ongoing global financial crisis, according to the estimate of the Japan External Trade Organization (JETRO).[68]

Taking Asia-Pacific as a whole, it should be noticed that China has evolved a future-oriented strategy to ensure its energy supplies from the resources-rich nations in the region. Beijing's "string of pearls" strategy, as called by the West, aims at developing a capacity to establish a forward presence along the Sea Lanes of Communications (SLOCs) for ensuring the connectivity between China and the oil sources in the Middle East. The "pearls" being broadly visualised are – Hainan with upgraded military facilities and a modern naval hub now, the Woody Island in Paracel archipelago off Vietnam, Chittagong (Bangladesh) container shipping facility, Sittwe (Myanmar) where China will help in constructing a deep water port and the Gwadar port in Pakistan.[69] Hambantota in Sri Lanka, where a port project is coming up with the Chinese assistance, can also be considered a "pearl".

Important Trends in China's Resource Diplomacy

Diversification of China's Energy Supply Sources

There are firm signals that the PRC's future energy policy direction will concentrate on diversifying the supply resources as a response to its perceived vulnerability to any over-dependence on resources in the politically volatile Middle East and Africa. Measures in this regard are already under China's implementation, as brought out above. Interestingly, the stress on the need for diversification has come from authoritative analysts in the PRC itself, saying that oil imports from the three main sources – the Middle East, Africa and Asia-Pacific, are not enough to ensure "sustainable oil supply" to the country. [70] The emerging alternate energy sources for China would include Latin America, oil and gas within the country, off shore zones and land territories nearer

---

[68] *People's Daily* online quoting *Xinhua*, February 26, 2009.
[69] US army War College, "Meeting the Challenge of China's Rising Power Across Asian Littoral", Monograph of Strategic Studies Institute, July 2006.
[70] *China Daily*, April 28, 2009, quoting Chinese analysts.

home like Russia. With the last mentioned in particular, China is establishing connectivity in various ways, for instance the building, now stalled, of a canal across the Kra Isthmus in Thailand to link the Indian Ocean to Pacific coast, Irrawaddy corridor in Myanmar connecting Yunnan province and the Gwadar port in Pakistan to link Xinjiang through the Karakorum highway.

Attention to Building of Overland Oil and Gas Pipelines

The PRC's reliance on oil and gas transport through land route is bound to remain important in the coming years. The primary reason is its awareness of the potential security problems in oil transport through distant sea-lanes and the still persisting inadequacy of its naval strength to protect such sea-lanes. Explaining this trend is the momentum being given by Beijing to its plans towards developing land pipeline routes, for example, China's pipeline connecting Kazakhstan (now partially operating), one linking Myanmar (under construction), another connecting Pakistan (visualisation stage) and yet another pipeline linking China with Russia began operation in December 2010.[71] China so far has 50,000 km of oil and gas pipelines and the figure will almost double to 90,000 km during the 12th Five Year Plan (2011–15).[72] The pipeline projects, as can be seen clearly, aim at reducing China's dependence on the sea borne energy trade, especially through the Malacca Strait. About 80 per cent of China's oil imports pass through the Strait, which is prone to piracy and maritime terrorism. It is also a sea point where the US and its allies are trying to control through joint naval exercises as well as programmes such as the container security initiative, proliferation security initiative and the regional maritime security initiative. Beijing may fear such vital energy supply channels could be cut at times of conflict against its interests.[73] Not surprisingly, President Hu Jintao himself described this as China's "Malacca Dilemma". China's attention to pipelines, however, does not mean ignoring sea-borne imports, which are bound to grow separately. Some China analysts point to the vulnerability of pipelines to sabotage and foreign military actions.[74]

---

[71] "China-Russia Oil Pipe Line Begins Operation", Caixinonline, http://english.caing.com, December 21, 2010.

[72] Xin Dingding & others, "China Faces New Risk Attacks on Pipelines", *China Daily*, January 6, 2010, quoting CNPC.

[73] Prof Zeng Xuegang, "China's Energy Corridors in Southeast Asia", *China Brief* No.3/2008, the James Town Foundation and Prof Fan Zhenjiang and Prof Ma Baoan, "Junshi Zhanlue Lun", Beijing, Defence University publishing house, Beijing, 2007.

[74] Andrew S. Frickson, No. 7.

Modifications in China's Approach towards "Pariah" States

It has already been pointed out above that China, since 2006, has been modifying its approach towards "rogue" regimes like Iran, Sudan and Myanmar; the three continue to be main energy exporters to China, but Beijing is becoming more and more vocal in faulting them respectively on the nuclear issue, human rights and democratic reforms. Interestingly, the US has taken a positive note of Beijing's changed approach towards Darfur issue relating to Sudan.[75] It may, however, be incorrect to take this shift in diplomacy as the start of a fundamental change in China's traditional position of extending economic assistance and arms aid to such regimes in return for the latter's energy supplies; it could only reflect a new perception of China's national interests[76] which demand that the country as a responsible international player, should play a constructive role in the world. The modification could, at the best, be a specific outcome of the need being felt by China's leadership to neutralise the western criticisms of China's hitherto followed "non-interventionist" policy towards such states, in total disregard of the latter's poor human rights records.

Changing Mercantilist Approach

So far China has been locking up energy resources around the world, by gaining outright ownership of the production bases located in key countries. This "mercantilist" stand contrasts with that of the west, which wants a liberalised world energy market with competition between the powers on a level playing field. The "mercantilist" stand could only lead to partial results for China; the PRC paid above market prices for overseas exploration and extraction projects, which has contributed only to a small 5 per cent of the country's imported oil demand, leaving the country to rely on the global market for the remaining 95 per cent.[77]

Signs of changes in Beijing's mercantilist approach are now appearing – the preference to the line of outright takeovers is slowly giving way to those favouring long-term contracts for crude supplies. More importantly, the

---

[75] *China Daily*, "US Envoy Defends China's Role in Darfur", April 12, 2007, as stated in "Energy Security and UN Diplomacy", *China Security Journal*, 4.3 (2008).

[76] Stephanie Kleine-ablbrandt & Andrew Small, "China's New Dictatorship Diplomacy", *Foreign Affairs*, January–February 2008.

[77] Henry Paulson, "The Right Way to Engage China", *Foreign Affairs*, September–October 2008.

repercussions of the same on the country's foreign policy are being felt, as Beijing increasingly realises that a "zero-sum energy competition" is giving rise to avoidable disputes with other powers like the US and Japan.[78] Evidences in this regard include China's growing engagement with the International Energy Agency (IEA), fresh efforts to solve disputes with Japan and a more co-operative regional approach in Southeast Asia in the matter of the security of the regional sea-lanes. China has joined Congo-basin Forest Partnership that promotes sustainable management of resources, contributed for the first time in 2007 to the International Development Association providing grants and credits to poorest countries and is now a donor member of the Inter-American Development Bank.

New Focus to Resource-based Financing in the Wake of Financial Crisis

China is utilising the opportunity of the fall in oil prices in the global market as a result of the ongoing financial crisis, to acquire energy assets abroad with the support of resource-based financing from its banks. Acquisitions already taken place includes CNPC's buying Canada's Tanganiyika Oil venture in Syria and the China Aluminium Corporation's getting 18 per cent share in the Australian mining company Rio Tinto.[79] Notable in this regard is a trend towards Beijing's efforts to find alternate sources for its trade surpluses in order to reduce its over-exposure to the US, happened as a result of its heavy investment in the US treasury bonds.

Signals on Military Support to Protect Maritime Interests

Signs are appearing towards a start in the support of China's People's Liberation Army (PLA) and Navy to the task of protecting the country's maritime interests under the overall PRC framework for energy security. For the first time since the founding the PRC in 1949, three PLA naval vessels participated in an operation outside the country in January 2009 – a UN sanctioned anti-piracy activity off the Horn of Africa. Also, vessels retired from the Navy are increasingly being pressed by China to patrol disputed

---

[78] Mikkal E.Herberg, Research Director, Asian Energy Security Programme, remarks at the US-China Economic and Security Review Commission, June 14, 2007.

[79] Peter Ford, "China Taking Advantage of Global Recession, Goes on a Buying Spree", *Christian Science Monitor*, February 21, 2009.

South China Sea islands and the Senkakus claimed by Japan.[80] At policy levels, the PRC's defence documents have begun to note the need for the armed forces to get involved in ensuring the country's energy security, for example, its Defence White Paper for 2006 referred to the "ongoing attempts to expand the ranges of PLA Navy and Air force" and "mounting security issues relating to energy resources."

This coincided with the appearance of several military viewpoints; a comment wanted the PLA Navy's transformation into an "open ocean defence navy" so as to improve "distant ocean mobile operation capabilities".[81] The 2008 Defence White Paper followed such sentiments by referring to "intensifying struggle for strategic resources". Also on the rise are official references to the PLA's undertaking of "historic long term missions" for protecting China's territorial and maritime interests through acquiring aircraft carriers, next generation weapons, etc.[82] Indications in China that such missions will have a "non-war" character, are worth noting.[83] Not to be missed in the same context, is a study by China's National Defence University, which recommended building capabilities by China to meet what it called "threats to strategic resource development and strategic passage ways."[84]

There had also been some voices in China favouring establishment of overseas bases. Beijing has, however, recently declared that the PRC does not have an agenda to set up such bases overseas and instead would co-operate with the UN-led anti-terrorism, anti-piracy and disaster relief missions.[85] The PRC's stated aim to protect its territorial and energy interests in the globe, presupposes, in the main, possession by the Chinese military of an "extended-range projection" capability. The Western estimates, however, say that Beijing's ability to project and sustain power at a distance is presently limited, but China may fill the gap in this regard through investing in military

---

[80] Ian Storey, "'Impeccable' Affair and Renewed Rivalry in South China Sea", *China Brief* 9.9, April 30, 2009. Two Chinese maritime survey ships patrolled Senkakus on December 8, 2008 and March 2009, AFP March 15, 2009.

[81] Rear Admiral Yao Wenhuai, "Build a Strong Navy and Defend China's Maritime Interests", *Guofang Journal*, No 7/07 and Daniel M.Hartnett, "The PLA's Domestic and Foreign Activities", testimonyatthe US-China Economy and Security Review Commission, March 4, 2009.

[82] Maj Gen Zhang Deshun, former PLA Navy Deputy Chief and NPC delegate, "China Says Navy Expansion no Threat to Others", *China Daily*, March 25, 2009.

[83] *Beijing Review*, "Naval ambitions", May 18, 2009, quoting Admiral Wu Shengli.

[84] Prof Fan Zhenjiang and Prof Ma Baoan, Junshi Zhanluelun, Beijing, Defence Publishing House, 2007.

[85] Rear Admiral (Retd) Zhang Deshun, former PLA Navy Deputy Chief of Staff, delegate to the National People's Congress, *China Daily*, March 11, 2010.

programmes like building new missiles, surface warships, fighter aircraft and aircraft carriers.[86] The bottom line, however, is that Beijing's intentions in this regard look beyond doubt.

Challenges before India

As its economy grows, India's energy consumption is rising; it is now the fifth largest energy consumer in the world and is expected to reach the fourth position soon. By 2030, India is likely to pass Japan and Russia to emerge as the world's third largest energy consumer.[87] With no prospects of improvement in the availability of domestic resources, inputs into India now contribute to 80 per cent of the oil consumed in the country.[88] To meet its future energy requirements, India's partnerships with other countries, which have surplus energy, are necessary. Signing of India-US civil nuclear energy co-operation agreement has been a step to increase the share of non-fossil fuel based energy resources in India's energy mix. The overall energy situation in India is in essence marked, like in China, by the continuing gap domestically between the energy supply and demand; it is the primary reason for India's reaching out to the world energy markets in order to get uninterrupted resource supplies essential for the country's sustainable economic growth. Increase in imports, with the surge in oil prices, has cost India a great deal of foreign exchange assets and has burdened its foreign trade balance. According to estimates by India, if oil prices rise for every $ 5, India's economic growth rate will drop 0.5 per cent, and its inflation rate would increase by 1.4 per cent.

China Factor

In pursuing its energy drive abroad, New Delhi no doubt faces a major challenge, against the background of India's simultaneous rise along with China, a nation conducting an aggressive resource hunt, backed by

---

[86] "The Military Power of the People's Republic of China, 2009", of the US Department of Defence and "China's Search for Military Power", Professor M. Taylor Fravel, Massachusetts Institute of Technology, National Institute of Defence Studies Symposium, Tokyo, 2007, Centre for Strategic and International Studies, Washington Quarterly 2008.

[87] Ma Jiali; "China, India Stoke Energy Bond", *China Daily*, February 2, 2010, quoting International Energy Agency.

[88] www.pib.nic.in, March 22, 2011 quoting Indian Minister Murali Deora.

its active diplomacy throughout the world. A Sino-Indian competition in accessing overseas resources looks natural. Their targets are almost the same resource-rich regions, particularly their respective neighbourhood that offers advantages in terms of logistics and cost (Iran, Bangladesh and Myanmar for India, and Russia, Central Asia and Myanmar for China). This is not to deny Beijing's willingness to co-operate with India in selected cases,[89] but it is also not hesitating to edge out India in a large number of other occasions,[90] implying deprivation of the latter from the much needed energy sources at particular locations. New Delhi should, therefore, work out replacement strategies to offset such losses.

Second, New Delhi should face the question why China is more successful than India in their competition to secure overseas energy supply sources. A primary reason seems to be the lack of a pro-active approach on the part of the Indian government unlike its Chinese counterpart, in providing finances to the Indian companies targeting overseas energy markets.

On the whole, China's success, in comparison to India, has been due to Beijing's strategy of mixing its energy search overseas with trade, aid, diplomacy and arms sales; this point should not be missed by India whenever it taps resource-rich nations in the world. On this account, it is not clear as to how much India can emulate the Chinese model, but New Delhi can certainly take measures to attract energy producing, but poorer nations in the world. Taking the case of Africa, where both India and China compete, reducing the tariffs for high value manufactured goods from such nations, could be an option for New Delhi. China has already implemented the same. Also, India's exports are more to Africa than vice versa, and hence the need for the former to address the resulting trade imbalance. New Delhi should in addition further activate the "Focus Africa" programme of its Exim Bank aimed at giving credits to the nations in the region.

Also advisable for India would be to learn from China's policy to diversify its energy supply sources, mainly as a step to reduce its dependence on the

---

[89] CNPC-ONGC joint bid for Petro-Canada Syrian oil fields in December 2005; SINOPEC-ONGC joint venture in acquiring Ominex De Columbia in August 2006. China and India are also co-operating in oil exploration in Sudan and Nigeria. China's CNPC is involved in a 1600-km natural gas pipeline spanning India's east to west coast.

[90] SINOPEC's outbidding of ONGC for an oil block in Angola in 2004, India's failure to beat bid by Chinese companies in Ecuador in 2005, the outbidding of ONGC by SINOPEC in acquiring Canadian Tanganyika oil company and China's outbidding India in signing a 30-year agreement to import natural gas from fields located in Myanmar in January 2009.

volatile Middle East. It will be in New Delhi's interests in this context to further improve its energy ties with Latin America, especially Venezuela as well as energy-producing nations in the neighbourhood like Myanmar and Iran. Also, India can take a leaf out of China's new stress to resource financing of its energy corporations to help them in mergers and acquisitions abroad in recognition of the advantages arising from the low oil prices as a result of the global financial crisis.

Next, India-China energy relations, definitely mutually beneficial in nature, may require a further boost. The two sides have already signed a memorandum for enhancing co-operation in the field of oil and natural gas in January 2006. Through their "Shared Vision" declaration (Beijing, 14 January 2008), both have expressed their commitment to make joint efforts to diversify the global energy mix and enhance the share of clean and renewable energy, so as to meet the energy requirements of all countries. Also, Beijing has offered New Delhi co-operation in the civil nuclear energy sector, for the first time. India and China should now start working together to take their bilateral energy co-operation forward under the framework of the prevailing strategic partnership between the two. Appropriate for them in this regard would be to take the cue from the ongoing US-China Strategic Economic Dialogue (SED), which has since led to the conclusion of a 10-year energy and environment co-operation framework between the two sides (June 2008).

The strategic and security impact of China's resource hunt overseas on India falls under a different category; New Delhi should not miss the implications for it arising from an important trend – the energy security factor will be a major determinant of China's foreign and even military policies. As the PRC is adding resources under a global strategy, its economy is bound to develop at a greater speed, enabling Beijing to accomplish without difficulty the stated goal of "medium level advanced nation" by 2050. Important for India to note is that China's economic development is also providing funds for the country's military modernisation; questions are being asked about the exact purpose of the latter. Indications are that Beijing is developing capabilities for use in conflict over resources on disputed territories in the region. In this connection, China is continuing its investment in military programmes designed to improve "extended range projection".[91] As energy supply requires connectivity, Beijing is creating a "string of pearls" to link China and the oil sources in the Middle East via India's neighbourhood. China is making

---

[91] Rear Admiral (Retd) Zhang Deshun, No. 83.

efforts to engage its South Asian neighbours in military and economic fields. Its drive to build port facilities in Pakistan, Bangladesh, Myanmar and Sri Lanka as well as plans to construct railroad lines to Nepal, reflect Beijing's concerted efforts to open and expand markets for their goods and services. Beijing also wants to control the Indian Ocean, a vital transit route for energy import sources from West Asia and Africa. It considers its presence in the Indian Ocean as a strategic leverage against India. Overall, the emerging environment is fuelling New Delhi's fears on China's intention to challenge India's traditional primacy in its neighbourhood.

In the Asia-Pacific region, India's counter-strategy is becoming evident. Perceiving a Chinese encirclement of India, New Delhi is projecting its own power in the region, through naval deployments and maritime diplomacy. It is trying to neutralise the growing Chinese influence in Myanmar through its own initiatives (for example, India-Myanmar Kaladan river transportation agreements of April 2008, involving India's upgradation of Sitwe, a place for refuelling for China's naval forces, to be connected to Eastern India ports). It is taking steps to expand its reach to areas close to the Malacca Strait. (For example, INS Viraat went to the Strait in 2005 and India and other powers held military exercises in an area close to the straits in September 2007). India's relations with South China Sea littorals have also grown, to the consternation of Beijing. China specifically objected to Vietnam's grant of exploratory rights to India near the disputed Paracel islands. India considers its presence in South China Sea as a deterrent against Beijing. In short, India's ongoing involvement in the wider East Asia under its Look East policy, is leading to its rivalry with China. India's foreign policy should aim at reducing any aggravation in this rivalry, particularly in the context of the continuing core issues dividing them like the boundary problem. China also has an equal responsibility in this regard.

India's response to China's resource diplomacy in the other regions – the Middle East, Africa, Central Asia, Russia and Latin America, is an evolving one. New Delhi should give to the geographically close Middle East something more in return for oil, such as transfer of technology.[92] It should take advantage of the trend in that region to forge closer commercial and political relations with India and China, to both of which energy ties with the Middle East are important. On Iran, New Delhi should take advantage of the limited Chinese presence in that country's energy sector.

---

[92] http://qo.worldbank.org/LKE09FGK90, 2009.

In Africa, India's foreign policy should become more resources based; fresh measures are necessary on India's part as a sequel to its own to Africa summit in 2008. In Central Asia, New Delhi does not enjoy direct access to the region's energy sources, but it should take remedial steps through diplomatic and other means. The case of India's ties with Kazakhstan is important for India due to the latter's strategic location in the Caspian Sea, considered the third largest oil reserve in the world, also with potential uranium deposits. New Delhi should take measures so as to match China's multi-dimensional relations with Kazakhstan as a member nation of the Shanghai Co-operation Organization. India's trade with Kazakhstan stands low at US $ 128 million (in 2007), in comparison to China's US 6 billion (in 2005).[93] India must address this imbalance.

New Delhi's relations with Moscow have been traditionally friendly. It should develop plans to speed up its access to the Russian oil and gas, as China does, regardless of India's lacking direct access to Russia's energy sources. Moscow-Beijing ties are robust and Indian diplomacy can capitalise on ties with Russia, for the purpose of building mutual trust in India-China relations. New Delhi can add more substance to the India-Russia-China triangular talks now in progress at the level of foreign ministers.

India has a lot to gain through energy relations with emerging destinations like Latin America, with Venezuela in particular. Venezuela President Chavez's stress on South-South relations along with a strong anti-US bias, need to be carefully handled by New Delhi through a diplomacy capable of addressing Washington's sensitivities. India should boost its trade with Latin America which just stood at the low level of US $ 3,000 million in 2005, as against China's US $ 40,000 million in 2004.[94]

Lastly, strengthening of energy relations with China by itself can bring rich dividends to India in the matter of its energy security. The Article 9 of the India-China Declaration, signed during Premier Wen Jiabao's visit to India in 2005, provides the basis for bilateral co-operation to explore and exploit oil and natural gas resources in the third-world countries.[95] But Sino-Indian energy initiatives can also become sources of conflicts, for example India's concern over China targeting the Indian Ocean, questioning Indian sovereignty over resource-rich Arunachal Pradesh, executing hydro-power

[93] www.mutiny.in, January 20, 2009.
[94] www.oecd.org, November 8, 2007.
[95] Paper submitted by Ma Jiali, (see Note 16)

projects on the river Brahmaputra like the one coming up at Zangmu in Tibet, with potentials to impact on the downstream flow into India's Arunachal Pradesh and undertaking power projects in the Pakistan Occupied Kashmir. India and China should, therefore, take conflict-resolution as a priority task; that can be done through bilateral political talks or through the medium of regional institutions.

Constraints for India other than China

The China factor alone is not sufficient to define the imperatives that have arisen for India with regard to its energy security. New Delhi's difficulties come from other sources, for example the lack of progress in obtaining natural gas from Iran through the proposed Iran-Pakistan-India (IPI) pipeline on which Iran and Pakistan have already signed an initial agreement in May 2009 without involving India as well as the stalled Turkmenistan-Afghanistan-Pakistan-India (TAPI) pipeline project as a result of the Talkiban insurgency in Afghanistan. On the IPI issue, New Delhi should find ways to find a balance between its energy ties with Tehran and strategic relations with Washington. Indian diplomacy would also require to be geared to face other challenges – New Delhi's strong disinclination to allow any strategic leverage to Pakistan following the 2008 Mumbai terrorist attacks, Iran's hard bargaining on gas prices and the chances of China joining the IPI project if India withdraws from it.

India is also coming under compulsions to confront a new geo-political situation, as oil flows from the Middle East are more and more shifting towards Asia. Importantly, Saudi Arabian oil supplies are moving towards India and China in the backdrop of the fall being seen in US dependence over Saudi oil. There is need for India, which has a "Look West" policy in parallel to a "Look East" policy, to leverage such a development with the aim to strengthen energy relations with the Gulf nations. New Delhi appears to be already aware of the same; India has been successful in bidding for oil blocks in Yemen, Qatar and Oman, besides starting FTA negotiations with the Gulf nations including Saudi Arabia, a G-20 member. The visits of Indian Prime Minister to Saudi Arabia in February 2010 and Deputy Chairman of India's planning commission to Bahrain in May 2010, were significant in the context of growing India-Gulf energy relations.[96]

---

[96] arabnews.co, February 26, 2011 and March 22, 2011.

To sum up, it can be said that the two rising powers, India and China, cannot avoid the influence coming from their self-interests and geo-political considerations over the respective energy policies; but at the same time, it would be prudent on their part to try to minimise the differences to the extent possible through diplomatic consultations and if necessary through multilateral mechanisms, on the basis of their realisation of the mutual benefits accruing from energy co-operation. One currently sees good prospects on this count, with both India and China recognising basically that "there is enough space in the world to accommodate the growth and ambitions of both."

Part III

China's India Policy

8

Sino-Indian Territorial Issues

The "Razor's Edge"?

David Scott

In terms of "the rise of China" and its "implications for India", the title of this book, the Sino-Indian territorial dispute represents an immediate arena in which India is having to face the uncomfortable implications from having an increasingly stronger neighbour. For India, the ability of China to deny India's hopes of territorial settlement on India's terms has become even clearer in the wake of China's rise in military power in and around her disputed territory, which remains the biggest amount of land still in dispute in Asia. As such,

> the 4056-kilometre (2520 miles) frontier between India and China, one of the longest interstate borders in the world, remains...not defined, let alone demarcated, on maps or delineated on the ground.[1]

Here, the judgement over a century ago, of Lord Curzon, British Viceroy of India 1898–1905 still seems relevant:

> the most urgent work of Foreign Ministers and Ambassadors...is now the conclusion of Frontier Conventions in which sources of discord are removed by the adjustment of rival interests or ambitions at points where the territorial

---

[1] M. Malik, "India-China Competition Revealed in Ongoing Border Disputes", *PINR* (Power & Interest News Report), October 7, 2007.

borders adjoin, ... frontiers are indeed the razor's edge on which hang suspended the modern issues of war or peace, of life or death to nations.[2]

Admittedly, the territorial issue has been officially decoupled from the wider Sino-Indian relationship; as with the People's Republic of China (PRC) rhetoric that

> China and India have already reached consensus on the border issue. Before it is completely resolved, both countries will endeavour to maintain peace and stability in the border areas and will not let the border issue affect the general picture of China and India's co–operation.[3]

However, in reality their territorial issues do affect their wider relationship, in PRC terms, "the existence of immense territorial disputes between China and India."[4]

In dispute terms, this chapter argues that, in International Relations (IR) theory terms, the territorial disputes between India and China involves *classical geopolitics* entwined with *critical geopolitics*. Each strand of geopolitics, in their different ways, both involve the respective "position" that India and China hold for themselves and for each other in their immediate and extended neighbourhood. Whilst each side argues from history, the chapter argues that in reality the evidence from history is rather ambiguous and inconclusive for both sides" territorial claims. Indeed, history is a sterile area to argue from, as one Indian commentator put it, "can we go beyond history to look at solutions which do not hark back to the past?"[5]

The chapter argues that, from the outside, resolution of the issue seems feasible enough in terms of simple seeming territorial tradeoffs involving Arunachal Pradesh and Aksai Chin; but is complicated by smaller geographic issues surrounding Tawang, and wider geopolitical issues surrounding Tibet and indeed, the balance of power in Asia between India and China.[6]

---

[2] Lord Curzon of Kedleston, *Romanes Lecture on the Subject of Frontiers*, 1907, http://www-ibru.dur.ac.uk/resources/docs/curzon1.html.

[3] Chinese Foreign Ministry cited in G. Cheng, "China Refutes Territory Grab Story", *China Daily*, January 13, 2010.

[4] Foreign Ministry spokesman Qin Gang cited in Ma Jiali, "Fanning the Flames", *Beijing Review*, July 12, 2009.

[5] V. K. Singh, "Resolving the Boundary Dispute", *Seminar*, 562, June, 2006, http://www.india-seminar.com/2006/562/562-vk-singh.htm.

[6] X. Liu, *The Sino-Indian Border Dispute and Sino-Indian Relations* (Lanham: University Press of America, 1994).

The two main areas of dispute along this Himalayan frontier are the *Western Sector* (Aksai Chin, around 37,250 sq km/14,380 sq mile); and the *Eastern Sector* (Arunachal Pradesh, around 83,740 sq km/32,330 sq mile). On the one hand, Arunachal Pradesh is inhabited by over a million people, Indian citizens, and includes important Buddhist centres like Tawang. On the other hand, Aksai Chin is a virtually uninhabited bleak barren plateau with no permanent settlements. It is the place "where not a blade of grass grows" as Jawaharlal Nehru once dismissively said; but where China's National Highway 219 runs through Aksai Chin as a key geopolitical infrastructure link for the PRC between its provinces of Tibet and Xinjiang. One further complication is China's occupation of the Shaksgam valley; around 5,180 sq kilometres/1,930 square miles, to which Pakistan relinquished its Baltistan-related claims in 1,963, but over which India maintains its own Kashmir-derived claims. Smaller pockets of disputed territory are found in the *Middle Sector* fringes of Himachal Pradesh and Uttar Pradesh. Elsewhere along the Himalayas, lingering uncertainty over China's recognition of Sikkim's incorporation into India in 1975 is entwined with continuing PRC claims to the "Finger Area" in the north of Sikkim, with 71 supposed incidents reported of the Chinese troop "incursions" in 2008. Nearby, territorial disputes between China and Bhutan around the Chumbi Valley triangulation point with India are of further concerns to New Delhi, given the Chumbi Valley's location looking down onto India's sensitive Siliguri corridor, which links India's north-eastern states with the rest of India.

Wider nuances arise with India's Foreign Secretary (2004–06) Shyam Saran, and his comments about *the logic of geography*. In front of one audience, it was a question for Saran of "geopolitical reality" in which

I would like to focus particularly on Asia, where the interests of both India and China intersect. It is said that the logic of geography is unrelenting. Proximity is the most difficult and testing among diplomatic challenges a country faces, to those who harbour any scepticism about this fact, it would suffice to remind that we share one of the longest [and disputed] land borders in the world with China.[7]

In front of another audience, it was again a question that

it is said that the logic of geography is unrelenting and proximity is the most difficult and testing among diplomatic challenges a country faces; frontiers with

[7] S. Saran, "Present Dimensions of the Indian Foreign Policy", http://meaindia.nic.in?/speech/2006/01/11ss01.htm; accessed on January 11, 2006.

neighbours are where domestic concerns intersect with external relationships. This is where domestic and foreign policies become inextricable and demand sensitive handling, it is important for us to look at the [disputed] boundary question from the long-term and strategic perspective of India-China relations, rather than as a mere territorial issue.[8]

The territorial issues between India and China form one of the biggest land disputes in Asia, and are of significance not only for the size of area under dispute, but also because the two disputants are the big countries most evidently on the rise in Asia. Alongside this *logic of geography*, there is then what Neville Maxwell called "the logic of power"; a *logic of power* whereby powerful states "in their expansive phases push out their frontiers until they meet the resistance of a strong neighbour or reach a physical barrier which makes a natural point of rest."[9]

In geopolitical terms, the current point of rest is along the Himalayas/Karakoram range, but in the long term where exactly is the "natural" point of rest between them? Amidst talk of mutual IR *security dilemma* dynamics, China's strengthening of military forces and related infrastructure in Aksai Chin and Arunachal Pradesh zones is now a spur to India's own more halting augmentation of military forces and related infrastructure. Meanwhile, both countries are seeking to expand their wider strategic space at a time when their immediate mountain borders remain unresolved.

Respective Claims

Both sides evoke but also dispute the historical record.[10] "Perceptual" differences, the stamping ground of IR *constructivism*, remain very different between India and China towards their own and each other's claims on the disputed territories.[11] The role of Tibet presents further related ambiguity

---

[8] Saran, "India and its Neighbours", http://meaindia.nic.in?/speech/2005/02/14ss01.htm; accessed on February 14, 2005.

[9] N. Maxwell, *India's China War* (London: Jonathan Cape, 1970), p. 19.

[10] See A. Lamb, *The McMahon Line: A Study in the Relations Between India, China, and Tibet*, 2 vols. (London: Routledge and Kegan Paul, 1966); D. Woodman, *Himalayan Frontiers. A Political Review of British, Chinese, Indian and Russian Rivalries* (London: Barrie and Rockliff, 1969); Lamb, *The Sino-Indian Border in Ladakh* (Canberra: Australian National University Press, 1973).

[11] Y. Vertzberger, "India's Border Conflict with China: A Perceptual Analysis", *Journal of Contemporary History*, 17.4 (1982): 607–31. Constructivist-ideational framework explicitly

in Sino-Indian relations.[12] Indian figures like K. Gopalachari, an advisor to the Indian team in the 1960 discussions with China, emphasised in 1963, in the bitter aftermath of India's 1962 military defeats at the hands of China, that

> the India-China boundary is not a complicated question left over from history, but one definitely settled by history; the Indian alignment of the 24000 mile boundary, one of the longest in the world, has been determined by geography, confirmed by tradition and custom, sanctified by treaties and reinforced by continuous exercise through the centuries of administrative jurisdiction appropriate to the areas concerned.[13] Ironically, the PRC uses the same criteria and lines of argument, complete with its repeated phrase of the issue as being "a question left over by history".[14]

History does not really settle the issue, as witnessed in the voluminous but inconclusive exchange of maps and documents in the 1960 negotiations. In reality, the picture has been a confused vague picture in the past, in which ethnic-tribal lines and power vacuums have generated blurred and unclear Tibetan borders.

China's territorial claims on Arunachal Pradesh stem from China's wider claims to Tibet, hence the PRC's styling of Arunachal Pradesh as *Zang Nan* "Southern Tibet". In terms of implications for India of China's rise, as Brahma Chellaney trenchantly put it, China "covets Arunachal as a cultural patio to Tibet – a classic attempt at incremental annexation".[15]

---

followed in L. Yang, "Looking Beyond the Border: The Sino-Indian Border Dispute and Sino-Indian Relations", *Working Paper* (Heidelberg Papers), 31, 2007.

[12] S. Zhao, "The Implication of Demilitarization of Tibet for Sino-Indian Relations and Asian Security", *Asian Affairs*, 22.4 (Winter 1996): 254–260; D. Norbu, "Tibet in Sino-Indian Relations: The Centrality of Marginality", *Asian Survey*, 37.11 (1997): 1078–1095; J. Garver, "The Tibetan Factor in Sino--Indian Relations", in Garver, *Protracted Contest: Sino-Indian Rivalry in the Twentieth Century* (Seattle: University of Washington Press, 2001), pp. 32–78; S. Thapliyal, "Tibet: The Real Issue", *India Defence Review*, 22.4 (October-December 2007): 80–86.

[13] K. Gopalachari, "The India-China Boundary Question", *International Studies*, 5 (1963): 33–42.

[14] E.g. "Statement of the Government of the People's Republic of China", October 24, 1962, *The Sino-Indian Boundary Question* (Beijing: Foreign Languages Press, 1962), pp. 1–5, p. 1.

[15] B. Chellaney, "China's Locus Standi on Arunachal?", *Times of India*, October 16, 2009. See also S. Hoffmann, "Rethinking the Linkage between Tibet and the China-India Border Conflict: A Realist Approach", *Journal of Cold War Studies*, 8.3 (2006): 165–94; D. Norbu, "Chinese Strategic Thinking on Tibet and the Himalayan Region", *Strategic Analysis*, 32.4 (2008): 374–80.

Despite the worried concerns of Vallabhai Patel over the implications of Chinese move into Tibet in 1950, Nehru moved ahead with the 1954 *Agreement on Trade and Intercourse between the Tibet Region of China and India*. This indicated Indian acceptance of PRC control over Tibet, with repeated use in the 1954 *Agreement*, eight times, of the phrase "Tibet region of China". It also included India's renunciation of forward military and economic rights enjoyed in Tibet by British India. More recently in their 2003 *Joint Declaration*, the formulation was that "the Indian side recognises that the Tibet Autonomous Region [TAR] is part of the territory of the People's Republic of China".[16]

In retrospect, some Indian figures have argued that this showed a recurring tendency for India to hand over "unilateral concessions" to China. However, there was some comment on the implications and sub-text of the 2003 *Joint Declaration* seeming to recognise the claims of the PRC rather than China *per se*; a qualified recognition whereby if the PRC collapses as a regime, then so could Indian recognition of Chinese claims to Tibet? There was also comment that China's favoured term "inalienable" was not applied to Tibet in the 2003 *Joint Declaration*. Of course, there are ambiguities in China's very claim on Tibet.[17] China claims that political links with Tibet go back centuries. In reality, Chinese control was first seen in the intervention of a Qing army in 1720 and arrival of a Chinese resident commissioner (*amban*). Since then, some degree of Chinese control was able to be enforced in Tibet when China was strong, but effectively lapsed (for most of the period) when China was weak.

As to the periphery around Tibet, it would seem that the *Western Sector*, Aksai Chin, was pretty well ignored by most settled surrounding powers in India and China. Admittedly, in 1865, a British surveyor W.H. Johnson employed by the Maharaja of Kashmir, had drawn up the so-called "Johnson Line" which had placed the Aksai Chin plateau in Kashmir, but the Chinese government rejected this demarcation, which remained nominal rather than implemented. A later British proposal was submitted in 1899 by Claude MacDonald, the British Minister to China, with Aksai

---

[16] "Declaration on Principles for Relations and Comprehensive Cooperation Between the People's Republic of China and the Republic of India", http://www.fmprc.gov.cn/eng/wjdt/2649/t22852. htm. accessed on June 25, 2003.

[17] M. van Praag, *The Status of Tibet: History, Rights and Prospects in International Law*, (Boulder: Westview Press, 1987); M. Goldstein, *The Snow Lion and the Dragon: China Tibet and the Dalai Lama* (Berkeley: University of California Press, 1997).

Chin allocated to China, but this was not followed through by either government.[18]

With regard to the *Eastern Sector,* Arunachal Pradesh has varied defensive and offensive strategic importance for India, as it (1) provides strategic depth to India's vulnerable Brahmaputra Valley and India's other North Eastern states; (2) provides security to Bhutan on its entire Eastern flank by geographical contiguity; and (3) in any future conflict with China and if India singly (or in coalition with some other power) develops offensive capabilities against China, it offers the shortest cut for India to China proper and to Tibet.

The problem for Indian claims is that some traditional and demographic links were present between Arunachal Pradesh and Tibet, with tax links maintained between Tawang and the Lhasa authorities well into the mid twentieth century.

Thus, the Imperial Gazetteer map *Political Divisions of the Indian Empire* (1909) showed the British India frontier as the southern (not northern) borderline of present day Arunachal Pradesh. Admittedly, more formal boundary lines between India and Tibet seemed laid down under the Simla Convention of 1914, which established the McMahon Line. The Chinese delegate from the Qing Empire, Chen I-fan, may have initially initialled the Simla Convention; but he then repudiated it, as did the central government in Beijing. The PRC has maintained a rejection of the Simla Convention as an unequal treaty and manifestation of imperialism on the part of British India;

> the so-called McMahon Line in the eastern sector is a line which the British imperialists attempted to force upon China by taking advantage of the powerlessness of the Chinese ... It is illegal and has never been recognised by the Chinese Government.[19]

British India did gradually move into the Himalayan slopes after 1914, calling it the North East Frontier Agency (NEFA); and this can be accurately summed by Mohan Guruswamy that India's claim to the north-eastern frontiers "does not rest on any great historical tradition or cultural affinity. We are there because the British went there."[20]

---

[18] R. Huttenbach, "A Historical Note on the Sino-Indian Dispute over the Aksai Chin", *China Quarterly,* 18, April-June (1964): 201–07.

[19] "Statement of the Government of the People's Republic of China", October 24, 1962, p. 1.

[20] M. Guruswamy, "Sino-Indian Ties. 20th Century Borders for Stable 21st Century Relations", *Issue Brief* (IPCS), 49, July 2007. See also P. Mehra, *The McMahon Line and After. A Study of the Triangular Contest on India's North-eastern Frontier Between Britain, China, and Tibet, 1904–47* (Delhi: Macmillan, 1974).

However, China now faces the problem that there has been continuous occupation of the *Eastern Sector* area by the Republic of India since 1950, albeit interrupted briefly in 1962 before Chinese troops withdrew their forces but not their claim. One of the mysteries remains why China withdrew their forces from the NEFA in 1962, given that it was claiming it as Chinese territory. It would seem that PRC concerns over maintaining their grip over Tibet made the key infrastructure role of the Aksai China the crucial element to retain, which is exactly what they did in 1962, with the NEFA perhaps considered as less important geopolitically for China's position in Tibet. Meanwhile, Indian re-occupation in the wake of the Chinese withdrawal in 1962 has led to the granting of full statehood in 1987 to the NEFA, now termed Arunachal Pradesh, and its subsequent participation in Indian politics. Such integration of Arunachal Pradesh within the Indian polity has not been recognised by the PRC; and it was no coincidence that in 1987, there were serious skirmishes at Sumdorong Chu in Arunachal Pradesh.

Faced with a rising India, whose closer security and defence links with the United States were signalled with their 2005 Defence Agreement, Chinese claims to Arunachal Pradesh have been re-invoked with increased vigour.[21] Hence, the widely publicised assertion in November 2006 by China's Ambassador to India, Sun Yuxi, that "in our position, the whole of the state of Arunachal Pradesh is Chinese territory. And Tawang is only one of the places in it. We are claiming all of that. That is our position."[22]

The clarification in 2007 by the Dalai Lama, that the 1914 Simla Agreement drawing the MacMahon Line to demarcate the Tibet-India border was signed by an independent government of Tibet, has strengthened PRC re-assertions of its own claims; as the Chinese are acutely concerned that the present Dalai Lama's position not only negates the Chinese claim on Arunachal Pradesh, but also questions the very legality of Chinese sovereignty over Tibet, and with it the PRC's incorporation of Tibet in 1950. Arunachal Pradesh's participation in Indian politics continues to attract Beijing's ire, witnessed in PRC

---

[21] J. Panda, "China's Designs on Arunachal Pradesh", *Comment* (IDSA), March 12, 2008; P. Stobdan, "Chinese Checkers in the Himalayas: Revisiting Sino-Indian Relations", *Strategic Analysis*, 32.5 (2008): 703–11, S. Dasgupta, "China Lashes out at India for Arunachal remarks", *Times of India*, November 11, 2008. See also B. Raman, "China: Media Anger on Arunachal Pradesh Continues Unabated, Raman, *Paper* (SAAG), 3260, June 18, 2009.

[22] Comments immediately picked up in the wider Indian media; e.g. "Close to Hu's Visit, China Claims Arunachal", *Hindustan Times*, November 14, 2006; "Trust Deficit to Shadow Hu's Visit", *Business Standard*, November 20, 2006.

denunciations in 2009 over the visit and campaigning in Arunachal Pradesh by national politicians like Manmohan Singh and Rahul Gandhi. Whilst Beijing expressed how it was "strongly dissatisfied" over what it considered "provocative" action by India, the Indian government merely reiterated how Arunachal Pradesh was an "integral part of India. We rest at that."[23]

India claims, simply enough in its eyes, that the Arunachal Pradesh border has already been agreed via the MacMahon Line drawn up and ratified in 1914 under the Simla Convention, which India sees as a sensible reflection of geography and history. Chinese administrations may have rejected the Simla Agreement, but Tibetan administrations did not. The Dalai Lama's acceptance of the MacMahon Line and of India's claim within it to Tawang, are a continuing feature of India's case, marshalled again following the Dalai Lama's visit, with Indian government permission to Tawang in November 2009, a visit denounced in the PRC.[24] China though argues that neither the Tibetan authorities nor the Dalai Lama have had, be it in 1914 or in 2009, the authority to dispose of territory and conduct foreign policy. In China's eyes,

> there has been no such a thing as "independent Tibet" since the Yuan Dynasty (1271–1368) established its suzerainty over the region. It was the invasion of Tibet by British forces in the late nineteenth century that made Tibetan sovereignty an issue. When the British forces withdrew after waging two wars, they tried to create an "independent Tibet" by convening the Simla Convention.[25]

As to the Simla Convention, the PRC continues to argue that it was an imperialist facade,

> UK representative Henry McMahon secretly signed the so-called "Simla Accord" with the local Tibetan government manipulated by "Tibet independence" forces during the "Simla conference" without the knowledge of Chinese representatives. This accord even incorporated a large area of territory in China's Tibet including the Tawang district to British India.[26]

---

[23] "Indian P.M's Visit a Provocative Move", *Global Times*, October 14, 2009; X. Zuo, "Indian PM Visit to Southern Tibet Spark's China's Ire", *People's Daily*, October 14, 2009; "Govt Says Arunachal Integral Part of India After Chinese Protest", *Times of India*, October 13, 2009.

[24] "India Covets Dalai Lama's Visit", *People's Daily*, November 9, 2009.

[25] "Leading Newspaper Op-ed Exposes Truths of Dalai Lama", *People's Daily*, April 4, 2009.

[26] "Dalai Lama Goes Further Down Traitorous Road", October 22, 2009, http://chinatibet.people.com.cn/6791227.html.

Status of Negotiations

In 1981, following the frozen relations prevalent after the 1962 war, border talks at the vice-ministerial level were initiated. Although Beijing had suggested sectoral swapping in 1960 and 1980, this "overall package" predisposition faced India's push for separate "sector-by-sector" agreements.[27] In 1988, more formal Joint Working Group (JWG) discussions were started with a twin mandate of ensuring "peace and tranquillity" along the Line of Actual Control (LAC) and working on a "fair, reasonable and mutually acceptable" Settlement of the boundary question. In September 1993, China and India signed the *Agreement on the Maintenance of Peace and Tranquillity along the LAC in the India-China Border Areas*, with a Sino-Indian Expert Group (EG) set up to assist the work of the JWG on the boundary question. The rhetoric was clear in its Article-1:

> the India-China boundary question shall be resolved through peaceful and friendly consultations. Neither side shall use or threaten to use force against the other by any means. Pending an ultimate solution to the boundary question....[28]

In November 1996, China and India agreed in their *Agreement on Confidence Building Measures in the Military Field along the LAC in the India-China Border Areas* to delimit their LAC and institute Confidence Building Measures (CBMs) along the frontier. The agreement included pledges on non aggression, prior notification of large troop movements, a 10-km no-fly zone for combat aircraft and exchange of maps to resolve disagreements about the precise location of the LAC.[29]

In June 2003, the India-China *Declaration on Principles for Relations and Comprehensive Co-operation between India and China* had the two countries agreeing "to each appoint a special representative to explore from the political perspective of the overall bilateral relationship the framework of a boundary settlement."[30]

---

[27] S. Ganguly, "The Sino-Indian Border Talks, 1981–1989: A View from New Delhi", *Asian Survey*, 29.12, 1989, pp. 1123–35.

[28] "Agreement on the Maintenance of Peace and Tranquillity along the Line of Actual Control in the India-China Border Areas", in M. Sali, *India-China Border Dispute: A Case Study of the Eastern Sector*, 1998 , Appendix II, pp. 289–92.

[29] See W. Singh Sidhu and J-D Yuan, "Resolving the Sino-Indian Border Dispute: Building Confidence through Cooperative Monitoring", *Asian Survey*, 41.2, pp. 351–76.

[30] "Declaration on Principles for Relations and Comprehensive Cooperation Between the People's Republic of China and the Republic of India", June 25, 2003.

Some ground rules for actual territorial negotiations seemed to have been achieved in April 2005 with the signing of the *Political Parameters and Guiding Principles for the Settlement of the India-China Boundary Question.*[31] However, the *Joint Declaration by the Republic of India and the PRC* (2006) and the *Shared Vision for the twenty-first century of the PRC and the Republic of India* (2008), which both expressed hopes that "such [boundary] differences are not allowed to affect the positive development of bilateral relations" in other fields, have perhaps pushed territorial differences but also territorial resolution to one side?[32]

To conclude, varied frameworks have been seen; some eight rounds of vice-ministerial talks from 1981–87, 14 JWG meetings from 1988–2003, and 13 rounds of Special Representative talks from 2003–09. Nevertheless, there seems to have been little substantive progress on territorial issues. Specific discussions on core territorial demands and delineation of forces have given way to broader, but some would say vaguer and less useful, political discussions of bilateral relations as a whole. In terms of general confidence, if anything, the situation has deteriorated between India and China, where the last few years have seen growing numbers of incursions, alongside infrastructure and military forces build up along the Himalayas, both on the Arunachal Pradesh and Aksai Chin borderlines. Despite some of the diplomatic rhetoric of engagement and global co-operation, strategic perceptions of each other have deteriorated, whilst public as well as elite distrust of intentions and military capacity has grown.

Even initial specific steps have been minimal and indeed appear somewhat grudging. In terms of establishing the LAC, maps have only been established with regard to the relatively minor *Middle Sector* (Himachal Pradesh/Uttar Pradesh fringes) where LAC maps were exchanged in November 2000. China then committed itself to an exchange of LAC maps of the *Western Sector* (Aksai Chin) in 2002 and the *Eastern Sector* (Arunachal Pradesh) in early 2003. However, in 2003 this was effectively overturned when China argued that the two countries should instead focus on achieving an overall final political package settlement. Equally well, the 2006 Joint Declaration pledge that "it was agreed to complete

---

[31] "Joint Statement of the Republic of India and the People's Republic of China", April 11, 2005, http://mea.india.nic.in/speech/2005/04/16ss01.htm.

[32] *Joint Declaration by the Republic of India and the People's Republic of China*, November 21, 2006, http://meaindia.nic.in/declarestatement/2006/11/21jd01.htm; "A Shared Vision for the 21st Century of the People's Republic of China and the Republic of India, January 15, 2008, http://www.fmprc.gov.cn/eng/wjdt/2649/t399545.htm.

the process of exchanging maps indicating their respective perceptions of the entire alignment of the LAC on the basis of already agreed parameters as soon as possible" also has shown no particular signs of being completed; with no LAC maps having emerged for those two major blocks of disputed territory, Aksai Chin and Arunachal Pradesh. This, in turn, makes the immediate implementation of the 1996 *Agreement on Confidence Building Measures in the Military Field along the LAC in the India-China Border Areas* difficult as the agreement refers to controlling military dispositions and deployments to certain distances from LACs, but yet those LACs have not been established.

The speed, or rather lack of speed, over negotiations is noticeable, a "glacial pace" given that current border discussions were first initiated in 1981.[33] The 2005 *Political Parameters and Guiding Principles for the Settlement of the India-China Boundary Question* talked of "an early settlement of the boundary question"

It did have its Article-7 provision that "in reaching a boundary settlement, the two sides shall safeguard due interests of their settled populations in the border areas."[34]

However, China's strong reassertion of its claims over Arunachal Pradesh, and especially Tawang, cut across such population principles. This population provision also seems undercut by the comments made to Pranab Mukherjee in June 6, 2007 by Chinese Foreign Minister Yang Jiechi, who stated that "mere presence" of settled populations would not affect China's claims.[35] Meanwhile, the 2006 *Joint Declaration* announced that "the Special Representatives shall complete at an early date the task of finalising an appropriate framework for a final package settlement covering all sectors of the India-China boundary," but as of yet there are no signs of any such "early finalisation" let alone "early settlement". Similarly, the *Working Group* set up at the 2007 Special Representatives meeting to prepare a "framework arrangement" has been equally barren on outcomes, so far.

Indian perceptions of Chinese motives remain highly critical. For Kapila, it was the opportunity for China "to keep alive the border dispute as a strategic pressure point against India."[36]

[33] S. Ganguly, "Border Issues, Domestic Integration and International Security", in F. Frankel and H. Harding, eds., *The India-China Relationship* (New York: Columbia University Press, 2004), p. 123.

[34] "Joint Statement of the Republic of India and the People's Republic of China", April 11, 2005.

[35] See P. Samantana, "China Draws Another Hard Line on Arunachal", *Indian Express*, June 7, 2007.

[36] S. Kapila, "China: The Strategic Reluctance on Boundary Settlement with India", *Paper* (SAAG), 2023, November 13, 2006.

For Malik it was a case that

> Beijing would not want to give up the "bargaining chip" that an unsettled boundary vis-à-vis India provides it with. An unsettled border provides China the strategic leverage to keep India uncertain about its intentions, and nervous about its capabilities, while exposing India's vulnerabilities and weaknesses, and ensuring New Delhi's "good behaviour" on issues of vital concern to China.[37]

Discussions, rather than negotiations have then settled down into a regular, but desultory fashion. The press communiqué from the 2009 Special Representative talks was still noticeably bland

> in a friendly and candid atmosphere, the two Special Representatives had an in-depth exchange of views on resolving the boundary question. Both countries agreed to press ahead with the framework negotiations in accordance with the agreed political parameters and guiding principle,

so as "to seek for a fair and reasonable solution acceptable to both. Prior to that, both should work together to maintain peace and tranquillity in the border areas."[38] Candid is often diplomatic euphemism for blunt differences of opinion, whilst the call for working together to maintain peace and tranquillity is a virtual admission that peace and stability has not yet been established. Equally euphemistic are PRC statements that both countries "should respect history and reality, take into account the feelings of both nations, make the most of their political wisdom and come up with a reasonable and mutually acceptable solution to their border issue."[39]

Such sentiments fail to give any tangible specifics on what actual solutions might be forthcoming.

Negotiating Strategies

One repeated emerging criticism of India's negotiating strategy is that "unilateral concessions" have been made too often by India, without similar concessions being made by China.[40] When PRC military forces started moving into Tibet in 1950, the Republic of India quickly moved to (a) give up

---

[37] Malik, "India-China Competition Revealed in Ongoing Border Disputes".

[38] "Press Release from Chinese Delegation: The 13th Meeting Between the Chinese and Indian Special Representative on Boundary Question", *The Hindu*, August 8, 2009.

[39] J. Ma, "Fanning the Flames", *Beijing Review*, July 12, 2009.

[40] A. Bhattacharya, "China's Claims Over Arunachal: Reflections on Chinese Foreign Policy and What India Needs to Do", *IDSA Comment*, November 21, 2006.

the Forward Rights inherited from the days of British India, which stemmed from the Simla Convention and Anglo-Tibetan Agreement of 1904; and (b) instead recognise Chinese control over Tibet in stronger terms than the hitherto used term "suzerainty". In effect, a "Tibet Card" was there to be played at a time of PRC uncertainties. A robust Indian intervention might have maintained Tibet as an effective buffer between India and China, or at least enabled concessions to be won by India on the Himalayan-Karakoram borders. This is the reverse logic behind recent Indian comments that

> China has failed to appreciate that if Arunachal is claimed to be the southern part of Tibet Autonomous Region (TAR), India cannot accept Tibet to be within China. India's formal position on Tibet articulated in 1954 and 2003 is therefore a tentative and unilateral diplomatic offer that can only be sustained and the circle completed once China recognises Arunachal as part of India.[41]

Re-invoking such a "Tibet Card" has been floated in some Indian circles in the past few years.[42]

Having lost that opportunity, the next criticism of Indian negotiating strategy is that, faced with an immediate PRC military presence in Tibet and renewed Chinese claims over Aksai China and Arunachal Pradesh, Nehru ignored the chance of a trade-off seemingly offered by China in 1960 whereby Aksai China would have gone to China and Arunachal Pradesh would have gone to India.[43] Instead, India refused to engage in sovereignty negotiations in the 1950s, maintained its claims to the fullest, neglected to build up its own military forces, yet still engaged in adventurist forward probing movements in the late 1950s. At the time, Nehru rejected the idea of territorial trade-off; India "will not concede one piece of territory in return for another in the same manner as a similar dispute between China and Burma was settled this year; there is no question of barter in these matters...facts are facts."[44]

His formal position was, in the formal *Indian Note* of June 16 1962, quite simply that "this boundary is well known and well recognised and has been so for centuries and cannot be the subject of any negotiations."

---

[41] S. Dutta, "Revisiting China's Territorial Claims on Arunachal", *Strategic Analysis*, 32.4 (2008): 549–91.
[42] R. Sikri, "India's Tibet Policy: Need for a Change", *Paper* (SAAG), 2649, March 28, 2008; V. Gumaste, "Why India Should Rake Up the Tibet Issue", *Rediff News*, October 15, 2009.
[43] See M. Miller, "Re-collecting Empire: "Victimhood" and the 1962 Sino-Indian War", *Asian Security*, 5.3, 2009, pp. 216–41 for talks and different perceptions then.
[44] As cited in the *New York Times*, April 26, 1960, p. 6; and the *Washington Post*, April 27, 1960, p. 7.

The trouble was the precise boundaries were not well known, were not well recognised, and had not been in shape for centuries. The irony is that the territorial agreement reached between Burma and China in 1960 involved China following the MacMahon Line alongside other mutual concessions and swapping of territory, as did the 1963 Agreement between China and Pakistan with regard to mutual concessions over claims and territory in the Karakoram reaches.

Nehru might have said "facts are facts" but the fact of the matter is that China's military superiority and continuing occupation of Aksai Chin created a very different subsequent set of facts in the wake of India's military defeat at the hands of China in 1962. The problem for consideration of negotiated resolution of the territorial dispute is that demands and offers have shifted. From the outside, an obvious trade off would be between the *Western* Sector and the *Eastern Sector*, which is where Noorani argued that "there is no territorial dispute which has been, and still is, more susceptible to a solution than India's boundary dispute with China. Each side has its non-negotiable vital interest securely under its control. India has the McMahon Line, China has Aksai Chin."[45]

In other words, China's *de facto* control of Aksai Chin could be reflected in agreed *de jure* sovereignty for China, and India's *de facto* control of Arunachal Pradesh could in turn be reflected in agreed *de jure* sovereignty for India. This had been Zhou Enlai's seeming suggestion in 1960, and was the "Package Plan'" floated by Deng Xiaoping during 1980. The problem is that the Indian government has never taken up such trade-off offers, with Chinese comments made about the weakness of the Indian governments in taking any compromise deal to the Indian public. The separate *sector-by-sector* approach advocated by India when discussions resumed in the 1980s, rather than *overall package* trade-off deals suggested by China, has not worked; it has merely led the PRC to maintain its particular claims in all sectors.

Another possible example of unilateral concessions was Rajiv Gandhi's visit to Beijing in 1988. Various concessions were made by him. He agreed that the settlement of the border dispute no longer was necessary as a precondition for improvement of bilateral relations. Second, he agreed that some members of the Tibetan community in India were engaged in anti-China activities, and third, he agreed that Tibet was an internal affair for China. Ganguly considered

---

[45] See A. Noorani, "On Maps and Borders", *Frontline*, October 11–28, 2008.

the results were "clearly asymmetric" as no support on the Kashmir issue was received from China, which "underscored the stark debility of India's negotiating capabilities vis-à-vis China." [46]

On the other hand, the earlier unequivocal support for Pakistan's case in Kashmir was moderated by a more neutral position by the 1990s, the PRC eventually announcing it was "not taking sides on Kashmir." [47]

A final example of "unilateral concessions" came in the 2003 *Declaration on Principles for Relations and Comprehensive Co-operation between India and China*, in which India explicitly recognised the sovereignty of China over Tibet. A careful look at the text shows one-way agreement, one-way obligations and one-way concessions. On the one hand, it stated that "the Indian side recognises that the Tibet Autonomous Region is part of the territory of the People's Republic of China and reiterates that it does not allow Tibetans to engage in anti-China political activities in India."

On the other hand, it went on to immediately say "The Chinese side expresses its appreciation for the Indian position and reiterates that it is firmly opposed to any attempt and action aimed at splitting China and bringing about independence of Tibet."

As can be seen, there was no recognition of Indian territory by China, not even return recognition by China of India's sovereignty claims over Sikkim, the Princely State reincorporated into the Republic of India in 1975, an incorporation which China had refused to recognise. [48] Indian commentators may have read the accompanying *Trade Memorandum* designating Natu La as a border trade post as recognition by China of India's sovereignty over Sikkim, but that was implied rather than explicit, *de facto* rather than *de jure*. [49]

Meanwhile, New Delhi has refused to lay out its formal position, other than the reiteration of its full claims of the Indian Parliament in November 1962, an unanimous vote to get China to vacate all Indian-claimed territories that China occupied. Specific territorial negotiations involving sensitive political

---

[46] Ganguly, "Border Issues, Domestic Integration and International Security", p. 122.

[47] "China Not Taking Sides on Kashmir", *People's Daily*, November 23, 2009. See J. Garver, "China's Kashmir Policies", *India Review*, 3.1 (2004): 1–24 for this shift.

[48] N. Ram, "Sikkim Story: Protection to Absorption", *Social Scientist*, 3.2 (1974): 57–71; G.S. Bajpai, *China's Shadow over Sikkim. The Politics of Intimidation* (New Delhi: Lancer, 1999).

[49] "Both sides reviewed with satisfaction the implementation of the memorandum on the border trade through the Nathula Pass between the Tibet Autonomous Region of the People's Republic of China and the Sikkim State of the Republic of India", "Settlement of China-India Boundary Question in Context of Long-term Interests, Overall Bilateral Relationship: Joint Statement", *People's Daily*, 12 April, 2003.

climb-downs or concessions might well be conducted in private out of the public gaze, yet there seems no indications of this either. India could then indicate some sort of territorial trade-off, short of this maximalist reiteration of its full claims, which China is unlikely to accept. Of course, India indicating a territorial trade-off would not necessarily meet with Chinese acceptance, given Indian suspicions that China is happy enough to avoid definitive frontier settlement, but at least it would clarify the issue, and in such an eventuality enable India to more straightforwardly strengthen her own presence and power towards China along the border. In IR terms, if *engagement* proved unsuccessful in leading to territorial settlement, then India could go for a degree of *internal balancing* through building up its military presence and power in Arunachal Pradesh and Ladakh. Some Indian commentators have suggested that "when the Agni-III is finally ready for deployment, it is likely that the Chinese will come down to the table for negotiations and there is likely to be further progress on the border dispute."[50]

It could also go for a degree of *external balancing* with others vis-à-vis China but that is a much wider issue. It could try adjusting its bigger policy on Tibet, in effect playing a "Tibet Card" to engineer geopolitical shifts in the future though it would be a much more high-risk strategy immediately bringing it up against China's perceived "core interest" of averting internal fragmentation.[51]

If India's strategy over the disputed territories has been hesitant, this has been exacerbated by the very opaqueness of the "Chinese whispers" coming from Beijing. What exactly does China really want, what is its bottom line? For example, are PRC reiterations of claims over the whole of Arunachal Pradesh, re-invoked with greater vigour since the 1990s just a maximalist initial tactic to end up with the Tawang pocket, thereby strengthening its control over Tibet, is a line of argument by Chinese commentators like Ma Jiali and others.[52] Are

---

[50] S. Kondapalli, "India-China Border Issue", *Seminar Reports* (ICPS), December 27, 2006.

[51] Indian P.M.'s "Visit a Provocative Move", *Global Times*, October 14, 2009; M. Li, "China's Core Interests Diplomacy Gains Ground", *People's Daily*, November 20, 2009.

[52] Ma Jiali, "Tawang is central to the resolution of the Sino-Indian border issue...If the border issue is not dealt well, the Chinese central government could face problems from local Tibetan people, who consider Tawang as part of Tibet...The Chinese government cannot afford to ignore popular feelings...Some Tibetans could use this issue to foment trouble in Tibet if Tawang is not returned to China", in "Return Tawang to China to Resolve Boundary Dispute," *Rediff News*, 7 March 2007, http://inhome.rediff.com/news/2007/mar/07china.htm. Also D. Rajan, "China: To Solve the Sino-Indian Boundary Problem, China-Russia Border Agreement Can be a Model, Feel Chinese Scholars", *Paper* (SAAG), 3247, June 11, 2009.

some suggestions in PRC circles of a different trade-off, Aksai Chin to India and Arunachal Pradesh to China, serious? Did China's acceptance in 2003 of Nathu La as an official border trade post between India and China represent full and definitive acceptance by China of Sikkim's incorporation into India and what is the significance of rising "incursion" incidents into Sikkim during 2008 by Chinese troops? These are the uncertainties that undermine Wen Jiabao's assertions in 2005 that "Sikkim is no longer the problem between China and India?"[53]

Is talk in the PRC that "China won't make any compromises in its border disputes with India" a tactical ploy by China to get India to make compromises?[54] If it is, then a trade-off deal is likely at some point. If it is not, then indefinite deadline/stand off is likely, unless one or the other disputant state attempts to decide it on the military battlefield.

One emerging line from the PRC, with implications for India, is PRC emphasis and definition of a "core interests" diplomacy, reflecting the rise of China "as the country becomes stronger, China is now on the trajectory to develop its own doctrine of diplomacy."[55]

This has been a development in the last couple of years, overlapping with rising friction along the disputed Himalayan reaches; generally what the PRC calls "the recalibration of its strategic focus in diplomacy to 'core interests,'" over which it is taking a more obstructive/assertive line.[56]

This sense of "core interest" can be primarily seen at stake for the PRC in Taiwan and also Xinjiang. It can also be seen with PRC statements with regard to Tibet, whereby "Tibet related issues remain a core interest of China that refers to state sovereignty and territorial integrity. This is neither a religious issue nor a human right issue."[57]

The question is how far China's "core interest" framework may be "expanding".[58] If such a "core interest" linkage is also invoked for Arunachal

---

[53] "Premier Wen Jiabao Meets with Journalists, Talking about 3 Achievements of His Visit to India", April 12, 2005, http://www.fmprc.gov.cn/eng/topics/wzlcflyeng/wzlcfzxxx/t191621.htm. Also "China Hopes to Have Border Trade Cooperation with Sikkim at an Early Date: Premier", *People's Daily*, April 13, 2005.

[54] "China Will Not Compromise on Territorial Issue", *Global Times*, August 7, 2009.

[55] Discussed in Zhang Haizou, "The Time has Come for Country to Set its Own Rules in Diplomacy", *China Daily*, March 12, 2009.

[56] Li Hongmei, "China's "Core Interests" Diplomacy Gains Ground", *People's Daily*, November 20, 2009. Also F. Ching, "China Reintroduces its "Core Interests'", *Opinion Asia*, November, 2009.

[57] "Chairman of Tibet's People's Congress Holds Talks with Australian Parliament", *People's Daily*, March 17, 2010.

[58] M. Richardson, "Assuaging China's Expanding "Core" Concerns", *Japan Times*, March 14, 2010.

Pradesh (or in PRC eyes *Zang Nan* "Southern Tibet') as "Tibet-related issues", then one would have less expectations of territorial agreements being reached between India and China, and more likelihood of armed resolution in the future. Such trends were the spur for Barat Verma at the *India Defence Review* to warn that for the PRC "the most attractive option is to attack a soft target like India and forcibly occupy its territory in the Northeast ... Beijing's cleverly raising the hackles on its fabricated dispute in Arunachal Pradesh to an alarming level, is the preparatory groundwork for imposing such a conflict on India;" a scenario dismissed in China as a "provocative and inflammatory illusion." [59]

Nevertheless, IR security dilemma dynamics may indeed lead to increasing military tension as both sides reinforce their military positions, and "war talk' about the disputed territories increases.[60]

Concerned voices are easy to find as "tensions over a boundary dispute between the two sides are escalating." [61] One reason for Indian concerns is the increasing number of "incursion" incidents along the border, though denied by China.[62] The official India leadership downplays such trends, India's Foreign Secretary Niripuma Rao thus asserting in September 2009 that "there has been no significant increase in intrusions across all sectors of the Line of Actual Control (LAC)," but that such India-perceived incursions were "because there is no mutually agreed or delineated border." [63]

This ignores the earlier increase in the previous year, whereby the number of India-perceived "incursions" by the PRC increased from 140 in 2007 to 280 in 2008, with a similar number in 2009.[64] Such incursion incidents involved not just the *Eastern Sector* around Arunachal Pradesh but now also the *Western Sector* around Aksai Chin/Ladakh; a particular widening development that Indian commentators like Bhaskar Roy have found "sinister" and which

[59] Bharat Verma, "Unmasking China", *India Defence Review*; 24.3 (July-September 2009) 3–9; cf. Chen Xiaochen, "Illusion of 'China's Attack on India Before 2012'," http://www.chinastakes.com/2009/7/illusion-of-chinas-attack-on-india-before-2012.html. accessed on July 17, 2009.

[60] M. Malik, "War Talk: Perceptual Gaps in "Chindia" Relations", *China Brief*, 9.20 (October 7, 2009): 6–9.

[61] H. Pant, "China, India: Back to the Boundary," *ISN Security Watch*, June 16, 2008.

[62] S. Ramachandran, "China Toys With India's Borders", *Asia Times*, June 27, 2008; though the PRC continues to deny such incursions, e.g. "China Rejects India's Allegation of Border Crossing Incidents", *Global Times*, June 11, 2009; "China Refutes Trespass Claims", *People's Daily/Global Times*, September 10, 2009.

[63] "No Significant Spike in Incursions; India, China in Touch: Rao", *IANS*, September 19, 2009.

[64] Following on from warnings by P. Das, "India Has to be Wary of Chinese Intrusions", *Strategic Comments* (IDSA), October 19, 2007.

Kanwal sees as "aggressive tactical posturing" on the part of China.[65] Admittedly, such border incursions, reflecting different perceptions of where the LAC actually is, have often been trivial in themselves; for example Chinese troops painting rocks in red paint or cross-LAC sheep grazing. Chinese troop movements near and around the narrow Siliguri corridor "chicken's neck" linking north-east India to the rest of India do though cause immediate geopolitical concerns to India.

Certainly, a substantive military build up along the Aksai Chin and Arunachal Pradesh borderlines has also been evident. Partly this has been an infrastructure race, in which India has been belatedly trying to catch up and match China's better established road, and now railway, infrastructure in these disputed borderlands.[66] It has also involved increasing military deployment, again by India to match China's already established forces in places like Linzi airbase. This is reflected in India increasing its ground forces in the border regions facing China.[67] In the *Eastern Sector*, this has also involved the Indian Air Force (IAF) deploying advanced long range Sukhoi Su-30 warplanes to Tezpur for potential cross-LAC operation complemented by six surface-to-air Akash missile squadrons.[68] In the *Western Sector*, this has also involved the IAF reactivating disused high altitude airstrips like Daulat Beg Oldi and Fukche.[69] Such reinforcements have been picked up in the PRC, and denounced as "unwise military moves".[70]

Brahma Chellaney expressed great caution, indeed scepticism, in 2006 about the state of play:

> Will India-China border talks ever end?[71] After a quarter century of unrewarding negotiations with Beijing, India ought to face up to the reality that it is being taken round and round the mulberry bush by an adversarial state that has little stake in an early border resolution; the more the talks have dragged on, the less Beijing has appeared interested in resolving the border disputes other than on its terms.

[65] B. Roy, "The Sinister Truth Behind China's Border Incursion Misadventure", *ANI*, September 18, 2009; G. Kanwal and M. Chansoria, "Breathing Fire: China's Aggressive Tactical Posturing", *Article* (Centre for Landwarfare Studies) 12, October 23, 2009.

[66] M. Rahman, "Arunachal Pradesh's Border Roads", *Article* (ICPS), 2924, July 29, 2009.

[67] "More India Troops in Disputed Territory", *People's Daily*, June 10 2009. Also R. Pandit, "Eye on China, is India Adding Muscle on East?", *Times of India*, July 2, 2009;

[68] Pandit, "Sukhoi Base in East to Counter China", *Times of India*, September 28, 2007; Pandit, "India to Deploy Akash Missiles in North-East to Deter China", *Times of India*, February 16, 2010.

[69] Ramachandran, "India Takes the High Ground Against China", *Asia Times*, June 14, 2008.

[70] "India's Unwise Military Moves", *People's Daily/Global Times*, June 11, 2009. In return see Pandit, "IAF Slams Chinese Objections to Airstrips in Ladakh, Arunachal", *Times of India*, October 15, 2009.

[71] B. Chellaney, "Will India-China Border Talks Ever End?", *Japan Times*, July 3, 2006.

It is time for it to draw the line, at least in the negotiations and to re-evaluate the very utility of staying absorbed in a never-ending process.[72]

Three years later, in the wake of the 2009 talks, his sense was the same, "the latest round of the unending and fruitless India-China talks on territorial disputes was a fresh reminder of the eroding utility of this process."

The PRC may indeed wish to keep the issue open as a way of distracting and threatening India but other dynamics may be leading the PRC to postpone decisive border negotiations. The PRC may well consider tightening its hold on Tibet itself as a greater priority, shaken during the disturbances that swept across Tibet and Tibetan areas in the spring of 2008? The PRC may also want to delay decisive border territorial resolution with India until it has resolved the Taiwan issue first? Garver also has wondered how far Beijing's apparent slowdown and readiness to avoid territorial resolution with India, is because of "understanding between Pakistan and China that neither will settle their territorial disputes with India independently of the other."[73]

Such a consideration point to the wider Pakistan-China-India triangle interplay around the disputed territories that stretch along the Himalayas from Arunachal Pradesh in the east to Aksai Chin and Kashmir in the west, which overlap with basic power balancing by the China-Pakistan "nexus" against India.[74] The overlaps between the varied territorial disputes was shown in 2009 when China gave visas for the entry of Kashmiri separatists to visit China, in the wake of India giving permission to the Dalai Lama to visit Arunachal Pradesh.

What is certain is that any quick decisive territorial resolution between India and China is unlikely. Following rising border frictions, the PRC media reported

China-India border dispute turns sour, with hard hitting nationalist blogs being noticeable in the Chinese official and state controlled media in the autumn of 2009.[75]

---

[72] Chellaney, "Why India is Clueless About China", *Rediff News*, September 7, 2009.

[73] Garver, "Sino-Indian Security Relation" in *Routledge Handbook of Asian Security Studies*, S. Ganguly, Andrew Scobell and Joseph Liow, eds. (London: Abingdon: Routledge, 2010), pp. 126–138, p. 131.

[74] K. Warikoo, ed., *Himalayan Frontiers of India : Historical, Geo-political and Strategic Perspectives* (London: Routledge, 2009); separate chapters on "Tibet and the Security of Indian Himalayan Belt", "India's Himalayan Frontier: Strategic Challenges and Opportunities in the 21st Century", "Strategic Dimensions of the Trans-Himalayan Frontiers", and "Great Game on Kashmir Frontiers".

[75] W. Qui, "China-India Border Dispute Turns Sour", *Global Times*, October 16, 2009; D. Rajan, "China: Nationalistic Blogs Raise New Issues Concerning Sino-Indian Border", *Paper* (SAAG), 3562, 24 December, 2009.

Admittedly, the Indian and Chinese leadership did again reaffirm dialogue in autumn 2009. However, this reaffirmation was in cautious terms "to gradually narrow differences on border issues between the two countries... to continue talks, with the aim of incrementally removing the barriers to a solution that was fair and acceptable to both sides."[76]

Despite the euphemistic headline from the official Chinese media that the two countries had reached "concensus on narrowing border differences'; in reality this merely indicated the existence of a gap without showing how and when it would be resolved. Talk of "gradually" and "incrementally removing" barriers to a solution flags up the slowness of any likely process, whilst offering nothing on what solutions could then emerge once such barriers have been, incrementally, removed.

What of solutions? Could outside arbitration be one way forward? Nehru himself had offered such a route in the immediate aftermath of war in the shape of the International Court of Justice (ICJ) at The Hague. However this was badly received in Parliament and Nehru then backed away immediately from this. In reality the ICJ seems ill equipped to deal with direct large-scale territorial disputes between major powers, whilst China's reluctance to have outside bodies disposing of sovereignty issues is higher even than India's.

One bilateral solution, which we can return to, involves a *logic of geography*, the "watershed/crestline" line along the Himalayas/Karakoram. It has a degree of clearness, "the advantage of having a border on such a prominent line as the high watershed of the Himalaya is that it is easily identifiable, historically traditional and politically neutral."[77]

It may also be sellable to both parties. Thus,

> as far as the Indian public is concerned, they have been brought up to believe that the Himalaya is the traditional boundary and they will be willing to concede any territory that lies beyond it without demur; such a boundary should also be acceptable to China as it is based on the same watershed principle which they have accepted in defining their boundaries with Myanmar, Sikkim and Nepal.[78]

This watershed principle was an angle suggested by Zhou Enlai in the abortive 1960 discussions. In effect, applying the watershed principle would leave Aksai Chin to China and almost all Arunachal Pradesh with India.

---

[76] "China, India Reach Consensus on Narrowing Border Differences", *Global Times*, October 24, 2009.
[77] Singh, "Resolving the Boundary Dispute".
[78] Ibid.

Admittedly, Tawang remains problematic. The Tawang District's 2,085 sq km is around 2.5 per cent of Arunachal Pradesh's entire 82,743 kilometres area, and its population of 38,924 is around 3.6 per cent of Arunachal Pradesh's 1,091,120 inhabitants (2001 figures), relatively small shares on paper. Neutralisation of the entire Tawang subdivision pocket might be an option. Within the Tawang District, given that the Tawang sub-district and the District capital Tawang (27°34'47"N) itself lies north of the Se la Pass and the Ka crest line (27°32'26"N), whereas the Lumla and Jang sub-districts lie on the southerly India-facing slopes of that crest line; could a division of Tawang District be carried out, with the Tawang sub-district allocated to China and the Lumla and Jang sub-districts allocated to India? However, local opinion at the District capital Tawang, population c. 20,000, would probably vote in favour of staying in "India" rather than going into the "PRC", though an independent "Tibet" option would provide an interesting third option. Having Tawang subdivision inhabitants relocate further south if they wished might be another solution, though ugly in political and human terms. Meanwhile, if the Dalai Lama's death was followed by any proclaimed rebirth at Tawang, a not impossible scenario, the situation would be still more complicated with the PRC.

Failing dramatic regime change scenarios of regime collapse/democratisation in the PRC, and re-establishment of a genuinely autonomous or independent Tibet, and Tawang notwithstanding, some sort of trade off involving Aksai Chin and Arunachal Pradesh seems the most likely way forward. In using relatively clear-cut neutral geographic principles, the deadlocked politics and unclear history could perhaps be sidelined? Such a trade-off would give neither side too much geopolitical advantage, but also ensure a degree of security for each? A *logic of geography* for the future for the national leaderships that would enable these two neighbours to get past the inconclusive divisive *logic of history* between them, and would provide a mutually satisfactory *logic of power* in terms of geopolitical equilibrium outcomes. Failing resolution of their territorial issues, the grinding tectonic plates along the Himalayas will continue to have their geopolitical counterpart as the two Asian giants look at each other across these disputed areas.

9

The Tibet Conundrum in Sino-Indian Ties

Elliot Sperling

The Tibet question in Sino-Indian relations is partly an unsettled inheritance from the Raj and partly an issue of persistent immediacy, one that has been able to renew itself and bedevil those relations into the present day. It has precipitated diplomatic and even military hostilities and still has the potential to claim lives in periodic (albeit low-level) border clashes. The question centres around two primary elements: the status of Tibet and the lack of common agreement on the border between the People's Republic of China (PRC) and India (i.e., the Indo-Tibetan border). One might think it would not be too difficult for India and China to isolate the two elements and deal with them separately, particularly since India has long accepted Tibet's status as a part of China. In truth, however, the matter of Tibet's status is inextricably linked to the border issue, which is rooted in the 1914 Simla Convention by which India and Tibet agreed to a frontier that, in the eastern sector, ran along the crest of the Himalayan range. And the force of the Simla agreement is dependent on recognition of the treaty-making authority of Tibet's traditional government. In 1950, however, with Tibet under attack from China, India acted to block United Nations (UN) action over Tibet by supporting the proposal of the United Kingdom in the General Assembly that no action be taken, in part because the British held that the status of the Tibetan government—the very government that had signed the Simla Treaty with India—was unclear. At best, the Indian delegate described Tibet as being historically associated with China while having enjoyed several decades of autonomy.[1] As a result, for decades a historical Catch-22 has hung over India's claim to the McMahon Line as the legitimate frontier between today's Arunachal Pradesh (the previous North East Frontier Agency) and Tibet. In fact, this was foreseen by then Indian Home Minister Vallabhai Patel.[2] Adding to the contradictions is the fact that India, although recognising Tibet as a part of China, has acquiesced since 1959 in the presence on Indian soil of a Tibetan Government-in-Exile (albeit no longer referring to itself nor formally recognized by India as such[3]) led by the Dalai Lama. Ultimately, the elements that make up India's Tibet conundrum cannot be easily divvied up and dealt with piecemeal; they are simply too closely intertwined.

A Tangled History

Although India agrees that Tibet is a part of China, the different interpretations of Tibet's status that emerged in the nineteenth century have dogged the Tibet issue into the twenty-first. In part this also relates to the change that occurred with the end of the Qing Dynasty in 1911, when the successor state, the Republic of China, laid claim to the non-Chinese dominions that had constituted a large part of what had been a Manchu Empire. The narrative by which Tibet is claimed as an historical part of China only took its most recognisable form in the middle of the twentieth century and even now seems to be going through a further elaboration. Whereas, contemporary China had for decades asserted that Tibet had been made an integral part of China by the Mongol rulers of the thirteenth-century Yuan Dynasty (as history, a somewhat problematic assertion), more recently official media have begun claiming Tibet as a part of China "since human activity began" on the Tibetan Plateau.[4] This assertion is not simply a bit of arcane hyperbole.

---

[1] See the record of the 24 November 1950 meeting of the General Assembly in Chanakya Sen, *Tibet Disappears* (Bombay: Asia Publishing House, 1960), pp. 102–103. On the Simla Convention and its historical background, see Alistair Lamb, *The McMahon Line: A Study in the Relations Between India, China and Tibet* (London: Routledge & Kegan Paul, 1966), 2 volumes.

[2] John W. Garver, *Protracted Contest: Sino-Indian Rivalry in the Twentieth Century* (Seattle: University of Washington press, 2001), p. 47.

[3] The Tibetan Government-in-Exile refers to itself as "the Central Tibetan Administration" in English, though government letters and documents continue to bear the emblem of the Tibetan government with its traditional motto.

[4] See Elliot Sperling, *The Tibet-China Conflict: History and Polemics* (Washington: East-West Center, 2004), p. 11; and "Tibet and China: the Interpretation of History Since 1950," *China Perspectives* 2009/3, pp. 33–35.

It commands notice due to the fact that the Tibet that is said to have been Chinese since prehistoric times is understood to include the territory claimed by the modern PRC, including modern-day Arunachal Pradesh.[5]

A more accurate assessment of Tibet's status vis-à-vis China would have to note that Tibet was integrated into the Qing Empire during the course of the eighteenth century, but its administration—like that of Mongolia, today an independent state—was kept separate from the administration of China. Although some writers who are sympathetic to Tibetan aspirations have tried to ascribe the perception of this integration to a misunderstanding of the relationship between Buddhism and politics at the level of the Qing court, the administrative record of the Qing makes Tibet's subjection to Qing rule indisputable.[6] The strength of that rule wavered, however, particularly as the Qing was forced to deal elsewhere with imperialist encroachments on its territory. As the effectiveness of the Qing writ in Tibet diminished, British India came to regard it as unsubstantial; a fact illustrated by Curzon's well-known remark that "We regard the so-called suzerainty of China over Tibet as a constitutional fiction..."[7]

With the collapse of the Qing Dynasty after the 1911 Revolution, the Dalai Lama declared Tibet's independence (an act obviously indicating a prior lack of such a status). But the new Chinese republic refused to recognise this and the country's status, as far as international recognition was concerned, seemed to be in limbo. The tri-partite Simla Conference was an attempt to rectify the situation, and indeed under the resulting Simla Convention an arrangement was worked out creating an Inner and an Outer Tibet, the latter understood to be free of Chinese interference, though under a nominally recognised Chinese suzerainty. The accord also denied China any rights under the convention unless it was formally signed,[8] something the Chinese government ultimately refused to do, even though its representative had initialled the document. Britain and Tibet did sign and as a result Tibet found

---

[5] Elliot Sperling, "Tibet and China: The Interpretation of History since 1950", *China Perspectives* 3 (2009), pp. 34–35. The borders said to delimit China are those of the Qing Dynasty at its height in the eighteenth century. See the map of these borders in Tan Qixiang 谭其骧, ed., *Zhongguo lishi dituji* 中国历史地图集, *Zhongguo bianjiang shidi yanjiu* (Shanghai: Cartographic Publishing House, 1987) vol. 8, plates 3–4.

[6] Elliot Sperling, *The Tibet–China Conflict: History and Polemics* (Washington: East–West Center, 2004) pp. 27–30.

[7] Parshotam Mehra, *The Younghusband Mission: An Interpretation* (Bombay: Asia Publishing House, 1968), p. 161.

[8] See the text of the Simla Convention in Lamb 1966, pp. 620–625.

itself dealing with British India for several decades without any implication of Chinese suzerainty or sovereignty (in later years a representative of British, and later independent, India took up official residence in Lhasa). And as noted, the border arrangements attached to the convention also created the frontier lines that today remain disputed between China and India.

Although China did not accept the border agreed to by Tibet and Britain, it focused most of its attention on the more important task of simply maintaining its claims to Tibet. For its part, Britain actually did little to alter the situation on the ground in those areas ceded by the Simla Convention. Tibetan aristocrats with holdings south of the McMahon line continued to collect taxes and largely administer their lands as before.[9] In practical matters of bilateral relations Britain dealt with Tibet as if it were independent, not referring to issues between India and Tibet to the Chinese government. At the same time, Britain did not designate its representatives in Tibet ambassadors, nor did it designate the legation they eventually set up in Lhasa an embassy. Prior to 1949, the Tibet issue came to the fore only intermittently between China and Britain and afterwards between independent India and China. Instances included China's questioning the status of Tibetan officials travelling abroad after World War II, as well as China's objection to Tibetan participation (as an independent country) in the 1947 Asian Relations Conference in New Delhi.[10]

Only after Indian independence and the 1949 Chinese revolution did India actively assert jurisdiction over territory south of the McMahon Line. Starting in early 1951, Indian troops were dispatched into the area of what is today Arunachal Pradesh to enforce Indian claims and to halt the collection of taxes and other payments by Tibetans from outside the region.[11] At the same time, the PRC, while not acting forcefully, did not relinquish China's previous claims to the region. But the contradictions that were to plague India's position were starting to emerge. When the People's Liberation Army (PLA) attacked the area under the Dalai Lama's jurisdiction in October 1950, the Tibetan government attempted to appeal to several countries and to the UN. India's response was to articulate hopes for a peaceful resolution

[9] Elliot Sperling, "The Politics of History and the Indo-Tibetan Border (1987–1988)," *India Review*, 7.3 (2008), pp. 230–231.

[10] Melvyn C. Goldstein, *A History of Modern Tibet 1913–1951: The Demise of the Lamaist State* (Berkeley: University of California Press, 1989), pp. 522–610.

[11] Elliot Sperling, "The Politics of History and the Indo–Tibetan Border (1987–1988)," *India Review* 7.3 (2008), pp. 230–231.

of the problem while seeking to avoid outside intervention for the sake of good relations with the new Chinese government.[12] Hence, India's support for the position of the United Kingdom which held that UN action was unwarranted because of the unclear status of Tibet. By that act, however, India placed itself in the untenable position of claiming a border agreed to by a Tibetan government whose status it was now accepting as unclear. This was a difficult balancing act at best: claiming a border with China that China categorically rejected while otherwise trying to maintain positive ties with China as if there were no major problems lurking in the background. But both India and China had a large number of other problems with which to deal and a modus vivendi was certainly in both of their interests. Accordingly, the two countries reached the well-known Panch Sheel Agreement (Agreement Between the Republic of India and the People's Republic of China on Trade and intercourse Between Tibet Region of China and India) in 1954 which essentially allowed India to continue the economic relations it had enjoyed with Tibet before 1951 within the context of China's newly established sovereignty over the area, a sovereignty that India formally recognised.[13]

The seeds of armed conflict were very much in place and the inherent contradictions in the relationship began to haunt India's relations with China from an early stage. In the Western Himalayan sector, China had taken steps to assert its claims even before it had attained full possession of Tibet. In its initial attack on Tibet in October 1950 one part of the invading force marched from the West and crossed through territory in the Aksai Chin,[14] the area that would see harsh fighting between India and China in 1962. At the time India seemed to be unaware of the Chinese incursion, an indication of the remoteness of the territory in question and India's tardiness in taking practical steps to realise what it claimed on paper.

Before long, however, the unresolved questions in Sino-Indian relations were exacerbated by China's ensuing difficulties in Tibet. Following the military defeat of the small Tibetan army, Tibet was incorporated into China in May, 1951, by the "Seventeen–Point Agreement on Measures for

---

[12] John W. Garver, *Protracted Contest: Sino–Indian Rivalry in the Twentieth Century* (Seattle: University of Washington Press, 2001), pp. 49–51.

[13] The text of the agreement, signed on April 29, 1954, as well as associated diplomatic notes, can be found in Lamb 1966, pp. 638–644.

[14] Tsering Shakya, *The Dragon in the Land of Snows: A History of Modern Tibet Since 1947* (New York: Columbia University Press, 1999), p. 278.

the Peaceful Liberation of Tibet," an instrument signed in Beijing (without the full authorisation of the Dalai Lama's government, but accepted by it nonetheless).[15] Not long after, following the entry of the PLA into Lhasa, the first signs of unrest appeared. During this period Tibet still retained its traditional government, albeit now under the sovereignty of the PRC, and Tibetans still easily transited into and out of India via Kalimpong. A Tibetan an expatriate community living in the Darjeeling-Kalimpong area made the situation inside Tibet known by sporadically disseminating reports. Sympathy for Tibet, as a victim of unprovoked aggression, prevailed in certain Indian circles in spite of Nehru's policy of friendship with China.[16] Not unsurprisingly, strong suspicions began to develop in China about Indian attitudes and intentions regarding Tibet, in particular a view that the policies and attitudes of independent India were influenced by the propaganda and machinations of anti-China (i.e., imperialist) parties.[17]

Revolt and War

In 1956, the Dalai Lama visited India for the celebrations to mark the 2,500th anniversary of the Buddha's birth. By that time open revolt had flared in the eastern portions of the Tibetan Plateau, in areas outside the jurisdiction of the Dalai Lama's government. The links between Tibetans there and Tibetans inside, what was to become the Tibet Autonomous Region in 1965, were close and the policies that had provoked a revolt and concomitant rising nationalism in the East did not leave the latter untroubled. During his visit to India, the Dalai Lama confided to Nehru his anxieties about what was happening and the fact that he was considering not returning to Tibet. Nehru signalled the state of affairs to China and the Chinese Premier Zhou Enlai arrived in Delhi shortly thereafter to meet with the Dalai Lama and attempt to assuage his concerns. The Dalai Lama ultimately returned to Tibet but the affair made it clear that India continued to maintain interests in Tibet. The greeting that the Dalai Lama received from Tibetan exiles in India added to China's unease with Indian policy.[18]

---

[15] Ibid, p 70.
[16] John W. Garver, *Protracted Contest: Sino–Indian Rivalry in the Twentieth Century* (Seattle: University of Washington Press, 2001), pp 44–52, etc.
[17] Thus the implications of the *People's Daily* editorial on Nehru in the aftermath of the 1959 revolt. See *Concerning the Question of Tibet* (Peking: Foreign Languages Press, 1959), pp. 265–267.
[18] On the Dalai Lama's 1956 visit to India and the events associated with it, see Shakya 1999, pp. 148–162.

In that regard, China was increasingly concerned about what it considered anti-China activities being carried out on Indian soil. In addition to the expatriate Tibetan community in the Darjeeling-Kalimpong area, there were agents of the Taiwan-based Kuomintang (KMT) regime as well as those who passed information to the US and others. The Chinese leadership viewed Kalimpong as a centre of espionage and sabotage and asserted that Nehru was well aware of the fact.[19]

The situation became ever more confrontational when the ongoing revolt in Tibet culminated in an uprising in Lhasa, the Tibetan capital, in March, 1959. In its aftermath the Dalai Lama fled south, crossing into India and setting off an exodus of Tibetans, the reverberations of which are still felt. From that point on a substantial Tibetan exile community has resided in India, its presence and its political agenda often becoming issues in Sino-Indian relations. Not long after leaving Lhasa, the Dalai Lama renounced the Seventeen-Point Agreement and declared the restoration of Tibet's independence. After crossing into India he established a government-in-exile. As noted above, India did not formally recognise the government and the Dalai Lama was ultimately quartered in Dharamsala, at the time a former hill station lacking convenient, quick access to the Indian capital. But the very presence of the exiles and their protection by India rankled in China. Chinese criticism of Nehru and his policies intensified, while at the same time sympathy for Tibetan suffering under Chinese rule added to a growing sense in political circles that India's abandonment of Tibet in 1950 had created a real threat along the northern border and fostered wide public sympathy for the Tibetans, making it a real issue in India's internal politics.[20]

The opposing elements inherent in the Tibet situation came together in the 1962 border war between India and China: the unsettled nature of the border, China's harsh rule in Tibet, general Indian sympathies for Tibet, and China's swift defeat of India's forces combined to harden hostile attitudes more than ever. Against this background, India began to take more concrete steps in contesting China's presence on the border. These included the creation and training of a Special Frontier Force to operate as part of the Indian army. Among some politicians, positions of studied ambiguity or even outright rejection regarding the question of China's rights to Tibet gained ground.[21]

---

[19] Ibid, p. 158.
[20] John W. Garver, *Protracted Contest: Sino–Indian Rivalry in the Twentieth Century* (Seattle: University of Washington Press, 2001), p. 57.
[21] Ibid, p. 63.

In addition, India began a brief collaboration with the United States (US) on the Tibet issue, in marked contradiction to earlier postures meant to distance India from the politics of the Cold War. Thus, the US helped train Tibetans for military purposes and provided intelligence to India while India, for its part, allowed the US to use its territory for monitoring purposes.[22] At this point relations between India and China could hardly have been worse; and the issues at the core of it all were related to the incorporation of Tibet into the PRC.

Tibetan Activism in India

Operating within the limits both of Indian law and the political pluralism of Indian society, the Tibetan exiles had significant leeway to promote the Tibetan cause. An assortment of Tibetan associations, including the Tibetan Youth Congress, the Tibetan Women's Association, and others, representing different constituencies in exile society, have operated for decades in Dharamsala with branches elsewhere in Indian cities and communities with significant Tibetan refugee populations. Similarly, shortly after the Dalai Lama's arrival in India, the Tibetan Government-in-Exile, even without territorial sovereignty, began functioning with a well formed bureaucratic apparatus that has grown to include a cabinet with various departments, an elected assembly, and, significantly, representative offices in various parts of the world. That this was permitted by India and that it has continued over the years was partly tactical, partly a result of inertia (once entrenched, it would have proven difficult, though not impossible, to shut down), and partly a result of the sincere sympathy for the plight of Tibet evinced by sectors of the Indian public and the Indian political class. As already noted, since Nehru's acquiescence to China's annexation of Tibet a sense of regret, if not of a moral wrong, has hung over the Tibet issue as far as a number of Indian political figures were concerned.

The Tibetan exile authorities have maintained open lines to those in power over the course of different Indian governments. Whether substantive or not, meetings between Indian leaders and the Dalai Lama or his representatives have served to maintain the visibility of the Tibet issue within India. Critical

---

[22] Kenneth Conboy and James Morrison, *The CIA's Secret War in Tibet* (Lawrence: University of Kansas Press, 2002), pp. 176–187, 206–209; and Steven A. Hoffmann, "Rethinking the Linkage Between Tibet and the China–India Border Conflict: A Realist Approach," *Journal of Cold War Studies* 8.3 (Summer 2006), pp. 187–88.

comments about the exile Tibetan position or comments supportive of Chinese policies in Tibet articulated by Indian political or media figures have occasioned verbal protests as Tibetans avail themselves of the democratic tools of Indian society. The rights to free speech and to peaceful assembly as well as the exercise of peaceful civil disobedience (with ensuing arrests and releases) have also been used by the exiles to organise demonstrations with which to confront visiting Chinese officials and dignitaries (producing, in turn, official protests from the Chinese side). Finally, the Government of India has continually maintained a liaison office in Dharamsala, seat of the Tibetan Government-in-Exile, staffed in some instances by personnel with foreign ministry backgrounds.

Tibetan exile society has successfully created a space for itself within India, though it is not without obvious limits. Although India provided military training for Tibetans, it has not permitted its territory to be used for armed attacks or incursions into Tibet. For that, however, the Tibetans had – for a brief period – a Central Intelligence Agency (CIA)-supported base in the Nepalese border area of Mustang from which raids into Tibet were launched. The base operated from 1961 to 1974[23] and the links between the Tibetan guerrillas there and the Dalai Lama's government in exile were not difficult to perceive; indeed, it was the Dalai Lama's brother, Gyalo Thondup, who was largely responsible for establishing the operation. During this time of overt hostility between India and China there was little reason for India to do other than turn a blind eye to these activities (which all parties pretended to keep covert). It is worth noting that China was itself supporting separatist movements in India's Northeast, funnelling arms and money to groups such as the Nagas.[24]

With regard to the military training of Tibetans, the most significant element was the establishment of the aforementioned Special Frontier Force within the Indian Army and the recruitment of Tibetans to serve in it. Established in 1963, the force was commanded by Brigadier S.S. Uban and based at Chakrata, just outside Dehra Dun.[25] Though it was supported at first by the US, joint co-operation in the training of Tibetan fighters continued only until the beginning of 1971 and the onset of the deep estrangement that characterized Indo-American relations for over two decades. Overall, the Tibetan force

---

[23] Ibid, pp. 196–204, 246–253.
[24] John W. Garver, *Protracted Contest: Sino–Indian Rivalry in the Twentieth Century* (Seattle: University of Washington Press, 2001), pp. 94–95.
[25] Kenneth Conboy and James Morrison, *The CIA's Secret War in Tibet* (Lawrence: University of Kansas Press, 2002), pp. 177–187.

remained a credible unit in the Indian Army and though it was never used for the purpose that many eager Tibetan recruits assumed it was meant to serve – the liberation of Tibet – the unit distinguished itself in the war for Bangladesh, earning a large number of citations while sustaining heavy casualties.[26]

If the Indian government was not substantively interested in the liberation of Tibet, it must be noted that the Dalai Lama himself had likewise abandoned that same goal in the early 1970s, a fact that must certainly have been known in Indian government circles. Still, the Dalai Lama had come into exile at the head of a movement for Tibetan independence and in spite of his decision to give up that goal it remained the publicly-stated aspiration of his followers and his government-in-exile until he made a public statement on the subject in 1988 in Strasbourg, explicitly proposing that Tibet remain an "entity" within China.[27]

Tibet and Post-Mao Regional Politics

The change in the Dalai Lama's policy was not unrelated to external factors, including a cutoff in US aid for the resistance in Nepal and the general improvement in China's relations with the outside world following the opening to the US in 1971–72. This trend intensified after the rise of Deng Xiaoping in the late 1970s. India too was part of this global tide of greater contact and interaction with China, though the start of renewed Sino-Indian diplomacy was not met with great happiness by many sectors of Tibetan exile society in India. Even after the Dalai Lama's public acknowledgement that he was opposed to seeking independence for Tibet, a somewhat odd ritual persisted for a while: Tibetans would criticise remarks from Indian political figures asserting their acceptance that Tibet was a part of China, while uttering nothing when the same position was articulated by the Dalai Lama.[28] In India's negotiations with China, the Tibet issue has been a persistent presence. High-level bilateral contacts resumed in 1979, with then Foreign Minister Atal Bihari Vajpayee's visit to Beijing. But the more significant event for Tibetan exiles was Prime Minister Rajiv Gandhi's 1988 visit to China.[29] In the atmosphere that

---

[26] Ibid, pp. 244–245.

[27] Tsering Shakya, *The Dragon in the Land of Snows: A History of Modern Tibet Since 1947* (New York: Columbia University Press, 1999), p. 423.

[28] See, for instance the editorial "India's Mistake, Tibet's Tragedy," *Tibetan Review* 32.1 (January, 1997), p. 3, disparaging Prime Minister Deve Gowda's reiteration of India's acceptance of Tibet as an integral part of China.

[29] John W. Garver, *Protracted Contest: Sino–Indian Rivalry in the Twentieth Century* (Seattle: University of Washington Press, 2001), p. 72.

ensued, India reiterated its recognition of China's unquestioned sovereignty over Tibet, a restatement of policy from the early Nehru years. Not unexpectedly some of the talk of Sino-Indian rapprochement elicited discomfort among segments of the refugee community.[30] The Tibet issue has also figured as an element in the jockeying between India and China over Nepal. The courtship of the Nepalese government by China has never been viewed dispassionately by India. Indeed, following the 1962 war, China went out of its way to extend friendship to Nepal, with a variety of aid programs and, perhaps most conspicuously (after having launched a 1960 operation against Tibetan fighters who had were using Nepalese territory as an operating base), by dealing patiently with the fact that a CIA-backed Tibetan force operated from the Mustang region and staged attacks against Chinese units in Tibet: all while strongly attacking India over the Tibet issue.[31]

Less subject to overt Chinese criticism was the fact that India continued to allow Tibetan refugees to remain in India where they inevitably gravitated to the already established strongly anti-Chinese exile communities. In the late 1970s and early 1980s China adopted a guardedly more open policy towards the exile community, hoping to encourage at least some of them to return to Tibet by permitting a number of family visits back and forth between Tibetans in exile and those in Tibet. Subsequently, such travel has come to be more restricted and as a result there is still an ongoing stream of Tibetans coming into Nepal and then travelling on to India in contravention of Chinese laws. These Tibetans add to the refugee community, and although India has long since stopped granting refugee status automatically to Tibetans who arrive within its borders, it has not returned them against their will to Tibet. It is understood, however, that along with those legitimately coming to India are some who provide intelligence to the Chinese authorities on the exile community.

In recent years, China has periodically tried to cut off the Nepalese route taken by almost all of the newer refugees, but up until recently this was done to little avail. Refugees still manage to get into Nepal and from there to cross the border into India, in a manner that can hardly be unknown to the Indian authorities. Indeed, the very high-profile escape in 2000 of the Karma-pa Lama, one of the

---

[30] "News in Brief," *Tibetan Review* 24.2 (February, 1989), p. 11: "Indian Prime Minister Rajiv Gandhi has been criticized by all Tibetan organizations for describing Tibet as "an autonomous region of China" during his recent visit to China. Of course, the an Indian leader was saying exactly what the Dalai Lama had been saying.

[31] John W. Garver, *Protracted Contest: Sino–Indian Rivalry in the Twentieth Century* (Seattle: University of Washington Press, 2001), pp. 147–149.

most revered lamas then in Tibet, took this route. Nevertheless, in the last few years it has become established policy for China to use its increased economic clout and ability to provide aid for Nepal to influence Nepalese attitudes on the Tibet issue, essentially to ensure that Nepal does not become a base for "anti-China" activities on the part of the Tibetan refugees resident in the country. And Nepal has accordingly adopted increasingly stricter police measures to suppress Tibetan protests against China, especially following the 2008 demonstrations in Tibet which elicited much international attention and sympathy. Border areas are now patrolled with greater security, in large part due to the financial and logistical support China is providing to Nepal.[32] Obviously, as noted, India does not look at China's greater presence in Nepal without concern. Less obvious, perhaps, is the fact that it is the Tibet issue that provides the basic context for China's presence there. Thus, Nepal, culturally and economically a part of South Asia, has become yet one more area in which India is being overtly challenged by China.

The Persisting Tibetan Element in the Border Issue

And this brings us back to the fact that attempts on both the Indian and Chinese sides to grapple with the question of improved relations always seem to run into problems with the border issue, and the border issue is intrinsically connected to the larger Tibet issue. Indeed, although India's recognition of Tibet as a part of China has long been an accomplished fact, for its part China has consistently declined to formally recognise Sikkim as a part of India with any absolute finality, as if that balances out any hints of illegitimacy about its annexation of Tibet.[33] Thus, talks on the border issue continue to be inconclusive and India remains, as noted at the outset, in the position of claiming validity for a border agreement signed by a Tibetan government whose status and competence it declined to support on the eve of China's annexation.

The centrality of the border issue to the Tibet issue and to Sino-Indian relations has manifested itself a number of times, most recently in November, 2009, when the Dalai Lama visited the Tawang district in Arunachal Pradesh. Tawang, which lies south of the McMahon Line, was very much a part of the realm of Tibetan culture: the sixth Dalai Lama was born there in 1683. The present Dalai Lama's visit, under Indian auspices, elicited sharp criticism from China, since it was a very public demonstration of the Dalai Lama's recognition of the validity

---

[32] Jim Yardley, "China Intensifies Tug of War with India on Nepal," *New York Times* February 17, 2010.
[33] "Border Games. Rectifying an Inconvenient History," TibetInfoNet Update – Special Report, November 8, 2009: http://www.tibetinfonet.nit/content/update/149; accessed February 18, 2010.

of the McMahon Line. More pointedly for Tibetans, it also highlighted the fact that in the face of the Dalai Lama's eventual demise (he was born in 1935) the Tibetan cultural world offers many regions outside the PRC from which a successor can be found.[34] In a sense, this also illustrates how China's logic about the traditional Tibetan presence in Arunachal Pradesh founders on the rocks of India's makeup as a state: there are other areas within India that are equally part of the Tibetan cultural realm and which have had important historical roles in that world – and yet their incorporation within India is not problematic. The presence of these areas – including Ladakh and parts of Himachal Pradesh – in India is not contested nor, (in contrast with Tibet) has that presence precipitated anything resembling armed revolt, years of resistance and, more recently, intense demonstrations of nationalist discontent. Ironically, though, China has offered to accept India's control of the area south of the McMahon Line in return for an acceptance of China's presence in those areas in the Western Himalaya that China both claims and controls.[35] India, however, has declined to link the two border issues. Power politics aside, it would be hard to imagine the population in Arunachal Pradesh willingly accepting a proposal placing itself under Chinese rule. While the border in the Western sector is more a question of demarcated lines rather than significant populations (unlike the state of affairs in the disputed Eastern sector), the civilisational issue – if one wishes to view things from that perspective – is not simple. The culturally Tibetan populations in the disputed areas harbour no manifest desire to throw off Indian rule, something that cannot be said of the population on the Chinese side vis-à-vis PRC rule. The fact of the Dalai Lama's presence in India, the manner with which he has been treated there, and the history of PRC problems with Tibetan Buddhism contribute to the larger picture, as does the Tibetan exile administration's public support for the Indian position on the McMahon Line.[36]

A pertinent illustration of the intertwined elements of the Tibet issue in Sino-Indian relations can be found in the aftermath of the border clashes around Sumdurong chu in 1986–87. In what can only have been a move to shore up

---

[34] The Dalai Lama has stated on several occasions that he would not be reborn in territory under China's control. See, for example, "Dalai Lama not to Reincarnate in China," Tibetan Review 34.8 (August, 1999), p. 7.

[35] John W. Garver, *Protracted Contest: Sino–Indian Rivalry in the Twentieth Century* (Seattle: University of Washington Press, 2001), pp. 100–106. See also Steven A. Hoffmann, "Rethinking the Linkage between Tibet and China–India Border Conflict: A Realist Approach", *Journal of Cold War Studies* 8.3 (2006), pp. 177 and 183.

[36] Edward Wong, "China and India Dispute Enclave on Edge of Tibet", *New York Times,* September 3, 2009 quotes the exile Prime Minister, Samdhong Rinpoche on the McMahon Line: "We recognize it because we agreed to it."

internal support within Tibet during a time of serious border tensions with India, in 1988 China printed and circulated a volume of memoirs, historical commentary, and even one rare historical text, all in a collection meant to prove India's claim to the McMahon Line to be in violation of the traditional boundary. Of course, the texts and even the memoirs related not to direct Chinese possession of the disputed area but to the customary Tibetan presence and administration (including taxation practices) there. Significantly, the volume never appeared in an English-language version, which would have been expected if the contexts were meant to bolster China's claims in the international arena. Rather, it appears to have been meant wholly for domestic propaganda purposes; indeed, it is doubtful if anyone in India (aside from a handful of Tibetan scholars) was aware of it when it appeared.[37] The memoirs bear the marks of heavy-handed Chinese political writing, with accounts of the arrival of Indian forces in the region in 1951 and even stories implicating India in the mysterious death of a Tibetan trying to collect traditional taxes there during the same period.[38] In effect this episode is symptomatic of a Chinese penchant for internal propaganda – in this case, unseen by outside observers – due to underlying insecurities about Tibetan loyalties on the Chinese side of the frontier.

China's militarisation of the Tibetan Plateau is another important piece of the complex relationship between India and China. Early on, following Tibet's absorption, China set out to build three major roads on the Tibetan Plateau. These roads made it possible for China to garrison and secure the area as never before. In addition, in 2006 a rail line between Beijing and Lhasa became operational. The actual number of Chinese troops stationed on the plateau is not public information and only approximations can be made. However, estimates place a total Chinese military force of possibly 400,000 in the Tibet Autonomous Region, out of which as many as 60,000 may be stationed in Lhasa. But it is impossible to know exactly how many soldiers are there at any specific time. Military exercises have shown that China has the capability of rapidly mobilising and airlifting significant forces into Tibet from surrounding provinces. The number of airfields on the Plateau is at least 25, but it is expanding; in 2010 a new airport was announced for Nagchu, some 230 kilometres to the north of Lhasa. In addition, China has significant nuclear launch facilities on the Tibetan Plateau.[39]

---

[37] Elliot Sperling, "The Politics of History and the Indo–Tibetan Border (1987–1988)", *India Review* 7.3 (2008), pp. 235–36.

[38] Ibid, p. 233.

[39] Elliot Sperling "The Tibetan question and security in Asia," in Sumit Ganguly, Andrew Scobell and Joseph Chinyong Liow, eds., *The Routledge Handbook of Asian Security Studies* (London: Routledge, 2010), p. 69.

China has been counting on the demise of the Dalai Lama to end the Tibet issue as a factor in its relationship with India and a perennial international public relations problem. Although a series of talks have occurred between representatives of the Dalai Lama and representatives of the Chinese government, beginning in 1979, they have long since become inconclusive (the most recent round concluded in January, 2010), and have served largely to deflect criticism from outside that China obstructs progress on the Tibet issue by refusing to speak to the Dalai Lama. That China has no intention of reaching an agreement with him has long been clear; the Dalai Lama's side, having decided to reach a negotiated agreement with China, long ago made the crucial concession: acceptance of Tibet as a part of China. Having achieved that, China now has little desire to see the Dalai Lama back in Tibet, especially as he could easily become the focus of Tibetan national aspirations, regardless of what he himself may want. One might also note that the lack of seriousness in the talks that is evidenced by what is not there: border issues. China has demanded that the Dalai Lama accept Tibet as a part of China, that he accept Taiwan as a part of China, and that he concede a number of other things as well (e.g., the legitimacy of socialist rule in Tibet). But it hasn't demanded that he accept the Tibetan borders that China claims, something that should otherwise be on the table in serious talks. In light of the exile government's articulated position that the McMahon Line is the valid border, a demand for recognition of China's position on the border question would be basic.

Ultimately, the Tibet issue will likely continue to complicate India's dealings with China. As things now stand, India may soon have a resident Tibetan refugee community that has reached no accommodation with China (because there is none to be reached) and which (as per Chinese strategy) is deprived of a leader whose international visibility made the Tibetan movement viable. At that point China may assume that the Tibet issue will cease to be a factor on Sino-Indian relations just as it believes the issue will quickly vanish as a problem in other areas of its international relations. But this is not necessarily how things will play out, for there will still remain the problem of India's claims to a border that was agreed to by a Tibetan government. In effect, the Tibet issue shows no sign of vanishing from Sino-Indian relations overnight.

10

China in South Asia

A Tightening Embrace

Harsh V. Pant

New Delhi has long viewed South Asia as India's exclusive sphere of influence and has sought to prevent the intervention of external powers in the affairs of the region. The notion of a Monroe Doctrine similar to the one proclaimed for the Western Hemisphere by the United States (US) in the nineteenth century was explored by Jawaharlal Nehru, India's first Prime Minister.[1] Henceforth, the security of its neighbouring states was considered to be intricately linked with India's own security. With India's rise in the global interstate hierarchy in recent years, tensions have emerged between India's purported role on the world stage and demands of the challenges it faces in its own neighbourhood. South Asia is a difficult neighbourhood and India's strategic periphery continues to witness continuous turmoil and uncertainty. The instability in Pakistan, Afghanistan, Bangladesh, Nepal, Sri Lanka and Myanmar is a major inhibiting factor for India to realise its dream of becoming a major global player. India's attempts to emerge as a global economic power is marred by the uncertainty in the region and this has even stalled India's attempts at building inter-dependencies and enhancing connectivity. India is surrounded by several weak states that view New Delhi's hegemonic status in the region with suspicion. The conundrum India faces is that – while it is seen as unresponsive to the concerns of its neighbours – any diplomatic

---

[1] C. Raja Mohan, "Beyond India's Monroe Doctrine," *The Hindu*, January 2, 2003.

aggressiveness on its part is also viewed with suspicion and often resentment. The structural position of India in the region makes it highly likely that Indian predominance will continue to be resented by its smaller neighbours even as instability nearby continues to have the potential of upsetting its own delicate political balance. However, a policy of "splendid isolation" is not an option and India's desire to emerge as a major global player will remain just that, a desire, unless it engages its immediate neighbourhood more meaningfully and emerges as a net provider of regional peace and stability.

The inability of India to assume a leadership role in its neighbourhood has been exploited by China that has made a concerted attempt over the last few years to fill the void. China is today more deeply involved in South Asia than it has ever been. This chapter examines the growing role of China in South Asia over the last decade and its implications for India. For a long time, only Pakistan among India's neighbours used China to further its strategic agenda vis-à-vis India. China-Pakistan collusion on the nuclear issue was probably the high point of this relationship. However, increasingly most of India's neighbours have made an attempt to court China as an extra-regional power in order to prevent India from asserting its regional supremacy. This strategy of using China to counterbalance India has been followed by Bangladesh, Sri Lanka and Nepal to varying degrees. And China has only been too willing to play this balance of power game as it not only enhances China's influence in South Asia but also keeps India bogged down in South Asian affairs, thereby preventing its emergence from the straightjacket of a mere "South Asia power" to a major global player, something that India has long desired.

Sino-Pakistan Ties: An "All-Weather" Friendship

Pakistan was among the first countries in 1950 to recognise the People's Republic of China (PRC) and break diplomatic ties with the PRC. Based on their convergent interests vis-à-vis India, China and Pakistan reached a strategic understanding in mid-1950s, a bond that has only strengthened ever since. Sino-Pakistan ties gained particular momentum in the aftermath of the 1962 Sino-Indian war when the two states signed a boundary agreement recognising Chinese control over portions of the disputed Kashmir territory and since then the ties have been so strong that the Chinese President Hu Jintao has described the relationship as "higher than mountains and deeper than oceans."[2]

---

[2] Issam Ahmed, "China–Pakistan Deal Raises Fear of Nuclear Proliferation," *Christian Science Monitor*, July, 2010.

Pakistan's President, Asif Ali Zardari, has suggested that "No relationship between two sovereign states is as unique and durable as that between Pakistan and China."[3]

Maintaining close ties with China has been a priority for Islamabad and Beijing has provided extensive economic, military and technical assistance to Pakistan over the years. It was Pakistan that in early 1970s enabled China to cultivate its ties with the West and the US in particular, becoming the conduit for Henry Kissinger's landmark secret visit to China in 1971 and has been instrumental in bringing China closer to the larger Muslim world. Pakistan enjoys a multifaceted and deep-rooted relationship with China underpinned by mutual trust and confidence. Pakistan has also supported China on all issues of importance to the later, especially those related to the question of China's sovereignty such as Taiwan, Xinjiang and Tibet and other sensitive issues such as human rights. China has reciprocated by supporting Pakistan's stance on Kashmir in return.

Over the years, China has emerged as Pakistan's largest defence supplier. Military co-operation between the two has deepened with joint projects producing armaments ranging from fighter jets to guided missile frigates. China is a steady source of military hardware to the resource-deficient Pakistani Army. It has not only given technology assistance to Pakistan but has also helped Pakistan to set up mass weapons production factories. Pakistan's military modernisation is dependent on Chinese largesse, with China supplying Pakistan with short-range M-11 missiles and helping Pakistan in the development of the Shaheen-1 ballistic missile.[4] In the last two decades, these two states have been actively involved in a range of joint ventures, including the JF-17 fighter aircraft used for delivering nuclear weapons, an Airborne Warning and Control System, and the Babur cruise missile (the dimensions of which exactly replicate those of the Hong Niao Chinese cruise missile). The JF-17 venture is particularly significant given its utility in delivering nuclear weapons. In a major move for China's indigenous defence industry, China is supplying its most advanced homemade combat aircraft, the third-generation J-10 fighter jets to Pakistan, in a deal worth around $ 6 billion.[5] Beijing is helping Pakistan build and launch satellites for

[3] Asif Ali Zardari, "Sino-Pakistan Relations Higher than Himalayas," *China Daily*, February 23, 2009.

[4] James Martin Center for Nonproliferation Studies, "Pakistan Profile," Nuclear Threat Initiative, January 2009, available at http://www.nti.org/e_research/profiles/Pakistan/index.html.

[5] Ananth Krishnan, "China's fighter jets for Pakistan," *The Hindu*, November 11, 2009.

remote sensing and communication even as Pakistan is reportedly already hosting a Chinese space communication facility at Karachi.[6]

China has played a major role in the development of Pakistan's nuclear infrastructure and emerged as Pakistan's benefactor at a time when increasingly stringent export controls in Western countries made it difficult for Pakistan to acquire materials and technology from elsewhere. The Pakistani nuclear weapons programme is essentially an extension of the Chinese one. Despite being a member of the Non Proliferation Treaty (NPT), China has supplied Pakistan with nuclear materials and expertise and has provided critical assistance in the construction of Pakistan's nuclear facilities. As has been aptly noted by Gary Milhollin, "If you subtract China's help from Pakistan's nuclear programme, there is no nuclear programme."[7]

In the 1990s, China designed and supplied the heavy water Khushab reactor, which plays a key role in Pakistan's production of plutonium. A subsidiary of the China National Nuclear Corporation also contributed in Pakistan's efforts to expand its uranium enrichment capabilities by providing 5,000 custom made ring magnets, which are a key component of the bearings that facilitate the high-speed rotation of centrifuges. China also provided technical and material support in the completion of the Chashma Nuclear Power Reactor and plutonium reprocessing facility, which was built in the mid 1990s. Although China has long denied helping any nation attain nuclear capability, the father of Pakistan's nuclear weapons programme, Abdul Qadeer Khan, himself has acknowledged the crucial role China has played in his nation's nuclear weaponisation by gifting 50 kg of weapon grade enriched uranium, drawing of the nuclear weapons and tonnes of uranium hexafluoride for Pakistan's centrifuges.[8] This is perhaps the only case where a nuclear weapon state has actually passed on weapons grade fissile material as well as a bomb design to a non-nuclear weapon state.

On the economic front, China and Pakistan have a free trade agreement with China accounting for around 11 per cent of Pakistan's imports. The two sides hope to exceed their 2015 bilateral trade volume target of US $15 billion. China's "no-strings attached" economic aid to Pakistan is appreciated more compared to the aid it receives from the US that often comes with riders

---

[6] C. Raja Mohan, "Dragon in Space," *Indian Express*, April 24, 2007.

[7] Gordon C. Chang, "Iran Tried to Buy the Pakistani Bomb. What was China's Role?" *Forbes*, March 17, 2010.

[8] R. Jeffry Smith and Joby Warrick, "A Nuclear Power's Act of Proliferation," *Washington Post*, November 13, 2009.

attached even as Chinese assistance is nowhere near what the US gives to Pakistan. Though Beijing did provide a soft loan of about $ 500 million to Islamabad to tide over its economic crisis in 2008, it did not end up giving a large-scale bailout package as was expected, thereby forcing Pakistan to go to the International Monetary Fund (IMF). China's economic co-operation with Pakistan is growing with substantial Chinese investment in Pakistani infrastructural expansion, including the noted project in the Pakistani deep water port in Gwadar. China is the largest investor in the Gwadar Deep Sea Port, which is strategically located at the mouth of the Strait of Hormuz. The two states have co-operated on a variety of large-scale infrastructural projects in Pakistan, including highways, mining, electricity generation and nuclear power projects. Over-riding Indian objections to its activities in Pakistan Occupied Kashmir (POK), China is busy undertaking a range of projects, the most significant one being the development of a strategic transport corridor between western China and Pakistan. It's Gwadar, however, that has attracted a lot of global attention. China's presence in the Bay of Bengal via roads and ports in Burma and in the Arabian Sea via the Chinese built port of Gwadar in Pakistan has been a cause of concern for India. With access to crucial port facilities in Egypt, Iran and Pakistan, China is well-poised to secure its interests in the region.

India has been the main factor that has influenced China and Pakistan's policies vis-à-vis each other. Whereas Pakistan wants to gain access to civilian and military resources from China to balance the Indian might in the sub-continent, China, viewing India as a potential challenger in the strategic landscape of Asia, views Pakistan as its central instrument to counter Indian power in the region. The China-Pakistan partnership serves the interests of both by presenting India with a potential two-front theatre in the event of war with either country.[9] In their own ways each is using the other to balance India as India's disputes with Pakistan keep India preoccupied, making it difficult for Delhi to attain its potential as a major regional and global player. China meanwhile guarantees the security of Pakistan when it comes to its conflicts with India, thus preventing India from using its much superior conventional military strength against Pakistan. Not surprisingly, one of the central pillars of Pakistan's strategic policies for the last more than four decades has been its steady and ever-growing military relationship with

[9] John W. Garver, *Protracted Contest: Sino-Indian Rivalry in the Twentieth Century* (Seattle: University of Washington Press, 200n1), p. 188.

China. And preventing India's dominance of South Asia by strengthening Pakistan has been a strategic priority for China. As Sino-Indian ties have deteriorated in recent times, Pakistan's centrality in China's foreign policy has only increased.

The fundamental underpinnings of the Sino-Indian bilateral relationship remain highly uncertain. China has tried hard to maintain a rough balance of power in South Asia by preventing India from gaining an upper hand over Pakistan. India's preoccupation with Pakistan reduces India to the level of a regional power, while China can claim the status of an Asian and world power.[10] It is instructive that even as India and China share similar concerns regarding Islamic terrorism in Kashmir and Xinjiang respectively, China has been rather unwilling to make a common cause with India against Pakistan. As India struggles to emerge as a global power with an ambitious foreign policy agenda, China can effectively scuttle Indian ambitions by continuing with its diplomatic and military support to Pakistan. Much to India's chagrin, China has given enough indications in the recent past that it wants to follow that path.

With the civilian government of President Zardari under intense pressure from the US to do more to fight terrorism emanating from Pakistani soil, there are calls in Pakistan to adopt a foreign policy which considers China and not the US to be Pakistan's strongest ally and most significant stakeholder. China's emergence as the leading global economic power coupled with recent attempts by India and the US to come closer has helped this suggestion gain further credibility. Washington has historically been accused of using Pakistan in time of need and then deserting it for a policy that favours stronger relations with India to serve its large strategic agenda. Pakistan remains angry about the US indifference towards it after using it to funnel aid to Afghan Mujahideen against the Russians in Afghanistan and then turning its back after the Soviet withdrawal. Where only around 9 per cent of Pakistanis view the US as a partner, around 80 per cent Pakistani population considers China a friend.[11] China is considered a more reliable ally which has always come to Pakistan's aid when India has seemed on ascendant to an extent where China has also supported Pakistan strategy of using terror as an instrument

---

[10] For an argument along similar lines, see Stephen P. Cohen, "Geostrategic Factors in India-Pak Relations," *Asian Affairs* 10.3 (Fall 1983): 24–31, 28.

[11] Ziad Haider, "The China Factor in Pakistan," *Far Eastern Economic Review*, October 2, 2009.

of policy against India. Not surprisingly, Pakistan has given China a "blank cheque" to intervene in India-Pakistan peace talks.[12]

China has provided Pakistan most of the ordinance that its Pakistan's Inter-Services Intelligence (ISI) supplies to terrorist groups operating in and against India. Most of the sophisticated communications equipment used by terrorists in India, especially in Kashmir, is made in China and has been routed through the Pakistani army. The terrorists who attacked Mumbai in November 2008 used Chinese equipment. Moreover, China continued to block UN sanctions against the dreaded Lashkar-e-Toiba (LeT) and Jamaat-ud-Dawa (JuD), the organisations that planned and executed the attacks in Mumbai despite a broad global consensus favouring such a move.[13] It was only in December 2008 that China agreed to ban JuD as tensions surfaced between Beijing and Islamabad on the issue of Chinese Uighur separatists receiving sanctuaries and training on Pakistani territory. Though counter-terror co-operation between China and Pakistan has gained traction and Pakistan has taken a number of steps to assuage the concerns of Beijing, the rise of Islamist extremism in China remains an irritant in an otherwise strong Sino-Pakistan relationship.

But with India's ascent in the global hierarchy and American attempts to carve out a strong partnership with India, China's need for Pakistan is only likely to grow. This has been evident in Chinese polices towards Pakistan on critical issues in South Asia. As tensions rose between India and Pakistan in the aftermath of November 2008 terror attacks in Mumbai, Pakistan's Chairman of the Joint Chiefs of Staff Committee went to China to seek support which was readily given. The visit resulted in the signing of a new agreement on military co-operation between the two nations with Beijing agreeing to expedite the delivery of F-22 frigates to Pakistan's navy. Beijing has justified its arms sales to Pakistan on the ground that India was buying similar weapon systems from the US. Given that India has entered into similar deals for military hardware from the US and Russia, China has defended Pakistan's desire for high capacity weapons systems as normal for an independent nation seeking to bolster its security.[14]

With the exception of China, other major global powers such as Britain, France, Germany and Russia supported the US-India nuclear deal as they

---

[12] "Pak now hand China a 'blank cheque', India says no way," *Indian Express*, February 23, 2010.

[13] For details, see Gordon G. Chang, "India's China Problem," *Forbes*, August 13, 2009.

[14] Saibal Dasgupta, "Arms sale to Pak justified as India buys from US: Chinese official," *Times of India*, December 22, 2008.

were eager to sell nuclear fuel, reactors and equipment to India. China, on its part, made its displeasure clear by asking India to sign the NPT and dismantle its nuclear weapons. The official Xinhua news agency of China commented that the US-India nuclear agreement "will set a bad example for other countries."[15]

Since the US-India deal is in many ways a recognition of India's rising global profile, China, not surprisingly, was not very happy with the outcome and indicated that it would be willing to sell nuclear reactors to Pakistan.[16] It was a not-so-subtle message to the US that if Washington decided to play favourites, China also retained the same right. China plans to supply two nuclear reactors to Pakistan in defiance of international rules. Chinese authorities have confirmed that the China National Nuclear Co-operation has signed an agreement with Pakistan for two new nuclear reactors at the Chashma site – Chashma III and Chashma IV – in addition to the two that it is already working on in Pakistan. This action of China will be in clear violation of the Nuclear Suppliers Group (NSG) guidelines that forbid nuclear transfers to countries not signatories to the NPT or adhere to comprehensive international safeguards on their nuclear programme. China has suggested that "there are compelling political reasons concerning the stability of South Asia to justify the exports," echoing Pakistan's oft-repeated complaint that US-India nuclear pact has upset stability in the region by assisting India's strategic programme.[17] The decision to supply reactors to Pakistan, a non-signatory to the NPT and with a record of dealing with North Korea, Iran and Libya, reflects China's growing diplomatic confidence and underscores its view of Pakistan as a prized South Asian strategic power.

Since 1962, the Chinese strategists had decided that they can deal with India on their own terms. But with the US entering the equations now, all kinds of uncertainties have been introduced into the Chinese planning. China's involvement in the construction of Gwadar has worried India due to its strategic location, about 70 km from the Iranian border and 400 km east of the Strait of Hormuz, a major oil supply route. It has been suggested that it will provide China with a "listening post" from where it can "monitor

---

[15] "Chinese Media Sees Red," *Press Trust of India*, March 3, 2006.

[16] Farhan Bokhari, "Pakistan in Talks to Buy Chinese Reactors," *Financial Times*, January 2, 2006.

[17] Mark Hibbs, "Pakistan Deal Signals China's Growing Nuclear Assertiveness," *Nuclear Energy Brief*, Carnegie Endowment for International Peace, April 27, 2010.

US naval activity in the Persian Gulf, Indian activity in the Arabian Sea, and future US-Indian maritime co-operation in the Indian Ocean."[18]

Though Pakistan's naval capabilities do not, on their own, pose any challenge to India, the combination of Chinese and Pakistani naval forces can indeed be formidable for India to counter. Recent suggestions emanating from Beijing that China is likely to set up military bases overseas to counter American influence and exert pressure on India have been interpreted in certain sections in New Delhi as a veiled reference to China's interest in having a permanent military presence in Pakistan. Even though it might not be politically possible for the Pakistani government to openly allow China to set up a military base, New Delhi fears that Islamabad might allow Beijing the use of its military facilities without any public announcements about it.[19] India's latest annual defence report conveys concerns regarding China-Pakistan collusion by underlining China's "assistance and cooperation with Pakistan..." as well as "the possibility of enhancing connectivity with Pakistan through the territory of Jammu and Kashmir illegally occupied by China and Pakistan."[20]

It has been suggested that the rapidly deteriorating situation in Pakistan and its long-term consequences for regional stability might result in greater co-operation between Beijing and New Delhi so as to stabilise the shared periphery between the two nations. The turbulence in Xinjiang has forced Beijing to pay greater attention to the sources of international terrorism in Pakistan with the prospect of Islamist extremism spilling over from Afghanistan and Pakistan into the restive Xinjiang province which saw riots between Han Chinese and the Muslim Uighurs in 2009. Yet concerns have only risen in India in recent times that China and Pakistan are co-ordinating their efforts on the border issue against India with China's position on the Line of Actual Control (LAC) becoming more aggressive than ever.[21]

Historically, China has supported Pakistan and other smaller states in South Asia to oppose what it viewed as India's hegemonic ambitions in the region. Now as India seeks to become a major global power, support for Pakistan assumes an even greater significance as Pakistan alone among South

---

[18] Ziad Haider, "Oil Fuels Beijing's new Power Game," Yale Global Online, available at http://yaleglobal.yale.edu/display.article?id=5411.

[19] Saibal Dasgupta, "China Mulls Setting Up Military Base in Pakistan," *Times of India*, January 28, 2010.

[20] Annual Report: 2009–2010, Ministry of Defence, Government of India, p. 6.

[21] "China's Positioning on the Border is Very Aggressive," *India Abroad*, April 3, 2010.

Asian states has the capability to constrain India to an extent that would help Beijing strategically. China has used its special relationship with Pakistan to pursue a classic balance of power politics vis-à-vis India. This policy has been rather successful in so far as India has found it difficult to emerge out of the straightjacket of being a South Asian power despite its long-standing perception of its own profile as a major global power. As recently as 2009, the US President could go to Beijing and acknowledge that China has a role to play in the India-Pakistan relationship.[22] It has been rightly observed that China's policy towards Pakistan is "an object lesson in how to attain long-term national goals by calm calculation, forbearance, and diplomatic skill."[23]

A rising India makes Pakistan all the more important for Chinese strategy for the subcontinent. It's highly unlikely that China will give up playing the Pakistan card vis-à-vis India anytime soon.

China and Bangladesh: Following the Sino-Pak Trajectory

Bangladesh is surrounded on three sides by India along a 4094 km long land border. This results in near total geographical domination by India except for the 193 km long land border that Bangladesh shares with Myanmar. India's overarching presence in South Asia, in fact, has been a cause for concern for all of its smaller neighbours. Bangladesh is no exception. For India, the struggle against Pakistan in 1971 was a strategic imperative; India further marginalised Pakistan by cutting it in half with the emergence of Bangladesh. India may have expected Bangladesh to remain indebted to it for its role in assisting Bangladesh to achieve independence, but this did not happen. After all, structural constraints are the most important determinant of state behaviour in international politics and Bangladesh soon began "balancing" against Indian preponderance in the region. Like other states in South Asia, Bangladesh has tried to counter India's regional hegemony through a variety of means.

Bangladesh's relations with Pakistan in the years immediately after independence were severely strained for obvious reasons, but their ties eventually began to improve quite dramatically. A major impetus for this was the desire of both countries to balance India's power and influence in the region. In 1974,

---

[22] For details, see the Joint statement by President Barack Obama and President Hu Jintao, November 17, 2009, available at http://www.whitehouse.gov/the-press-office/joint-press-statement-president-obama-and-president-hu-china.

[23] S.M. Burke, *Pakistan's Foreign Policy* (London: Oxford University Press, 1973), p. 213.

Pakistan and Bangladesh signed an accord to recognise each other and two years later established formal diplomatic relations. The two states have maintained high-level contacts ever since. It has been correctly observed that popular fears of Indian domination in both countries outweigh any lingering animosity between them, resulting in closer Pakistan-Bangladesh ties.[24] Thus, Bangladesh started cultivating Pakistan in an effort to counterbalance India because it sees India as its main potential threat. In contrast, India's foreign policy obsession with Pakistan has led it to ignore Bangladesh. The former Pakistani President General Pervez Musharraf reportedly used his 2003 visit to Bangladesh to forge covert military ties with Dhaka and obtain authorisation for Pakistan's premier intelligence agency, ISI, to operate from Bangladeshi territory. Growing closeness to Pakistan has enabled Bangladesh to also come close to China, Pakistan's closest ally in the region.

Bangladesh has made a systematic attempt in recent years to woo an extra-regional power – namely, China – to prevent New Delhi from asserting regional supremacy in its relations with Dhaka. This strategy is not typical of Bangladesh's foreign policy but other states in the region – including Pakistan, Sri Lanka and Nepal – have used China to try to counterbalance India. Bangladesh has been more than willing to play off Pakistan and China against India. China on its part has made a serious effort in recent years to wean Bangladesh away from India's influence, thereby further enhancing its own role in South Asia.

Since China and Bangladesh established ties in 1976 their bilateral relationship has grown steadily, culminating in the signing of a "Defence Co-operation Agreement" in 2002 that covers military training and defence production. It was aimed at bolstering Bangladesh's defence forces. Much like Pakistan, the armed forces of Bangladesh are predominantly equipped with Chinese military hardware. This agreement is the first ever signed by Bangladesh in its history. It was a period when Bangladesh was under pressure from India for allowing its territory to be used for anti-Indian activities. Bangladesh might have felt the need to engage China more substantively to signal to India that it can't be pushed too much on the issue. Dhaka has emerged as the prime buyer of weapons made in China that include 122-mm Howitzers, rocket launchers, small arms like pistols and sub-machine guns

---

[24] Kathryn Jacques, *Bangladesh, India, and Pakistan: International Relations and Regional Tensions in South Asia* (New York: St. Martin's Press, 2000), p. 161.

along with regular 82-mm mortars.[25] Bangladesh's missile launch pad near the Chittagong Port has also been constructed with assistance from China. It successfully test-fired land attack anti-ship cruise missile C-802A, a modified version of Chinese Ying Ji-802, with a strike range of 120 km in 2008 with active participation of Chinese experts.[26]

China has also provided Bangladesh with substantial resources to bolster its civil service and law enforcement agencies. The two states have signed an agreement on peaceful uses of nuclear energy in the fields of medicine, agriculture and biotechnology.[27] China is now Bangladesh's largest source of imports even as Bangladesh is the third-largest trade partner of China in South Asia. Bilateral trade has increased from $ 1.1 billion in 2002 to $ 4 billion in 2008 reaching nearly $ 5.5 billion in 2010 with China emerging as Bangladesh's largest trading partner. There is a growing Chinese investment in a range of sectors in Bangladesh, especially in the field of small and medium-sized enterprises. China is investing in important infrastructure development projects and is providing duty free access to Bangladeshi products in its markets. Energy-hungry China views Bangladesh's large natural gas reserves as a potential asset to be tapped and, much to India's discomfort, Bangladesh supports China's entry into the South Asian Association of Regional Cooperation (SAARC). It was at the invitation of Bangladesh that China was given an observer status in SAARC. China has offered to help in the construction of nuclear power plants in Bangladesh to help meet the country's growing energy needs even as it is making a push towards the development of natural gas reserves of Bangladesh. While Bangladesh has granted China exploration rights for developing natural gas fields of its own, friction in India-Bangladesh ties has precluded co-operation between India and Bangladesh on the issue of energy. Energy co-operation between China and Bangladesh is growing with Chinese oil companies helping in the development of oil and gas reserves in Bangladesh with the potential of Bangladesh exporting oil to China. There is ambition in Dhaka to construct an oil pipeline from Chittagong to Kunming in China. China is also helping Bangladesh in the construction of a deep water port at Chittagong and is investing in the deep sea port at Sonadia, further heightening Indian fears of "encirclement."

[25] Pranab Dhal Samanta, "Breaking 10-year Silence, China Reveals It's No 1 Arms Supplier to Bangladesh," *Indian Express*, September 9, 2007.

[26] Sumit Sen, "Bangladesh Building Missile Arsenal," *Times of India*, September 12, 2008.

[27] Tarique Niazi, "China's March on South Asia," *China Brief*, Vol. 5, No. 9, April 26, 2005.

In this context, it is interesting to note the proposal to revive the Stilwell Road (also known as the "Old Burma Road') which stretches from the Indian state of Assam through Bangladesh and Myanmar, extending all the way to Yunnan Province in southern China. In 1999 China, India, Myanmar and Bangladesh all came together in what is known as the "Kunming Initiative" to push this proposal forward, mainly because of the potential trade advantages that would be derived from linking those countries to Southeast Asia via a long land route.[28] But India has been reconsidering this proposal, fearing that it might give a fillip to insurgents in north-eastern India who receive support from Bangladesh and also allow Chinese goods to potentially flood Indian markets. Bangladesh has offered transit rights to China as it seeks to establish road and rail links between Chittagong and Kunming through Myanmar, something India is not very comfortable with. After agreeing to allow New Delhi to use the Chittagong and Mangla port facilities, Bangladesh has offered the same to Beijing. Dhaka has also sought Chinese assistance for its proposed deep sea port in the Bay of Bengal.[29] China is not only funding the development of Bangladesh's Chittagong port but also the construction of highway linking Kunming, in south-western Yunnan province to Chittagong via Myanmar to give access to China to make use of the port.

By courting Bangladesh, China will be able to get a strategic toe-hold in India's eastern flank. The development of Chittagong port along the line of Gwadar in Pakistan is aimed at facilitating China's entry into the Bay of Bengal. Though Chittagong port is apparently being developed for commercial purposes, it could easily be used for staging Chinese naval assets. China's access to Chittagong port will bring it closer to Myanmar oil fields. Close Sino-Bangladesh relations also further enhances Indian vulnerabilities in the critical North-eastern region. There are growing fears in India that Indian security would be gravely damaged if Dhaka decides to grant military basing rights to China. A close strategic relationship with Bangladesh will allow China to link its electronic listening systems at Coco Island in Myanmar and the staging systems in Bangladesh to monitor Indian naval and missile activities even as the prospect of Chinese ships

[28] Ramtanu Maitra, "Prospects Brighten for Kunming Initiative," Asia Times Online, <http://www.atimes.com/atimes/South_Asia/EB12Df04.html>
[29] *The Assam Tribune*, March 23, 2010.

operating in the Andaman Sea would seriously constrain Indian power projection.[30]

While Sino-Bangladesh ties have burgeoned under non-Awami League political dispensations in Dhaka, even Awami League has been careful in courting China and in not appearing to have moved under the Indian orbit of influence. The military co-operation between the two has continued to gather momentum irrespective of who is in power in Dhaka. A close relationship with China is one of the most potent ways by which Dhaka can demonstrate its autonomy from Indian domination.[31] It is Sheikh Hasina, considered reliably pro-India, who has described China as the "most dependable and consistent friend of Bangladesh" ever since the two states established their diplomatic ties more than three decades ago.[32] Given the growing closeness between China and Bangladesh, it is not surprising that the term "all weather friendship" – usually reserved to describe China's ties with Pakistan – is now also being used to underline the changing nature of Sino-Bangladesh bilateral relationship.[33]

China in Sri Lanka: The LTTE and After

If New Delhi has consistently sought to exclude a hostile third-party presence from Sri Lanka, growing Chinese presence in the country poses a serious challenge to Indian policy.[34] Colombo's centrality between Aden and Singapore makes it extremely significant strategically for Indian power projection possibilities. After initially following India's lead in international affairs, even demanding that the British leave from their naval base at Trincomalee air base and air base at Katunayake in 1957, Colombo gradually gravitated towards a more independent foreign policy posture. And it was India's enthusiasm for China that made Sri Lanka take China seriously but after the Chinese victory in its 1962 war with India, Colombo started courting Beijing much more seriously. Beijing, for its part, viewed New Delhi's role in the Sri Lankan affairs not only as a means to "control" Sri Lanka and achieve

---

[30] Vijay Sakhuja, "China-Bangladesh Relations and Potential for Regional Tensions," *China Brief*, July 23, 2009.

[31] J.N. Dixit, *Liberation and Beyond: Indo-Bangladesh Relations* (New Delhi: Konark, 1999), p. 283.

[32] "Hasina Meets Wen to Deepen "Comprehensive Partnership'," *Press Trust of India*, March 18, 2010.

[33] "Who is greater friend? India or China? Dhaka Debates," *Indo-Asian News Service*, March 19, 2010.

[34] Dhirendra Mohan Prasad, *Ceylon's Foreign Policy under the Bandarnaikes (1956-65): A Political Analysis* (New Delhi, S. Chand, 1973), pp. 304–88.

"regional hegemony" in South Asia but also to "expel the influence of other countries."[35]

Under the Indo-Sri Lankan agreement of 1987, the two sides agreed that neither would allow its territory to be used against the security interests of the other and Colombo guaranteed that foreign military and intelligence personnel in Sri Lanka would not hurt Indo-Sri Lankan ties. This merely confirmed Beijing's suspicions that India desires to be the pre-eminent external actor in Sri Lanka.[36] Sri Lanka's support to China on issues related to the question of China's sovereignty including Taiwan and Tibet and China's support for issues related to Sri Lankan territorial integrity, has reinforced Sino-Sri Lankan bilateral relationship. But given Beijing's inability to project power substantively in South Asia till the early 1990s, it could only be a marginal player in the Indo-Sri Lankan dynamic and was forced to accede to India's central role in Sri Lanka, especially as India seemed willing to pursue coercive diplomacy till late 1980s.

With the Sri Lankan military declaring victory over the Liberation Tigers of Tamil Eelam (LTTE), New Delhi has been forced to dramatically recalibrate its strategy toward the island nation and has been desperately seeking a voice in the rapidly evolving situation in Sri Lanka.[37] Colombo has promised to undertake major development in the former Tiger-controlled areas in the north and has pledged to protect the rights of the minority Tamils. Yet, the death of Tamil leader Velupillai Prabhakaran sparked incidents of violence across the Indian state of Tamil Nadu, underlining the balancing act that New Delhi must perform.

When the Mahinda Rajapaksa regime decided in 2007 that the time for a steady military offensive against the LTTE had come, not only was the LTTE bereft of significant outside support but the Sri Lankan government was assured of the Chinese support.[38] With India constrained in providing military assistance to Colombo, limiting its arms transfers to defensive uses, due to the sensitivities of its Tamil population, China and Pakistan emerged as main arms suppliers to Sri Lanka. Colombo astutely cultivated the two

---

[35] Garver, *Protracted Contest*, pp. 308–9.
[36] For a detailed examination of this accord, see Shelton U. Kodikara, "Genesis of the Indo-Sri Lankan agreement of 29 July, 1987," *Contemporary South Asia*, Vol. 4, No. 2 (July 1995), pp. 171–185.
[37] For a discussion of the factors responsible for the defeat of the LTTE, see Harsh V. Pant, "End Game in Sri Lanka," Yale Global Online, February 23, 2009, available at http://yaleglobal.yale.edu/content/end-game-sri-lanka
[38] Ibid.

nations over the last several years to keep India in check. Like most of India's neighbours, Colombo tried to balance India's regional predominance by courting extra-regional powers. China is emerging as a major player in this context giving Sri Lanka greater strategic room to manoeuvre. For China, its ties with Colombo give it a foothold near crucial sea-lanes in the Indian Ocean as well as entry into what India considers its sphere of influence. China not only supplies military hardware and training, but helps Colombo in gas exploration and building a modern port in Hambantota. China's arms transfers include fighter aircraft, armoured personnel carriers, anti-aircraft guns, air surveillance radars, rocket-propelled grenade launchers and missiles, strengthening the position of the Sri Lankan Army against the first terrorist organisation to boast of an army, navy and air force along with a small submarine force. Sri Lanka's victory over the LTTE would not have been possible without the crucial support it received from China. To begin with China only provided political and diplomatic support to Sri Lanka in its fight against the Tigers and Colombo was equally reluctant to seek Beijing's help for fear of antagonising India. But when Rajapaksa decided to launch an all-out offensive against the Tamil rebels after being humiliated with the discovery of LTTE air prowess, it decided to court China more actively in the defence sphere. When India made it clear that it could not send offensive weapons and weapon systems such as radars and the West decided to suspend military aid on account of human rights concerns, China decided to come to the rescue of the Sri Lankan government. Sri Lanka signed a $ 37.6 million deal in 2007 to buy Chinese ammunition and ordnance for its army and navy even as China supplied Sri Lanka fighter jets to counter LTTE's air prowess. Chinese military supplies to Sri Lanka are estimated at $ 100 million per annum with China supporting Sri Lankan defence forces in boosting its capabilities for high–tech aerial warfare and restructuring and reorienting the military. China has encouraged the Sri Lankan military's participation in multilateral regional military activities and Sri Lanka was accepted as a Dialogue Partner to the Shanghai Co-operation Organization (SCO) in 2009.

China has also displaced Japan as Sri Lanka's major aid donor with an annual aid package of $ 1 billion. Bilateral trade between China and Sri Lanka has doubled over the last five years with China emerging as the largest trading partner of Sri Lanka. Chinese investment in the development of infrastructure and oil exploration projects in Sri Lanka has also gathered momentum. China is providing interest-free loans and preferential loans at subsidised rates to Sri Lanka for the development of infrastructure. It is the first foreign country to have an exclusive economic zone in Sri Lanka. China is involved in a range of infrastructure development projects in Sri Lanka – constructing power plants, modernising Sri Lankan railways, providing financial and technical assistance in launching of communication satellites, etc. China is financing more than 85 per cent of the Hambantota Development Zone to be completed over the next decade. This will include an international container port, a bunkering system, an oil refinery, international airport and other facilities. The port in Hambantota, deeper than the one at Colombo, is to be used as a refuelling and docking station for its navy.[39] Though the two sides claim that this is merely a commercial venture, its future utility as a strategic asset by China remains a real possibility to India's consternation. For China, Hambantota will not only be an important transit for general cargo and oil but a presence in Hambantota also enhances China's monitoring and intelligence gathering capabilities vis-à-vis India.

India's political and economic influence in Sri Lanka is gradually shrinking even as courting China gives Colombo greater room for diplomatic manoeuvring vis-à-vis New Delhi. It was India's hands-off policy towards Sri Lanka because of the strong domestic Tamil sentiment against supporting Sri Lankan counter-insurgency that allowed China to move in. As the Tamil Tigers came close to defeating the Sri Lankan forces, the island nation asked India for assistance and all India could do was offer financial assistance even as Colombo turned first to Islamabad and then to Beijing for military supplies. By doing this India gave the Rajpaksa regime a free hand in defeating the LTTE and with this India's strategic space in Sri Lanka shrank to an all-time low despite its geo-strategic advantage and economic clout.[40] Beijing's diplomatic support helped Colombo to deflect Western criticism of its human rights record in defeating the LTTE.

India has expressed its displeasure about growing Chinese involvement in Sri Lanka on a number of occasions. In 2007, India's National Security Advisor openly criticised Sri Lanka for attempting to purchase Chinese-built radar systems on the grounds that it would "overreach" into the Indian air space.[41] India has meanwhile failed to exert its leverage over the humanitarian troubles that the Tamils trapped in the fighting have been facing. New Delhi's

---

[39] Sutirtho Patranobis, "China Creates a Pearl in Sri Lanka," *Hindustan Times*, September 16, 2009.

[40] Ashok K. Mehta, "Colombo Looks Beyond Delhi," *The Pioneer*, March 18, 2009.

[41] "Come to Us for Weapons: Narayanan to Lanka," *Indian Express*, June 1, 2007.

attempts to end the war and avert humanitarian tragedy in North-East Sri Lanka proved utterly futile.

Sri Lanka has emerged stronger and more stable after the military success in the Eelam war and the two elections at the national level. To counter Chinese influence, India has been forced to step up its diplomatic offensive and offer Colombo reconstruction aid. With the LTTE now out of the picture, the Indian government is hoping that it will have greater strategic space to manage bilateral ties. However, where New Delhi will have to continue to balance its domestic sensitivities and strategic interests, Beijing faces no such constraint in developing even stronger ties with Colombo. As a consequence, India is struggling to make itself more relevant to Sri Lanka than China.

China and Nepal: Growing Reach in an Era of the Maoists

Despite being a tiny landlocked state, Nepal has a pivotal position in the South Asian geo-strategic environment as it shares a border of 1,236 km with China and 1,690 km with India.[42] For both China and India, therefore, Nepal holds great strategic value.

"A yam between two rocks," was how the founder of Nepal, Prithvi Narayan Shah, described the kingdom. For China, Nepal's strategic significance lies, first and foremost, in its close proximity to Tibet. Nepal, according to Beijing, constitutes a vital part of an inner security ring that cannot be allowed to be breached by any global or regional power.[43] The Chinese occupation of Tibet in 1950 significantly increased Nepal's strategic importance for China. Ensuring Nepal's neutrality on the issue of Tibet, and securing active Nepali co-operation to prevent Tibetans from launching anti-China activities, was Beijing's primary objective in Nepal. For China, the growing influence of India had grave implications for its security considerations, especially as regards Tibet. Thus, preserving the balance of power in southern Asia in its favour became the principal strategic objective of Beijing's Nepal policy. Securing Nepal's active co-operation to prevent its rivals" use of the country

---

[42] This and other geographical details regarding Nepal can be found at the Central Intelligence Agency website, see https://www.cia.gov/library/publications/the-world-factbook/geos/np.html

[43] For a detailed discussion on Tibet's strategic importance for China, see Rama Kant, "Nepal's China Policy," *China Report*, Vol. 30, No. 2, pp. 164–166.

for anti-China activities became the primary Chinese strategic objective in Nepal.[44]

For India, Nepal remains the principal strategic land barrier between China and its own resource rich-Gangetic Plain. India's strategic stakes in Nepal dramatically increased with the Communist victory in China and the country's subsequent occupation of Tibet in 1950. Since the middle of the nineteenth century, Tibet, rather than Nepal, had served as India's buffer with China. The role of this buffer passed on to Nepal after the Chinese annexation of Tibet. It became imperative for New Delhi to deny China direct access to Nepal because of the vulnerability of India's Gangetic Plain containing critical human and economic resources.[45]

Nepal's strategic importance has led Beijing to focus its policies on preserving and enhancing the Himalayan state's independence and neutrality by trying to reduce its dependence on India in the political, economic and security arenas. China's policy options, however have been severely circumscribed by the special security relationship between India and Nepal as underlined in the 1950 Peace and Friendship Treaty between the two.[46] In the early years of the Cold War, Beijing, wary of an alliance between the US and India against it, acceded to India's pre-eminent position in Nepal, and followed its lead on its relations with Nepal. Diplomatic relations were established between China and Nepal only in August 1955. China, in deferment to India, agreed to handle its relations with Nepal through its embassy in New Delhi. Nonetheless, Beijing continued to engage Nepal by providing economic aid and strongly supporting Kathmandu in its disputes with New Delhi on the issue of trade and transit, thereby increasing its influence among Nepalese elites.

With a rise in China's economic and political profile, it became more assertive in Nepal. By late 1980s, China's engagement with Nepal had taken on more substantive dimensions. It signed a secret intelligence sharing agreement with Nepal in 1988 and agreed to supply arms to Nepal. This arms agreement elicited a strong reaction from India which imposed an economic blockade on Nepal in 1989-90.[47] This did not prevent economic and bilateral

---

[44] Narayan Khadka, "Chinese Foreign Policy Towards Nepal in Cold War Period: An Assessment," *China Report*, 35.1, pp. 62–65.

[45] Garver, *Protracted Contest*, p. 140.

[46] The full text of the 1950 Treaty of Peace and Friendship is available at http://meadev.nic.in/economyibta/volume1/chapter38.htm

[47] For details on the Indian economic blockade of Nepal, see Garver, Protracted Contest, pp. 155–162.

interactions between China and Nepal from gathering momentum in the next decade. Despite its 1950 treaty with India, Nepal began importing Chinese weaponry and cultivated extensive military co-operation in a move to reduce dependence on India. When the US, the UK and India refused to supply arms to the regime of King Gyanendra, China responded by dispatching arms to Nepal despite sharing ideological affinity with the Maoists. China supported the Nepalese King Gyanendra's anti-democratic measure in the name of political stability but was nimble enough to shift its support to the Maoists as they gained ascendancy in the Nepalese political establishment. It became the first country to provide military assistance to the Maoist government.

Over the years, China's policy towards Nepal has been guided by its larger strategic game-plan vis-à-vis South Asia. In the initial years of the Cold War when Beijing was worried about a possible coming together of India and the US, it treated Nepal cautiously so as not to hurt Indian interests. However, once China gained confidence and international recognition, it went all out to expand its influence in Nepal. By supporting Kathmandu's position during most disputes between India and Nepal, Beijing was able to project itself as a benevolent power as against the supercilious attitude of India towards its smaller neighbours. It was also able to upgrade its military ties with Nepal, despite India's stiff resistance. As ethnic tensions have risen in Tibet in recent times, China has sought to curb the activities of Tibetan refugees in Nepal. China's interest and presence in Nepal, however, has gradually expanded and now goes far beyond the Tibet issue. China is projecting its "soft power" in Nepal by setting up China Study Centres (CSCs) that are being used to promote Chinese values among the Nepalese populace that is otherwise tied culturally to India. These centres are emerging as effective instruments in promoting Chinese perspectives on key issues concerning Nepal. China is constructing a 770 km railway line to connect the Tibetan capital of Lhasa with the Nepalese town of Khasa, a move that would connect Nepal to China's national rail network. China is also constructing a 17 km long road through the Himalayas linking Tibet to the Nepalese town of Syabrunesi which will not only connect Tibet to Nepal but when completed will also be the first direct Chinese land route to New Delhi. China views Nepal as a vital bridge toward South Asia. China has increased its aid to Nepal substantially in the last few years and the trade volume between the two is growing though the trade balance continues to remain heavily in favour of China, something that China is trying to address by providing duty free access to Nepali goods in China. China's strategy of providing aid without any conditions and support for building infrastructure is enhancing China's role even as Chinese products are flooding the Nepalese market replacing Indian ones. By projecting India as a factor of instability and an undue beneficiary of Nepal's resources, China has used Nepalese sensitivities vis-à-vis Indian influence to good effect, thereby further undercutting Indian influence in Kathmandu. India's overwhelming presence remains a source of resentment towards India in Nepal. China appears attractive because it can claim that unlike India it is not interested in the internal affairs of Nepal.

The success of a democratic Nepal at peace with its neighbours is essential for the entire region. What is, however, of far greater importance for India is the trajectory of Nepal's foreign policy. India was concerned that the rise of the Maoists in Nepal could marginalise India in the Himalayan Kingdom's foreign affairs. The Maoist-led government indeed made a decisive shift towards Beijing when it suggested that Nepal would maintain equidistance from both China and India.[48] The Maoist leader Prachanda, after becoming the Prime Minister, broke the long-standing tradition of Nepalese heads of state making their first foreign trip to India, and decided to make China his first destination, ostensibly to attend the opening ceremony of the 2008 Olympic Games in Beijing. China also pushed the Maoist government towards signing of a new treaty replacing the 1960 Peace and Friendship Treaty between China and Nepal. The Maoist government made clear its intention to re-negotiate the 1950 treaty with India, but before they could accomplish their objective, the government fell.

While it was the fear of the unknown that haunted India after the win of the Maoists, it was clear that other political dispensations in Nepal too, and the monarchy in particular, had not been particularly well-disposed towards India for the last several years. Nepal under the Maoist dispensation has been no different than Nepal under its discredited monarch who did his best to play off China against India to increase his longevity in power. Recent events in Nepal – culminating in the resignation of Maoist Prime Minister Prachanda and threatening resumption of the Maoist-military confrontation – have again created problems for India. Maoists have spoken of a "foreign hand" behind the events, and few Nepalese take this as anything but an allusion to India. The resignation of the Maoist-led government in Nepal has plunged the Himalayan kingdom into crisis and India is being blamed for pulling

---

[48] "Nepal for Equidistant Ties with India, China," *India Abroad*, June 23, 2008.

strings from behind the scenes. New Delhi will have to allay concerns that it is interested in controlling Nepalese politics while quietly nudging Nepalese political parties into forming a stable government and working to counter China's growing influence. As Tibet develops economically and transport links emerge between Nepal and China, China's ability to project power in Nepal is only likely to increase significantly.

Conclusion

India's growing willingness to look beyond the confines of South Asia is also shaping the current trajectory of its foreign and security policy. India was long viewed by the world through the prism of its conflict with Pakistan. As India has emerged as an economic powerhouse supported by its democratic institutions, its strategic weight in global politics has grown to a point where it is being viewed as one of the six members of the global balance of power configuration, alongside the US, China, the EU, Japan and Russia. Indian foreign policy, as a result, is more ambitious in its scope today than it has ever been, evident in India's engagements with states in Africa, Latin America and the Middle East as well as with the traditional power centres. Yet, it is in Indian's own neighbourhood that India seems to be rapidly losing ground to China. India's long-term challenge in South Asia is about the impact of a rising China on the geopolitics of the subcontinent.

China's strategy towards South Asia is premised on encircling India and confining her within the geographical co-ordinates of the region. China has started building a circle of road-and-port connections in India's neighbouring states and is deepening its military and economic engagements with them, allowing it to envision a larger role for itself in the Indian Ocean region. The Chinese strategy of containing India within the confines of South Asia through the use of its proxies started off with Pakistan and has gradually evolved to include other states in the region including Bangladesh, Sri Lanka and Nepal. China is investing in several modern ports around India that can be used for strategic purposes. It is entering markets in South Asia more aggressively through both trade and investment by improving its trade and investment relations with South Asian states through treaties and bilateral co-operation. China's actions have conveyed to India that even as India tries hard to break out of the straitjacket of being a South Asian power by forging a strategic partnership with the US, China will do its utmost to contain India by building up its neighbouring adversaries.

Not surprisingly, China's quiet assertion in India's backyard has allowed various smaller countries to play China off against India. In South Asia, most states are now using the China card to balance against the pre-dominance of India. This is a standard strategy adopted by small states in regional systems that are dominated by two or more major powers.[49] Small states seek to preserve their sovereignty by resorting to strategies that seek to balance great powers locked in an incessant security competition. Such states promote their national interests by not explicitly aligning with any one major power, but pursue policies that preserve their independent existence. Such is the case with the states in South Asia too. Forced to exist between their two giant neighbours, the smaller states in South Asia have responded by a careful balancing act.

As India's material power capabilities have increased over the last two decades, it has become more confident of its rising power and status, and has pursued a more pro-active foreign policy, moving away from the idealism of the past to a greater "strategic realism." This has allowed New Delhi to more vigorously pursue its interests globally and challenge China's rising pre-dominance in the Asia-Pacific region and the Indian Ocean region in particular. As a consequence, not only have the Sino-Indian relations become overtly conflictual but the centrality of South Asia in China's foreign policy has also come under sharper relief.

India's structural dominance in South Asia makes it a natural target of resentment among its smaller neighbours. And therefore most of these states have sought to balance Indian influence by courting China. India's challenge is two fold: First, it must engage its neighbours in a productive manner that will allow it to realise its dream of emerging as a global power. Second, it must prevent China from gaining a strategic foothold in South Asia and preserve its influence in the region. India's interests in nudging its neighbours towards political moderation, economic modernisation, and regional integration are in tune with those of the broader international community. Yet, for all the talk of India as a rising global power, the country has found it difficult to emerge as a leader in its own backyard. New Delhi doesn't seem to have a clear neighbourhood policy and by not being proactive, it has ceded the strategic space to other actors, most significant of which is China. China's

[49] For an example of how smaller South Asian states have used China as a leverage in their dealings with India, see Manish Dabhade and Harsh V. Pant, "Coping with Challenges to Sovereignty: Sino-Indian Rivalry and Nepal's Foreign Policy," *Contemporary South Asia*, 13.2 (June 2004), 157–169.

presence looms large over the subcontinent, emerging as the single most important external power in the region. China's growing reach in South Asia has weakened New Delhi's influence, alarming Indian policymakers. These actions are in keeping with China's long-standing policy of preventing India from joining the ranks of major global powers and keeping it contained to the confines of South Asia.[50] It is to be expected that China will try to counter India's rise by using Pakistan as a countervailing factor and cultivating India's other neighbours in order to emerge as an un-tethered hegemon in Asia. This strategy seems to be working at the moment when India finds itself largely isolated in its neighbourhood. And it remains far from clear if India has yet found a way of asserting its supremacy and containing rapidly growing China's profile in the region.

[50] Harsh V. Pant, *The China Syndrome: Grappling with an Uneasy Relationship* (New Delhi: HarperCollins, 2010), pp. 37–71.